"*Things that Matter* is an insightful and expertly edited collection of essays from active participants in one of Australasia's most significant theological colleges. It constitutes an important updated institutional history and highlights well the flourishing of the diverse contextual theologies that have been developed at UTC over many decades."

—GLEN O'BRIEN
Professor of Christian Thought and History,
University of Divinity, Melbourne, Australia

"*Things That Matter* is a profound testament to the power of faith, community, and theological formation. More than just a history, this book beautifully weaves personal narratives with deep reflections on identity, vocation, and hospitality within Christian discipleship. As someone shaped by UTC, I know firsthand the transformative role of theological education and the bonds that sustain faith leaders. A compelling and heartfelt read, this book is an inspiring resource for those shaping the church's future."

—CHARISSA SULI
President, Uniting Church in Australia

"This is an important and timely book. It provides critical insider perspectives on what happened to theological education when a denominationally run theological college established formal links with a university. In ten wide-ranging essays, it considers what was lost and gained as the college negotiated the issues involved in embracing the intellectually open approach of the university, while simultaneously responding to the opportunities and challenges of theological and multi-cultural diversity within the church, college, and wider community."

—JUDITH RAFTERY
President, Uniting Church National History Society, Adelaide, South Australia

"Theological colleges occupy a highly contested place in the Uniting Church. Considered studies of what they are and the manifold work that they do, however, are rare. This book helps to correct that by exploring, in some detail, many aspects of the work of United Theological College over the last twenty-five years. The authors variously analyze what matters: what has mattered, what no longer matters, what should matter. It matters, too, that members and leaders of the Uniting Church engage the insights of these high-quality essays."

—GEOFF THOMPSON
Associate Professor of Systematic Theology, Pilgrim Theological College

Things That Matter

Things That Matter

Essays on Theological Education on the Occasion
of the Fiftieth Anniversary of United Theological College

Edited by
WILLIAM W. EMILSEN
and PATRICIA CURTHOYS

Foreword by Stephen Pickard

WIPF & STOCK · Eugene, Oregon

THINGS THAT MATTER
Essays on Theological Education on the Occasion of the Fiftieth Anniversary of United Theological College

Copyright © 2025 Wipf and Stock Publishers. All rights reserved. Except for brief quotations in critical publications or reviews, no part of this book may be reproduced in any manner without prior written permission from the publisher. Write: Permissions, Wipf and Stock Publishers, 199 W. 8th Ave., Suite 3, Eugene, OR 97401.

Wipf & Stock
An Imprint of Wipf and Stock Publishers
199 W. 8th Ave., Suite 3
Eugene, OR 97401

www.wipfandstock.com

PAPERBACK ISBN: 979-8-3852-1880-6
HARDCOVER ISBN: 979-8-3852-1881-3
EBOOK ISBN: 979-8-3852-1882-0

VERSION NUMBER 042225

Revised Standard Version of the Bible, copyright © 1946, 1952, and 1971 the Division of Christian Education of the National Council of the Churches of Christ in the United States of America. Used by permission. All rights reserved.

New Revised Standard Version Updated Edition. Copyright © 2021 National Council of Churches of Christ in the United States of America. Used by permission. All rights reserved worldwide.

Contents

Foreword by Stephen Pickard | vii
Contributors | xi
Introduction | xv

1. UTC at the Intersection of Church and University | 1
   Ross Chambers

2. A Quarter Century of Systematic Theology | 24
   Ben Myers

3. Formation for Ordained Ministry at UTC | 40
   Peter Walker and Nicole Fleming

4. Community of the Heart | 54
   Rebecca Lindsay

5. Multiculturalism, Theological Learning, and Community at UTC | 68
   Seforosa Carroll and Carolyn Craig-Emilsen

6. Pasifika Voices Flourishing in the Presence of Others | 90
   Clive Pearson

7. Things That Matter to Koreans | 110
   Myung Hwa Park

8. Camden Theological Library:
   Not Simply an Excellent Theological Library | 126
   William W. Emilsen

9. Lifelong Learning:
   The Contribution of Visiting Scholars and Conferences | 145
   Mark Hillis

10. With Heart and Mind: Research and Publications at UTC | 169
    John T. Squires

Index | 201

Foreword

IT IS DIFFICULT TO resist the conclusion that theological education is essentially a site of contest. To be involved in this worthy and time-honored enterprise is to be inescapably embroiled in issues to do with power, who has power, how is it deployed, and for what purposes. Just ask any principal, dean, or director of a theological institution under the scrutiny of the wider church and responsible for the management of resources, budgets, curricula, and people. Perhaps it has ever been thus. Why is this so?

In the late nineteenth century, John Henry Newman identified theology as one of the three fundamental powers of the church.[1] Theology (Newman's system of philosophy) offered a critical stance in relation to the other two powers, the worship/sacramental tradition (liturgy) and ecclesiastical rule (polity and political power). He argued that these latter two powers required a third power (theology) as an essential hermeneutic for the ongoing faithfulness of the church to the gospel. Without this third power the church was subject to tribal ritualism/superstition (today seen as introverted self-absorption) or an unfettered abuse of ecclesiastical power (today, executive management and fiscal control). Church history bore testimony to the conflict that often occurred between these three indispensable elements of the life of the church. Newman considered that the theological vocation was essential to preserve and foster a critical and reforming spirit.

Newman's simple schema has proven resilient and relevant in an anxious, cash-strapped ecclesial environment heavily dominated by business corporate models and bureaucratic rule. In such a context the theological voice is easily muted—the theologian, wounded, lying on the roadside

---

1. John Henry Newman, *Lectures on the Prophetical Office of the Church Viewed Relatively to Romanism and Popular Protestantism*, vol. 1 of *The Via Media of the Anglican Church*, 3rd ed. (London: Basil Montagu Pickering, 1877), xl–xli.

waiting for a good Samaritan to come with aid; the student, a fellow traveler on an uncertain and unstable track. Yet the stakes are high. Leaders of theological institutions are acutely aware that theological education has become, if it wasn't before, a contested site for the people of God. The reason is clear. Theological institutions, precisely because they have such potential impact on the shape of ecclesial identity and mission, become sites of contest. Disputes about theological education revolve around issues concerning purpose. Are such institutions fundamentally training institutes for ordained and/or lay mission fieldwork? Or are they places for more rigorous theological reflection to build an informed and intelligent engagement of the church with society? Or is there perhaps a third way—a mediating tradition that attempts to straddle both, offering something quite unique and nourishing for the life of the church?

The essays in this volume, covering a quarter century of theological education at United Theological College, are testimony to the power of this third mediating way in theology. It is the way of practical wisdom. Indeed, UTC stands in a long tradition of theology as the active pursuit of wisdom and its radical and transformative impact. It is clearly not an optional extra nor a luxury the church can ill afford nor the preserve of an elite—clergy, seminarians, the experts, or "professionals." It is a task for the baptized, enshrined in their baptismal vows and a corollary of their diverse ministries in the world. Yet how, it may be asked, is it ever possible for the people of the church to fulfill their vocation and ministry unless they are equipped to engage in critical reflection upon their vocations in order that they might more clearly embody the faithfulness of Christ in the world? To live a life of faith is to be a pilgrim seeking deeper understanding of the ways of God with the world. On this account theology has a significant function; therefore, it ought to occupy a fairly central place in the life of the church. For the sake of the mission of the church, theology belongs within the orbit of the fundamental powers Newman spoke of that energize and guide the people of God.

Given the increasing diversity of the cultures that make up contemporary Australia, a significant challenge for theological education is to find authentic Australian voice(s), if it is to contribute to the needed transformation of the church and bear witness to the coming kingdom of God. Such a polyphonic voice includes the peoples and cultures of Asia and Oceania and the liquid continent that this encompasses. How, then, will theology and theologians play their part in the equipping of the whole people of God for such an exciting, rich, and complex task? What structures will best serve the future church? In a resource-depleted church, what new possibilities are there for theological education that is truly for all the people? What is required is a mission-shaped theological education. The orientation to mission is a fundament for theological education today. Indeed, the future capacity to enhance the mission of God in the world is directly related to the task of theological education. On this account, theological education is not an undertaking that is self-serving and hermetically sealed from the wider church and society, nor is it restricted to those who are preparing for ordained ministry as such. Rather, theological education is an agent of mission pointing to the coming kingdom, a task in progress as the church prays, "May your kingdom come. May your will be done on earth as it is in heaven" (Matt 6:10 NRSV).

To place theological education within the orbit of mission is both important and timely. However, what does mission actually mean when it comes to theological education? Might the heart of this concern be the learning of wisdom for the sake of God's mission in the world? The appeal to wisdom offers a sharper focus for the missiological purpose of theological education. Wisdom is inherent in the church's witness. It is not a wisdom "of the world" but of a different order, concentrated in the proclamation of Christ crucified—"the power of God and the wisdom of God" (1 Cor 1:20-25). As Daniel Hardy once stated,

> We are the place in which the wisdom of God appears. And as Christians, we are formed in the wisdom of Christ by learning. And . . . it is true for every Christian person. And hints of such things are found much more widely.[2]

This final comment is tantalizing, for it suggests that wisdom is not confined to the church but is present and active in the created order. This is one reason why theological education ideally needs to be in conversation with other disciplines of knowledge and learning in a public university. The truth is out there in the world beloved of God. For Hardy, "formation in wisdom by learning" was the hermeneutical key to theological education. Its origins

> go very deeply into God's life and purposes, which are never far from us, or indeed from God's world. God's own life is one whose mystery is shaped as a *Spirit-filled truth and holiness in Christ crucified*. It is by this life that we—as well as the world surrounding us—are shaped.[3]

This fundamental dynamic of wisdom in the world and human life implies that learning wisdom is inherent in Christian faith; it is not an optional

---

2. Daniel Hardy, *Finding the Church* (London: SCM, 2001), 170.
3. Hardy, *Finding the Church*, 170.

extra; it is unavoidable; and it is present across cultures and peoples of the world. The real challenge is to respond appropriately to the movement of God's wisdom, and it is precisely here that theological education has a critical role in the life of the *ecclesia* of God. Furthermore, it is a broad compass, focusing upon the particularities of faith and theology through time and across space, but also open to other kinds of learning that display God's wisdom at work in the world. In the Christian tradition, this following of God's wisdom draws us into the world of Scripture, the traditions of interpretation, the exercise of reason and spiritual discernment, and an attentiveness to the remarkable diversity of people of the world—their sufferings, creativity, and hopes. The essays in this book remind me of the missional calling of theological education, the priority of the search for wisdom, and the inherently contested nature of the theological task.

Reading these essays has been a great delight, and it is an honor to have been asked to write this foreword. My own sojourn as an Anglican at UTC, as both a lecturer in theology and evangelism (1991–1997) and vice principal (1996–1997), was a rich and fruitful time. It was such a privilege to work with colleagues from many denominations and students from many cultures, a number of whom are contributors to this book. The essays are testimony to the remarkable developments at UTC over the past quarter century: new strategic alignments, an enriched focus on multicultural ministry, a scholarly practical wisdom, deeper foundations in the life of the church, and a compassionate focus on the needs of wider society. Celebrating half a century of such engagements at UTC is one thing. Contemplating the next quarter century is quite another. I am left with questions: How will the church, and therefore places of theological education like UTC, respond to AI and its impact on critical thinking, assessment, and formation in wisdom? How will new resources be generated? What new possibilities will arise for being the church in an uncertain and fragmented society? Will theological education straddle the tension between kairos time, the time that remains for fresh initiatives, and kronos time, with its focus on securing imagined futures? Can theological education be a positive and welcome power in the worshiping and political life of the ecclesia of God? In short, how might UTC undertake a humble yet persistent prophetic task regarding the things that matter?

Rt Rev. Professor Stephen Pickard
Charles Sturt University
Canberra

Contributors

Seforosa Carroll is an Australian Fiji-born Rotuman theologian. She is an interdisciplinary theologian whose research falls into the categories of public, contextual, and practical theologies. Seforosa is currently academic dean and lecturer in cross cultural ministry and theology at the United Theological College (UTC). Seforosa has served in several placements within the UCA as well as with the World Council of Churches in Geneva.

Ross Chambers is an emeritus professor at Charles Sturt University where he was dean of the Faculty of Arts, 1991–2001, then deputy vice-chancellor (academic), 2002–2012. In these roles he was closely involved in the establishment of the School of Theology at the university and in its subsequent operation. Since retirement from the university, he has served as chair of the Council of UTC and as a member of the Uniting Mission and Education board of the NSW (New South Wales) and ACT (Australian Capital Territory) Synod of the Uniting Church. He has been a member of the Uniting Church since the Union and is currently a member of the Port Macquarie congregation where, at present, he is the chair of the church council.

Carolyn Craig-Emilsen is an interviewer and oral historian. She worked for ABC Radio in the mid-1970s and later as a freelance interviewer and documentary producer. Between 1978 and 1994 Carolyn was employed by Macquarie University as a manuscript editor on the *Macquarie Dictionary*, as a founding producer of Sydney Educational Radio (2SER-FM), and as a lecturer in Mass Communication. From 1994 to 1996 she was the director of communications for the National Assembly of the UCA. Carolyn taught critical thinking/reasoning and was the study skills tutor at United Theological College from 2004 to 2013.

Patricia Curthoys works as a professional historian, primarily on Australian history projects. She has worked for academics, state and local government, and other cultural institutions as well as nongovernment organizations. She is an associate of the Centre for Applied History at Macquarie University. Patricia was the 2023 Australian Religious History fellow at the State Library of New South Wales, working on a project on religion, race, and gender in mid-nineteenth-century New South Wales.

William W. Emilsen taught church history and world religions at United Theological College for twenty-two years and was an associate professor in the School of Theology at Charles Sturt University until his retirement in 2014. His recent publications include the biography *Charles Harris: A Struggle for Justice* (2019) and the edited collections *Sacred Ways and Places in the Blue Mountains* (2019), *Growing Up Uniting* (2021), and *Eugene Stockton: Blue Mountains Hermit* (2023). His research interests include Aboriginal history, the life and thought of Mahatma Gandhi, the history and culture of the Blue Mountains region, and the history of the Uniting Church in Australia. William is an ordained minister of the Uniting Church and is a member of the Leura Uniting Church in the Blue Mountains.

Nicole Fleming is the dean of candidates at United Theological College, Sydney. Nicole is enthusiastic about encouraging candidates for ordained ministry to integrate academic learning with ministry practice. She studied theology at Charles Sturt University, social development at the University of New South Wales, and leadership at the University of Divinity (Melbourne). Nicole is an ordained minister of the Uniting Church in Australia.

Mark Hillis is an ordained Uniting Church minister. He has served with the Synod of NSW and ACT and the National Assembly in educational leadership roles plus a number of pastoral ministry placements. He was the sessional lecturer in Christian education at United Theological College and an academic associate at Charles Sturt University from 2006 to 2020. In Mark's student days he was the first elected Senior Student of the United Theological College.

Rebecca Lindsay lives with her family on Gadigal and Bidjigal land in Sydney's southeast. She teaches Hebrew Bible / Old Testament at United Theological College, part of the Charles Sturt University School of Theology. This is also the place where she began her formal theological education, inside classrooms and outside of them on green chairs. Rebecca's research explores the entanglements of settler colonialism and biblical interpretation in the lands now called Australia.

Ben Myers is professor of theology and literature at Alphacrucis University College. His publications include *Milton's Theology of Freedom*; *Christ the Stranger: The Theology of Rowan Williams*; *The Apostles' Creed: A Guide to the Ancient Catechism*; and numerous journal articles on theology and literature. He taught systematic theology at UTC for nearly a decade (2009–2017) and, before that, served as a research fellow at the University of Queensland. He is an adjunct of the Centre for Religion, Ethics, and Society at Charles Sturt University and has had international appointments as a member-in-residence at the Center of Theological Inquiry in Princeton and as a visiting fellow at the Forschungszentrum Internationale und Interdisziplinäre Theologie at Heidelberg University.

Myung Hwa Park is the minister of the Leura Uniting Church. Myung Hwa graduated from Ewha Womans University in Korea and spent three years in Pakistan as a missionary before she came to Australia. In 1990, she became the first Korean woman minister ordained in the Uniting Church in Australia. She has ministered to Tongan, Aboriginal, and English-speaking congregations and was the first Culturally and Linguistically Diverse (CALD) woman to serve as moderator for the Synod of NSW and ACT. Myung Hwa is a leader in the Korean National Conference and has a special interest in ecospirituality.

Clive Pearson is a former principal of United Theological College and head of the School of Theology at Charles Sturt University. He has published extensively in the fields of cross-cultural and diasporic theologies, the theology of climate change, and various expressions of public theology. From 2017 through to the end of 2023, he was the editor in chief of the *International Journal of Public Theology*. The particular areas of doctrine around which his work has been focused are theologies of providence, theodicy, sin, Christology, and ecclesiology.

John T. Squires is an ordained Minister of the Word in the Uniting Church in Australia. John was senior lecturer in biblical studies (1990–2010) and vice-principal at UTC in Sydney (2006–2010), director of education and formation and principal of Perth Theological Hall in Western Australia (2017–2018), and in presbytery minister roles in the Mid North Coast (2011–2016) and Canberra region (2019–2022). He is currently the editor of *With Love to the World* and blogs regularly on *An Informed Faith*. He lives at Dungog in the Hunter Valley, north of Newcastle, NSW.

Peter Walker is the principal of United Theological College, Sydney. He studied history and theology at the University of New South Wales, McGill University, and Charles Sturt University. Peter teaches Christology and Christian theology of religions and has a research interest in Christian-Muslim relations and theologies of religious diversity. Peter is an ordained minister of the Uniting Church in Australia.

Introduction

IN 2000 GEOFFREY BARNES published a fine history of United Theological College in Sydney titled *Doing Theology in Sydney: A History of United Theological College, 1974–1999*. This book makes no attempt to revise Barnes's history. *Things that Matter* is a collection of essays on theological education at United Theological College (UTC) for the years 1999 to 2024. The essays are written in a variety of styles. Some are reflections, almost intimate and personal. Others verge on the biographical or draw heavily on interviews and surveys, thus allowing the voices of former and present students and faculty to be heard. Most, however, are thematic rather than strictly historical, though nearly all of them are consciously written against a background of flux in theological education in Australia and, particularly so, within the Uniting Church.

The editors, together with Principal Peter Walker, have tried to make wise choices about what should be included in this volume, about what is important and what is less so. Readers will undoubtedly discern omissions, but the ten topics selected here, we believe, have been of central importance to the college's existence, evolution, and influence over the past quarter century. Some of the topics are perennial like teaching, formation for ministry, library services and resources, research, and publications. Others are more distinctive of the period. For example, out of the many factors that might have been chosen, few would disagree that the educational conjuncture of the college with Charles Sturt University (CSU), discussed by former Deputy Vice-Chancellor (Academic) Professor Ross Chambers in the opening chapter, has probably had the most significant impact. Apart from the resources that have come from the university to the college, CSU has had a profound influence: enlivening the college, strengthening the educational experience of students, fostering talented research students, and creating confident lay and ordained leaders willing to engage with the realities of secular society. The college's entry into the university was the realization of a long-held dream for many of the founders of the college. As far back as the mid-1960s, linking with a university was seen by the first and longest-serving chairperson of the UTC Council, Professor James Tulip, as "the doorway to the future." He told an ecumenical conference of theological educators at that time that it had "enormous potential for greatness," and the church that responded positively to "the pulse of life" among its students would be blessed like the two obedient servants in the parable of the talents (Matt 25:14–30).[1]

A second example of a distinctive topic arising out of the period under review is the manner in which the college has successfully embodied learning in a multicultural community. The standard story of what is happening in our church is that it is becoming more diverse. Certainly this diversity has been true of the student body at UTC for most of the past twenty-five years. Though not without its challenges, the coming together of people to study from different cultures and across all sorts of boundaries has been a powerful unifying force at the college. The UTC community treasures learning from each other's culture and supporting one another, as so beautifully depicted in Rebecca Lindsay's chapter, "Community of the Heart." UTC's inner dynamic has little to do with programs or policies or assembly statements. It has more to do with creating a place where, in the words of the closing paragraph to Carroll and Craig-Emilsen's chapter, the "community has embraced the intersections between learning, culture, and faith and has worked consistently at sustaining an ethos which has encouraged deep spiritual growth and lifelong learning."

The contributors to this volume have had a long connection with UTC. Together they bring a comprehensive and critical insider's perspective on the college's history, going back to its foundation and right up to the present. Eight of them did their primary theological education for ordination at UTC, including Peter Walker, the present principal, and Mark Hillis, who was Senior Student when the college began and who was also given the honor of leading the Prayers of the People at the inaugural ceremony. Four of the contributors were former members of the faculty, including a former principal, Clive Pearson, and two others, Emilsen and Squires, who each taught at UTC for more than twenty years. Four of the current faculty and three sessional lecturers have also contributed. Finally, there is Ross Chambers, the long-serving chair of the UTC Council, and coeditor Patricia Curthoys, both historians who joined in the contributors' web of obligation to remember the College's past. Whether full-time or part-time, retired

---

1. James G. Tulip, "Theological and Tertiary Education in Australia," *Tulip Papers* 49.27 (1966). The Tulip Papers are in the possession of Tulip's son, William Tulip.

or moved on to a new placement within the church or a new position in another institution, all of the contributors to this volume have retained an active interest and deep affection for the college.

Too often history is written as obituary, sweet words said over the deceased. This is not the case in *Things That Matter*. The contributors to this volume write "with heart and mind" (to borrow the title of John Squires's chapter), and they do so out of the passionate belief that their subject *really does matter*—for theological education of course, but more than that. It matters for the Uniting Church and its place and influence in society. They are deeply concerned about memory loss and the tendency to privilege, indeed flatter, the present. Professor Bruce Mansfield, who wrote the foreword to Barnes's *Doing Theology in Sydney*, reminded his readers that "self-scrutiny" is the main aim of institutions that commission written histories at important anniversaries.[2] Self-scrutiny, like all spiritual matters, requires honesty, courage, and digging through the nitty-gritty realities of the past. While *Things That Matter* seeks to avoid the triumphalist temptation to eulogize the past, it nonetheless has been written in the hope of encouraging people to look at the college's history anew, expecting to be surprised and, just maybe, to reflect on what has happened.

In celebrating UTC's fiftieth anniversary with *Things That Matter*, we are mindful of what Margaret Bendroth calls the "great conversation" that has taken place before us.[3] *Things That Matter* builds on and, hopefully, enriches that conversation. Ultimately, however, the Christian tradition is a long conversation about the declaration that "Jesus is Lord," one in which the college has been a lively and creative participant now for fifty years.

---

2. Bruce E. Mansfield, foreword to *Doing Theology in Sydney: A History of United Theological College, 1974–1999*, by Geoffrey Barnes (Adelaide, SA: Openbook, 2000), 3.

3. Margaret Bendroth, *The Spiritual Practice of Remembering* (Grand Rapids: Eerdmans, 2013), 93–95.

1

UTC at the Intersection of Church and University

Ross Chambers

In 1999 United Theological College (UTC) became a participant in the School of Theology at Charles Sturt University (CSU).[1] Its participation was initially for the purpose of offering fourth-year honors degrees, postgraduate programs, and higher degrees such as the PhD. Participation also had the purpose of increasing support for research through accessing university research services and funding. In November 2006 participation was extended to undergraduate programs in a further agreement. As a result, UTC withdrew from the Sydney College of Divinity. Since that time all academic awards at UTC have been awards of CSU and the academic activities of UTC have been undertaken under the standards, quality assurance, accreditation, and other academic governance arrangements of the university, an

1. Much of the detail in this paper is based on the author's knowledge of, and access to, internal Charles Sturt University data. In addition it refers to the Deed of Agreement (in several iterations) and deliberations of the Uniting Mission and Education Board and College Council and CSU bodies, which are not captured in the bare resolutions. It also has some element of the reflections of a participant in much of what has been described. The author wrote a major report on the School of Theology commissioned by the university in 2015. It is an internal document, although shared with the heads of colleges. Professor Chambers was also the original author of all the early iterations of the deed and oversaw the discussions behind these, including those behind the 2006 deed. —Eds.

Australian public university established by an act of Parliament in 1989. From that time the academic programs of UTC were no longer those of a private higher education provider but those of a public university established within the Australian university system. In the Australian context, where theological education and formation for ordination had been based in nonuniversity colleges, the NSW (New South Wales) Synod of the UCA (Uniting Church of Australia) had come to require university theological education to meet the academic requirements for ordination and had done so in collaboration with not a private, faith-based university but a public university.

CSU had taken the decision to include theology within its course profile soon after its establishment. The decision was made against a background of changes in the Australian university system, in community attitudes, and in some theological colleges and churches, which made the inclusion of theology in a university's profile both possible and more desirable. One important factor was that in some colleges, including UTC, the culture and values underpinning teaching and scholarship in the academic component of formation had come to align with those of universities. Free inquiry and the expectations that there would be a link between teaching and research and that teaching would be based in current scholarship formed part of their ethos. Admission, assessment, and graduation requirements for the academic programs were based on academic considerations alone (rather than the expectation that students' views would be consistent with those of the denomination). Collegial, peer-reviewed processes for assessment, curriculum development, and quality assurance were well established. Faculty in these colleges were expected to hold doctoral qualifications. Many, in fact, had undertaken their doctoral research in leading international universities. The sectarianism which had characterized much of theological education throughout European-Australian history, and which had been a (possibly *the*) major factor in inhibiting the establishment of faculties of theology in Australian universities, had declined in these colleges where curriculum was intentionally ecumenical and where faculty were often drawn from a variety of denominational backgrounds. These developments had made links with such colleges attractive to universities, especially in research and doctoral programs. Links at the undergraduate level were less common.

A further very important factor was that, notwithstanding a decline in church attendances and the history of secularism in Australian public life, religion in the late twentieth and early twenty-first century seemed to have increasing salience. Faith-based organizations, especially the major churches, were providing a very high proportion of social services and an increasing proportion of children were being educated in faith-based schools. The growing diversity of the Australian population meant that the implications of a multifaith society had become a feature of public discourse. Universities with faculties of education or social work and related disciplines were recognizing the need to engage with faith-based organizations, including those where many of their graduates would find employment. Some had come to see preparing students for life in a multifaith society as important. This period saw the development of multifaith chaplaincies at several universities. In this context, then, a link with the best scholarship in the religious traditions of society was attractive. Importantly, and related to the developments outlined above, there was growing demand for theological education from people who were not seeking ordination. This included not only lay members of denominations and those working in faith-based schools and human services, but also people from the more general population. Already by the nineties, at some colleges, such students well outnumbered ordinands. Levels of enrollment seemed likely to be sustainable.

The factors set out above were very much at work in the decision by CSU to include theology in its course and discipline profile. Later, they also led the university to establish a school of Islamic Studies. For a newer university, which had been created from Colleges of Advanced Education, whose profile was focused on professional education, theology was highly relevant to its large education and social work faculties. It was also, however, a way of bringing into the university well-established traditions of humanities scholarship. The School of Theology when created had, for instance, the highest proportion of staff with PhDs of any school at CSU. As will be seen below, the school for many years also had the highest number of research publications per staff member of any school.

Two other factors were important in the creation of the school. The first was that CSU, given its history and discipline profile, was welcoming of the professional aspects of theological education. The Canberra-based, Anglican theological college, St. Mark's, which became the first college to join the school, had held discussions with the ANU (Australian National University) and the University of Canberra about possible links. These universities were interested only in what were regarded as the properly "academic" disciplines within theology, not in the more professional, formation-oriented teaching.

A second important factor was that CSU was successful in approaching the Commonwealth for approval to apply Commonwealth funding to undergraduate theological studies. Approval was given on the basis that the offering of theology would not be subject to any faith test, wording consistent with the Australian Constitution and meaning that admission, assessment, and graduation requirements should be academic only. This approval meant that CSU became the first Australian university to be able to apply the full range of university funding to theology and related disciplines. A student at CSU in theology could undertake their studies on the same funding basis as a student in any other discipline.

An additional factor in the development of the School of Theology at CSU was the university's comfort and experience with multiple campus locations. The university was based in several regional campuses as well as in Manly, Sydney, and had well-developed systems for operating across campuses. It was happy to take on additional campus locations, such as UTC at North Parramatta.

Interest at UTC and the NSW Synod in joining the School of Theology at CSU, which had been established in 1995 through an agreement with St. Mark's National Theological Centre in Canberra, was the result of several factors. Awareness of the arrangements in the agreement with St. Mark's was an immediate factor. More broadly, interest reflected the commitment in the Uniting Church, expressed in its *Basis of Union*, to the "ministry of scholarship."[2] This had supported the maturing of UTC as an academic institution with a commitment to scholarly values and a university ethos, particularly one that valued the link between teaching and research, which would provide opportunities for research degrees and which offered its academic programs on the basis that there would be "no faith test" in admission, assessment, or eligibility for graduation. There was a view that the college was already working at university level and that it was appropriate that this be recognized. More broadly, there was a view that theology could and should take its place within the discourses of contemporary society as these developed in the modern, public university. It was important not only that theology contribute to these but also that it listen to and engage in dialogue with other disciplines and ideas. The experience of some leaders within the college helped shape these views. The chair of the College Council at this time, Professor Bruce Mansfield, was at the same time the deputy chancellor of CSU and had been the deputy vice-chancellor of Macquarie University. Another influential member of the council, Professor Jim Tulip, was a member of the Department of English at the University of Sydney.

More pragmatic factors were also at play. Participation in the School of Theology would give access to university funding and to university services such as student support, marketing, IT infrastructure, student administration systems, and staff development programs. Under the agreement that established the School of Theology, participating colleges received the share of funding for student enrollments that, under the university's funding

---

2. Uniting Church in Australia, *Basis of Union*, para. 11.

formula, went to schools of the university. They also received funding for library services and had access to infrastructure funding, research funding, and teaching development funding on the same basis as other schools of the university. All this was expected to have a significant benefit for resourcing the college and in reducing the costs to the synod of the college. It should be noted, however, that it was understood that some (albeit significantly reduced) synod funding would still be required for the college to operate effectively and in support of synod needs and expectations of the college.

An important issue in relation to funding was that acceptance of Commonwealth funding would be linked to a fundamental and, for some, controversial change in financial support for those in formation for ministry. Under the new arrangements the ordinands, not the synod, would become individually responsible for student fees, in particular the Higher Education Contribution Scheme (HECS), which students receiving a Commonwealth Supported Place (CSP) were expected to make. HECS was not an up-front fee paid at enrollment but a debt to the Commonwealth that would be repaid through the taxation system once the student's, or former student's, income reached a threshold. A self-funding element would be introduced to the formation process.

Further pragmatic considerations were the transaction costs and processes involved in gaining and maintaining accreditation as a nonuniversity higher education provider. These were substantial and recurring, involving a NSW government agency, the Higher Education Board (HEB). Each award required HEB accreditation and reaccreditation on a regular basis. Universities, on the other hand, were "self-accrediting" institutions. They were responsible for accrediting academic programs and awards through their academic boards (members of which were drawn from within the university), for determining their course and discipline profiles, and for maintaining standards and systems of quality assurance. Processes for approval, accreditation, and monitoring were simpler and much less costly.

Finally, and perhaps most importantly, the synod, when discussing the decision to participate in the School of Theology, conceived such participation as a form of mission and public engagement. Participation would be a step into the public sphere given the importance of universities in modern societies, into dialogue with contemporary culture, and into a space where increasing numbers of younger people might be met. (By the late nineties over twenty-five percent of school-leavers were attending university.)

THE DEED OF AGREEMENT

The School of Theology at CSU was established within the university under a Deed of Agreement between the university and St. Mark's National Theological Centre in Canberra, a theological college within the Anglican Diocese of Canberra and Goulburn. The deed provided for other parties (particularly other theological colleges) to join the school subject to the agreement of the parties to the deed. UTC joined the school through this provision. The deed did not have a fixed term. It envisaged an ongoing relationship, although there were provisions for parties to withdraw from the agreement. The deed provided for periodic review of its terms. Under this provision St. Mark's, UTC, and CSU have renewed the Deed of Agreement with minor revisions in 2013 and 2020.

Two commitments lay at the heart of the deed: a shared vision of a university-based, ecumenical school of theology supporting broad access to theological education; and recognition of the needs and requirements both of the faith community served by the relevant college and of the university.

The development of the deed was shaped by consideration of the ongoing status of the participating colleges. In discussions leading to the deed, it became a shared view that it was important that a college should retain its identity and its connection to its faith community. The alternative, that the college would become part of the university, was quickly ruled out. There were several reasons for this. It was agreed that, in some important respects at least, theology was an expression of, or was needed to develop in dialogue with, the life of a community of faith and that an ongoing connection to the community was important. Full incorporation into a university had the potential to break this connection. It was also recognized that colleges had roles in their faith communities in addition to the provision of academic programs and scholarship. These, including preparation and assessment of potential candidates for ordination and contributions to the councils of the church, could not properly be exercised by a public university. More pragmatically, university funding would not and should not be used to support these roles. An ongoing financial commitment from the faith community would be necessary.

An issue at the heart of these discussions was the appointment and oversight of faculty. If appointed to, and employed directly by, a university, it would not be possible to include considerations of faith in the appointment. This would need to be on the grounds of academic suitability alone. The resolution of these discussions formed the basis of the deed. Faculty would be appointed to colleges by the relevant denomination. Those faculty who were appropriately qualified in terms of CSU position qualifications and standards would then be approved by the university as academics in the School of Theology and, while "not being employees of CSU," would "have the status and privileges of academic staff of Charles Sturt University and be subject to the responsibilities and accountabilities of academic staff."[3] The current version of the deed (2020) has tightened this process to require the colleges to include the university in selection processes for faculty who are intended to contribute to the School of Theology.

In essence, under the deed the parties agreed to establish a School of Theology within Charles Sturt University. The school would offer university award programs, including research degrees, and undertake scholarly and research activities. Participating colleges would contribute appropriately qualified staff, infrastructure in the form of teaching spaces and academic offices, and IT. The libraries of the colleges would also support the teaching and research of the school. The university would provide funding to the school for teaching and research on the same basis as other schools of the university, together with a loading to recognize the infrastructure, IT, and library contributions. The school would compete for research, infrastructure, and development funds on the same basis as other schools. It would be supported by the university's staff development programs, student administration and student support systems, library, IT, marketing, and communication systems.

As a school of the university, the School of Theology would have the same governance arrangements as all schools. There would be a head of school appointed by the university from the staff of the school, a school board and assessment committee, and a theology courses committee. These would all be responsible to a faculty of the university that was in turn responsible to the academic board. Staff of the school would be eligible to serve on university, faculty, and school boards and committees on the same basis as other academic staff. The school would be subject to the university's academic regulations, codes of conduct for staff, and quality assurance processes. Academic staff of the school would be subject to the same performance requirements as other academic staff. Important examples of the latter included requirements in relation to research outcomes and in relation to teaching development. Staff of the school would be expected to complete CSU's teaching induction programs and other required learning and teaching development programs.

An interesting feature of the deed is that the treatment of the libraries at UTC and St. Mark's differs. The library at St. Mark's is integrated into the CSU library services system. It uses the CSU cataloging system, the CSU

---

3. Chambers, "Deed of Agreement," appendix A, §8.8, §3.6.

online serials and e-books system, and the CSU borrowing system. It receives operational funding from CSU. The NSW Synod chose to keep the Camden Theological Library housed with UTC as a synod library separate from the CSU system, thus foregoing resources available to St. Mark's library. The Camden library is available to support staff and students of UTC and the School of Theology, and these can also access the CSU library, including that of St. Mark's. The library maintains separate systems and its own collection, including serials. Behind this decision was the preference of the synod to maintain the Camden Library as a resource for all church members. Where a library became part of the CSU system, access to some resources, especially online serials and e-books, would be restricted by licensing arrangements to staff and students of the university. A further distinctive feature of the deed regarding libraries was that, in recognition of the use made of the Camden library by the School of Theology, the university made annual special purpose grants to it. These grants formed the basis for the development of the important Korean theological collection within the library. Such grants recognized the presence of significant numbers of Korean students at UTC, the strong Korean presence in the NSW Synod, and the links which developed between the school and theological faculties in Korean universities. In more recent versions of the deed, a contribution to the libraries at both St. Mark's and UTC has been included in their university funding.

Under the deed, the synod was required to provide infrastructure for the work of the school (offices, teaching spaces, library, and some IT) and appropriately qualified academic staff. The synod directly, and its educational bodies such as the Ministerial Education Board (MEB), were not represented in any of the academic governance processes and committees established under the deed. These operated within the university and only involved accredited academic staff. As a result, the role of the synod in the academic programs involved informal influence and links only. At the same time, the MEB was responsible for assuring the church that the academic programs would meet the requirements for formation for ministry and, where appropriate, for continuing professional development and lay education. This situation would require effective communication between synod bodies and their staff and the faculty of UTC, especially senior faculty such as the college principal.

Under the deed, the synod as the employer of staff appointed to the school was also ultimately responsible for the performance and conduct of these staff. The deed provided that staff appointed to the school would be subject to the performance expectations of academic staff of the university and the university's code of conduct. Where there were concerns with regard to these, the university was to draw this to the attention of the synod for appropriate action. The university also had the right to withdraw accreditation of staff. The deed thus established a potentially complex system of supervision and performance review for staff. An additional factor in this context was that faculty of the college had duties unrelated to their university duties, including contributing to synod-based education and formation programs. Finally, where faculty were ordained ministers of the UCA, they were subject to the church's arrangements for oversight of ministers, including the process known as "Vital Ministry." As in the case of aligning academic processes and synod expectations, the college principal would be at the intersection of university and synod expectations in the management of performance and the allocation of duties.

TEACHING AND LEARNING

The School of Theology has consistently performed very well on CSU's measures of teaching quality. It returns the best scores within the university in surveys of students' satisfaction with teaching and learning. This is perhaps not surprising in that the school has been able to retain good staff-student ratios when these have been deteriorating in other disciplines and in the university system generally as an outcome of declining Commonwealth funding per student. At UTC, faculty staffing costs have not relied solely on university funds. These are supplemented by synod contributions. Again, in contrast to the university system generally where high levels of casual staffing have developed in response to funding pressures, the school has not had to rely on casual staffing for teaching. Students at UTC are taught in small groups by highly qualified academics and have ready access to staff outside class sessions. The college has been intentional and successful in building a sense of shared community amongst students and staff, thanks in part to the activities of an active Students Association. A strong cohort effect, another important factor in student engagement and satisfaction, has been a result. The only CSU quality measure where the school has struggled sometimes is the ratio of course units to academic staff. This has often exceeded the ideal of two units per staff member per session, a reflection of the relatively low numbers of faculty and students in comparison with other disciplines and the range of units which need to be offered.

Distance Education and Off-Campus Study

The desire of St. Mark's to make theological education available through off-campus study (generally referred to in the 1990s as "distance education") was an important factor in the development of the agreement to form the school. CSU was Australia's largest distance education provider with well-developed systems and expertise to support off-campus teaching and off-campus students. Distance education was offered by the school from its beginnings both at the undergraduate and postgraduate levels. It came to form a significant element in St. Mark's student enrollments. The Deed of Agreement of 1999, under which UTC initially joined the School of Theology, gave access for UTC to distance education for postgraduate programs. These became an important part of the offerings of the college, including opening new ways to support the continuing professional development of ministers. It also made possible participation in offering programs at graduate diploma and master's level for graduates from other disciplines (often referred to as "entry-level postgraduate programs").

The revision of the deed in 2006, under which UTC came to participate in undergraduate programs of the school, allowed St. Mark's to continue as the principal provider of distance education offerings at the undergraduate level. This recognized the importance to St. Mark's of its distance education student load as well as the investment it had made in developing learning materials for off-campus study. This revision did permit UTC to use distance education for specific Uniting Church purposes. These provisions have been retained in subsequent revisions of the deed. This approach had significant implications for UTC. It was unable to engage with demand in the broader community for theological study by distance education. In addition, Uniting Church members interested in study by distance often came to view the school's distance programs as "too Anglican."

Recently, however, new modes of teaching have gone some way toward addressing access to UTC programs for those unable to study on the UTC campus in person over a teaching semester. The college has used "intensives" where students gather for a short period (four to five days) to participate in lectures and tutorials covering the full unit of study. They then complete assessment tasks and further reading from their off-campus locations over the remainder of the semester. Intensives have proven popular and effective. While mostly offered at the UTC campus, some have been offered in other locations, notably Port Macquarie where CSU has a campus and Canberra. Use is now also being made of Zoom and similar technologies to allow a student to access a form of face-to-face teaching. Experiments with this approach had begun before the COVID pandemic, but the use of this format was greatly accelerated during the years of restricted on-campus access. UTC programs can now be accessed through lectures and tutorials offered over Zoom. This has improved access for regional communities and has supported the development of programs of "regional formation," which allow candidates for ordination to undertake formation within regional settings rather than being required to attend the UTC campus as full-time students. This approach to teaching has also reinvigorated postgraduate programs and single-unit offerings. These developments have been accompanied by the strengthening of library and other student support services for off-campus students, including some outstanding work in the library to create online databases and access to e-books and serials.

Curriculum and Course Profile

The decision in 1999 that UTC participate in the School of Theology gave the college access to teaching at postgraduate level, including by distance education, to research higher degrees (RHDs), including the PhD, and to offering a fourth-year honors program. The last represented a new element in Australian theological education where previously classes of honors had been awarded on the basis of performance in the three-year bachelor of theology. The fourth-year honors program in Australian universities is an extension of a three-year program which provides research training involving advanced course work and the preparation of a dissertation (usually fifteen thousand words). It is the major pathway to gaining a place in RHD programs. Graduates with Class 1 Honors are permitted to proceed directly to doctoral studies. Since 1999 the theology honors program has been very successful, indeed amongst the most successful honors programs at CSU. It has enabled students to add depth to their undergraduate studies, has stimulated interest in research, and has seen many students proceed to RHD programs.

Since 1999 UTC has offered, through the School of Theology, a suite of postgraduate programs of three types: programs of advanced study to master's level in theology (master of theology) for graduates in theology; programs in ministry to the master's level (master of ministry) for graduates in ministry and practical theology; and programs in theological studies (MA in theological studies) for graduates in other disciplines. Graduate Diploma and, in some cases, Graduate Certificate programs are articulated with the master's programs. These programs have supported UTC's contribution to continuing professional development for ministers and others working in the church. Following changes to the Uniting Church's standards for formation for ministry, which allowed more flexible pathways in formation taking account of candidates' prior learning, the graduate diploma and masters programs in theological studies have become a pathway to meeting the academic requirements of formation, alongside the bachelor of theology. Until recently the School of Theology also offered a doctor of ministry program, a doctorate by advanced coursework and dissertation. Such doctorates are well established in other professions and provide an opportunity for development of advanced professional practice. The doctor of ministry was discontinued in 2018 following a review of doctoral programs, partly because of low demand and partly as a result of a decision to concentrate resources for higher degree studies on research degrees.

The years since 2006 have seen significant changes to the structure and curriculum of the bachelor of theology. These provide a very good illustration of the interaction between the college, the wider UCA, and the university. Some changes have come about because of CSU degree requirements. All CSU undergraduate degrees are required to include studies of indigenous Australian history and culture, especially as these bear on professional formation. Likewise, all undergraduate degrees are to include professional ethics. One result of these requirements is that the bachelor of theology at UTC includes these elements as part of the formal award program. At other UCA colleges they are included in formation as part of the non-award program. The shape of the degree has also been influenced by revisions to the UCA's standards for formation for ministry introduced in 2018. The revised standards adopted a focus on outcomes (knowledge, skills, attitudes) rather than specifying the content of formation programs, including the academic component of these. This gave colleges greater flexibility in designing programs to support the acquisition of the standards. Included in the UCA's Standards is a requirement that students have the capacity to engage with the multifaith character of contemporary Australian society. UTC has, more than other UCA colleges, been able to include studies related to this in the bachelor of theology program thanks in part to collaboration with the Islamic Studies school at CSU, which is also located in Sydney.

The past two decades have seen a shift in the structure of the bachelor of theology. At the time the School of Theology was created, the degree had a structure similar to an arts degree, offering majors and minors in the theological subdisciplines and giving students flexibility to choose their majors. More recently the structure of the degree has come to resemble that of professional programs such as social work, in which choice has been restricted and a program of study, designed to support the acquisition of the outcomes set out in the UCA's Standards, is required. Completion of majors in the subdisciplines is no longer a focus. The degree has thus become a professional degree shaped by contemporary conceptions of ministry.

While the curriculum and degree structure changes outlined above may have strengthened alignment between the academic formation program and the church's vision for ministry, they have had other less positive consequences. The *Basis of Union* of the UCA includes a specific commitment to valuing the "ministry of scholarship."[4] One function of a theological college has been to prepare people to exercise this role. The strength of the PhD program at UTC is an important element in this. The changes to the bachelor's degree structure, however, have made the pathway to advanced study and preparation for the ministry of scholarship more difficult. The UCA's Standards still require "a mature knowledge of Christian tradition and the Biblical witness,"[5] but this has not been taken to mean either a requirement for a major in a subdiscipline or a requirement for biblical languages. (UTC is the only UCA college to have retained a language requirement, albeit a minimal one.) Students completing the bachelor program may not have the depth of study or, in the case of biblical studies, the languages required for honors and PhD study. Where a student wishes to pursue such a path, it is now necessary for the college to design an individual program within the framework of the degree.

Subdisciplines

The units that make up the bachelor of theology and the postgraduate programs remain grounded within the traditional subdisciplines: theology, especially systematics; pastoral and liturgical; biblical studies; and church history. All these continue to be represented within the faculty. There have, however, been significant changes in emphasis. Pastoral and liturgical studies are now located within a broader framework of "practical theology," which also includes elements of ecclesiology and ministry practice. The most recent appointments in theology have been linked to a specific focus: one in "preaching and theology," the other in cross-cultural theology. Perhaps surprisingly, given the commitment of the UCA to social justice and to practical ministry, ethics (or theological ethics) has not emerged as a distinct field. It has continued to be taught within systematic theology. Also perhaps surprisingly, given the strong emphasis on the contextualization of theology and the church, formal studies of the Australian context have not developed, although contextualization might be said to be a thread running

4. Uniting Church in Australia, *Basis of Union*, para. 11.
5. Uniting Church in Australia, *Standards*, §4.

through much of the program. A lectureship in mission was established at UTC in 2014 as a result of collaboration with the Alan Walker College of Evangelism.

STUDENTS AND DEMAND

Demand for the programs of the School of Theology has remained stable and sustainable within funding arrangements. It should be noted in this context that most students are not ordinands and that numbers of the latter have rarely exceeded ten commencing students a year. Students in the school are mature aged. Recent school-leavers are rare. The average age of cohorts at UTC in formation and at undergraduate level has consistently been around forty or more. Until recent changes in teaching practices, described above, nonmetropolitan students were not well represented at UTC. Enrollments at the college do, however, reflect the diversity of the Uniting Church in other respects, especially with regard to cultural and linguistic background. The Pasifika and Korean communities of the Uniting Church in NSW are strongly represented in the student body. In terms of gender, women have slightly outnumbered men.

The nature of the student cohort at UTC has made possible a significant enhancement to support for students' learning through the permanent placement of a learning and study skills officer. This position, established in 2011, is funded through CSU and has a focus on induction of new students and support for students whose first language is not English. The CSU funding, in turn, comes from Commonwealth funding given to universities for supporting the participation of students in university education who come from underrepresented or disadvantaged educational backgrounds.

In 2015 CSU arranged a review of the programs which was to consider the falloff in "market share" in theology. Across the higher education sector, demand for theology had grown, but CSU's share had fallen. The review identified some possible factors in this. Much of the demand seemed to be for programs that had a particular denominational or theological focus. The school's programs were intended to be ecumenical in character and based in a broad conception of the Christian tradition of scholarship and thought. At the same time, the failure to fully integrate units from UTC and those from St. Mark's in the distance offerings had weakened the ecumenical character of the distance program. The review also identified opportunities for strengthening enrollments, including international education, indigenous education, programs to support the education needs of the church-based social service providers, and subdegree pathway programs for lay education.

The opportunities have been pursued with limited success. In international education, the links with Korean theological faculties and universities, which developed in the first decade of the century in postgraduate studies with some success, have not continued. This was partly a result of changes in Korean government requirements but also an outcome of internal school and university factors. Likewise, the opportunities for students at UTC to include study-abroad and student-exchange programs with Korean Christian universities aligned with the UCA have not proved popular. The major international development for the School of Theology, following the recommendations, has been the participation of St. George's College, an Anglican college in Hong Kong, as a member of the school. As noted below, however, international research collaboration has been strong.

Indigenous education has not developed as hoped. This is especially noteworthy as CSU is recognized within the Australian university sector for its strengths in this. It was the first Australian university to have an enrollment of more than one thousand indigenous students, has well-developed support structures and pathways for those students, and strong engagement with its indigenous communities. UTC created a scholarship program for indigenous students and has supported small numbers over recent years. An ambitious proposal developed by indigenous Christian leaders to offer a masters program for indigenous communities, which combined theological studies with community development studies, was put to the school but failed to receive approval. It was eventually taken up by the University of Divinity.

Discussions with the faith-based human services sector, which is very large in Australia, and particularly with Uniting, the human services organization of the Synod of the UCA in NSW, have been pursued for many years. One positive outcome has been the development of programs to meet the needs of chaplains as part of the ministry programs. The vision of developing collaborative programs that would assist the staff of organizations such as Uniting to reflect theologically on their work has not been realized.

Behind the initiatives above and their relative lack of success lay some difficulties in the university sector and in the church during the past decade or so. During this time universities experienced growing financial pressures and a significant increase in external Commonwealth audit and compliance regimes, including with regard to international education. One outcome of this was greater caution in taking on initiatives and a tendency to look for savings and streamlining of programs and offerings.

These factors were also experienced within the church in the second decade of this century. The synod faced serious financial challenges, partly as a result of the Global Financial Crisis. Its response to these included a review of all activities and functions. This led to a prolonged period of uncertainty, including about the future of UTC and arrangements for theological education and the commitment of the synod to the ministry of scholarship. The College Council, which had a degree of autonomy in oversight of the college and representing the college to the synod and which included faculty and student members, was abolished. Its functions were taken over by the synod's Mission and Education Board or given to managers and directors as part of a move to adopt corporate structures within the synod. Faculty experienced these developments as a loss of agency and transparency and lack of clarity about synod expectations and future directions. For a period, the position of the principal was disestablished, and its role split between the executive director of Uniting Mission and Education and a member of faculty who was designated the academic dean, with responsibility for managing the college's participation in the university. As a result, faculty were no longer represented within the councils of the church. For some years, then, there was little encouragement for new initiatives, especially external or public-facing initiatives. The dominant discourse around the college and theological scholarship emphasized an instrumental role, preparing ministers and lay leaders, rather than the broader value of theological and biblical scholarship and the importance of public engagement.

A distinctive feature of UTC was that, unlike other UCA colleges and many other theological colleges including St. Mark's, it was not directly responsible for lay education and continuing professional education of ministers and other leaders. A structural separation of these responsibilities had long existed in the NSW Synod. The most recent structural review, in 2018, retained this arrangement, creating a Directorate of Vital Ministry, with responsibility for lay education and continuing professional education, alongside the college. This separation has, at times, seemed to be linked to a view that higher education programs and programs based in current theological scholarship are not relevant to lay people or ministers and leaders. This is a somewhat surprising view given the levels of lay enrollment in UTC courses and the fact that the Uniting Church has one of the highest proportions of members with higher education qualifications amongst the denominations. There has also been at times overt suspicion or disapproval of ministers undertaking postgraduate and doctoral programs in preference to what are seen as more immediately relevant short courses and workshops. The structural separation has also made more difficult the development of integrated "ladders of learning" where someone can progress from short courses and single-unit studies to undergraduate and postgraduate programs. Notwithstanding this historical and cultural background, the college has, especially in recent years, worked hard with colleagues in

Vital Ministry to have UTC offerings incorporated into lay education and continuing professional education programs and to encourage ladders of learning. Several factors have assisted this, including an increase in practical theology studies within the college, the development of Zoom classes, and greater flexibility within the CSU system to support the offering of short courses and certificate programs.

RESEARCH

One of the changes to the activities and ethos at UTC following the decision to participate in the School of Theology was that research and research training programs from bachelor of theology (honors) to PhD were established. These experienced strong demand and became a significant part of teaching loads at UTC. Many students came from within the UCA, and the programs contributed to the ministry of scholarship across a range of sub-disciplines. Biblical studies and applied theology were especially prominent in the topics pursued by students. Applied theology included dissertations aligned with evolving priorities of the UCA, especially ecotheology, gender, multicultural theology, and contextual theology. Another significant group of students were faculty from bible colleges and other theological colleges. Such faculty had previously needed to enroll in overseas institutions to undertake doctoral studies. The research higher degree programs have thus influenced Australian theological education more broadly. At its height in the years 2010 to 2014, the theology graduation ceremonies saw around ten PhDs awarded each year, and in one memorable case sixteen. Since that time numbers of doctoral candidates have declined to more modest levels. This is partly as a result of the increase in opportunities for doctoral study in theology within Australia and partly because of changes to Commonwealth policy, which have had the effect of restricting numbers of doctoral places.

The discipline of theology (which includes faculty of the School of Theology as well as members of the university's research centers in theology, some of whom are not members of the school) has consistently had one of the best research records within CSU in terms of number of publications. Despite other demands, especially from teaching and church activity as well as from the increasing audit and compliance processes of the contemporary university, faculty have maintained a commitment to scholarship, research, and publication. Research seminars, where faculty and research students present works in progress to their colleagues, have been a regular feature of the life of the college.

Research in theology has benefitted from the research policies of the university. Theology was one of the first fields of research to be identified for inclusion in a "designated research area." Such areas were supported by the establishment of a research center to which a director was appointed along with support staff, including a research manager, and special funding and priority access to PhD places were provided. The designated research centers were created with the purpose of building critical mass of staff and resources in areas of research excellence, especially those which were well aligned with the university's mission and in which the university might make distinctive contributions. Research centers were expected to foster multidisciplinary research around identified problems or foci. This meant that a center would not simply support a discipline or disciplines per se but would support an identified focus to which a discipline would contribute. Until 2022 the focus of the center based in theology was "public and contextual theology" with the center being known as PACT. While not all faculty were able to align their research with PACT, most could do so, including those in biblical studies. The primary multidisciplinary focus of PACT was Christian-Muslim dialogue and related issues of the place of religion in a modern multifaith society, involving faculty from the School of Islamic Studies at CSU as well as from theology. This aspect of PACT was particularly highly regarded within the university as distinctive to CSU, as the only Australian university with schools of both Christian theology and Islamic studies, and as addressing an important contemporary issue. Among other achievements PACT fostered the "scriptural reasoning" movement in Australia, bringing scholars from Christian and Muslim traditions together to share readings of Scriptures. PACT attracted funding from the Department of Foreign Affairs to support dialogue with Islamic scholars in Indonesia. PACT has also worked with a wide range of disciplines including ethics, social policy, economics, social services, philosophy, and law. PACT made, by invitation, a submission to the Ruddock inquiry into the need for religious freedom legislation.

Following a review of its research centers in 2022, CSU determined to continue to support a center which included theology and Islamic studies but to bring these together with applied and professional ethics, a field in which CSU was very strong and was highly rated in external reviews. As a result, PACT was disestablished, and the Centre for Religion, Ethics, and Society (CRES) came into being. While the focus of CRES may not be as relevant as that of PACT to some faculty and theological subdisciplines, interfaith dialogue, religion in multifaith societies, and the role of religion in the public sphere in a pluralistic society remain strongly supported, as does collaboration between theology and fields such as economics, social policy, and social philosophy. An intention of CRES is to bring theology into dialogue with contemporary ethical thought and its applications.

A factor in establishing CRES was concern with the ranking of theology in the external reviews of university research conducted by the Australian Research Council. Theology had not succeeded in achieving the rankings expected of it, and it was hoped that a link to a field—ethics, in which CSU was consistently highly ranked—might help address this. Research in theology at CSU has many indicators of high quality: books with prestigious university publishers; visiting fellowships at leading universities and invitations to speak at prestigious conferences; international recognition for staff by the major professional associations. On the other hand, there has not been success against key measures used in Australia. These include research income, research higher degree activity, publication ranking, especially journal ranking, and impact. Higher degree activity is strong in theology. Since the adoption in recent years of "impact" as a measure, theology has been able to identify significant impact through its contributions to interreligious dialogue and, to a lesser extent, public discourse. It can also point to some consultancy activity, especially with church-based human services organizations. Research income remains problematic for theology partly because there are usually few costs other than the time of faculty. Most importantly in the evaluation of research publications, which is based on a combination of ranking of journals and publishers, numerical measures of citation and impact, and peer review by ARC panels, theology has not fared well. This has been a major source of concern to the university and, even more so, to faculty. Several factors seem to have influenced this. Theology as a discipline in Australia has been slow to determine a robust system of ranking for journals and publishers. This is, in part, because so much of the discipline lies outside the university system. Peer evaluation has been undertaken by panels broadly based in religious studies and the sociology of religion whose members may not have experience with theology and its methodologies. Of special significance may be that faculty in theology recognize the importance of writing for a lay audience as well as a scholarly audience. Their publications thus include work that would not be highly ranked against scholarly criteria. CSU and senior staff in theology have been active in recent years in advocating the establishment of a separate theology panel as part of the research assessment process.

A very successful and lively characteristic of research in theology has been international collaboration. PACT was a founding member in 2002 of the Global Network for Public Theology (GNPT) along with Princeton, Stellenbosch, Edinburgh, Bielefeld, and Chester universities. The network now has more than twenty members. It publishes the *International Journal of Public Theology*, the editor of which is based in PACT. There has been strong collaboration with universities in South Korea, especially those with links to the UCA. The School of Theology has worked closely with the Pacific Theological College in Fiji and for many years provided accreditation for doctoral programs there. Finally, in more recent years, PACT has been a collaborator in a major research program based at the University of Heidelberg focused on dialogue between theology and other disciplines and professions.

AT THE INTERSECTION OF CHURCH AND UNIVERSITY

UTC's participation in the School of Theology and the life of the university did not mean that it ceased to participate in the life of the church, especially the Synod of NSW and ACT (Australian Capital Territory). The expectation of UTC itself and of the church was that participation in the School of Theology would enhance UTC's contribution to the life and mission of the church. UTC exists and functions at an intersection of church and university. Both the synod and the university, in endorsing UTC's participation in the School of Theology, had and continue to have expectations of UTC. The latter has responsibilities towards both. It is subject to governance and management of both church and university.

To what extent has the participation of UTC in the School of Theology been successful in meeting the expectations of synod, university, and the UTC community itself? How has participation in the School of Theology shaped UTC, its identity, mission, and activities? Has it been possible for it to meet the expectations of both the university and the synod?

Participation in the school might have had risks for the identity of UTC, notwithstanding the fact that the terms of the deed were intended to preserve the integrity of the participating colleges and their connection to their faith communities. UTC has, however, retained a distinct identity in the school. Reasons for this include the structures established by the deed, the ongoing demands on the college from the church, and the determination of St. Mark's to retain control of most distance education offerings. As will be argued below, in some ways UTC has strengthened its "Uniting Church" identity in recent years. At the same time, the academic programs of the college in teaching and research have clearly become university, as opposed to more broadly higher education, programs. Faculty work under the requirements and standards of the university and participate in the university's collegial and academic management programs fully.

A greater threat to the identity of the college in the years of participation in the School of Theology has, in fact, come from the synod. The disestablishment of the College Council, which had preserved a relatively autonomous role for the college within the synod, led to the college being positioned as part of Uniting Mission and Education (UME) and being overseen by the UME Board. For a time under these arrangements, the position of principal of the college was also disestablished, with duties shared between an academic dean (who managed the link with the university) and the executive director of UME. The principal had provided a college voice within the councils of the church. Since that time, however, the identity of the college within the church has strengthened, firstly as one of four divisions with UME, then, following the disestablishment of UME, as a direct report to the executive of the synod. As part of this process, the position of principal was reestablished. It is currently part of the executive management structure of the synod. The Ministerial Education Board has been established to provide oversight of the college and of the lay education and continuing professional education programs of Vital Ministry. Its principal responsibilities are to ensure that the college functions in compliance with the requirements of the UCA Assembly regarding formation for ministry and to ensure that the college meets the requirements of the deed. Alongside these developments, however, has been an ongoing discussion within the UCA nationally about the creation of a national theological college. It is still unclear what this would mean for the UTC and for its participation in the school. Currently the discussion is focused on a national network model.

Changing oversight and management arrangements within the synod have been linked to strengthening the alignment of the college with synod priorities and strategies. One result of this has been a significant change in the denominational affiliation of faculty. In 1999 the faculty was drawn from diverse denominational backgrounds. For some years now the faculty has been predominantly drawn from the Uniting Church. A further significant result has been that the role assigned to the college by synod has emphasized internal educational requirements, including formation. Synod has seemed in this context to be hesitant in endorsing an outward-facing public engagement mission for the college, in contrast to the hopes expressed in 1999. The changes over the years have also heightened the difference for faculty between the ethos of the university and that of the church. Within the university, faculty work within strong, collegial processes in which they contribute to decisions about teaching, curriculum, standards, and research. Within the church, faculty are overseen by management structures in which they have few formal opportunities for input. Collegial or conciliar boards have largely disappeared.

UTC and the school are highly regarded within the university. The quality of teaching and faculty, the levels of research and research higher degree activity and their international links, and the sustainability of student demand and the funding model all mean that UTC is meeting the expectations of CSU. The university continues to support a designated research center linked to theology and has embraced interreligious dialogue as a core contribution to Australian society. It is supporting attempts to improve the ranking of theology in ARC research assessments. Theology has established a firm place within the university's profile.

The church continues to provide significant funding to the college alongside university funding. Its expectations of UTC's participation in the school seem over time to have become more limited. The emphases on public engagement and on research capacity, which were prominent in the initial decision to participate, are less obvious now in internal church discourse. Likewise, discussion of pathways in formation that might be less academically demanding has arisen in recent years, and priorities for lay and continuing professional education have not emphasized formal university study. Participation in the school has allowed the synod and its college to provide high-quality, nationally accredited academic programs to support the academic requirements of formation and that access Commonwealth funding and draw on the university's systems and resources. It has also supported the recruitment of high-quality faculty attracted to working in a university as well as a church context. The college itself maintains a strong commitment to research, to public engagement, and to supporting the "ministry of scholarship," while at the same time aligning itself more closely with synod priorities.

FINAL REFLECTIONS

The Deed of Agreement succeeded in creating structural and cooperative arrangements that have preserved the identity of colleges participating in the School of Theology as institutions based in a faith community, while at the same time creating a school within the university that has been able to provide teaching and learning and research of a high quality. This has meant that theology at UTC has come to have a distinctive place and a distinctive ethos. Other arrangements between theological colleges and public universities in Australia have faltered in recent years. Theological colleges, including other UCA colleges, remain outside the public university system. Theology at UTC has taken a place within the discourse of contemporary intellectual and cultural life of a modern public university. It brings Christian thought and scholarship to the problems and agendas addressed in universities. It is in dialogue with the other disciplines and professions, learning and at times being challenged through this, but also contributing its own insights and perspectives.

Major elements in the Formation Standards of the UCA are that ministers will understand the Australian context in which they work, assist the church to speak to that context, and be able to bring faith effectively into the public sphere. UTC's participation in the School of Theology has brought faith and formation for ministry into lively engagement with contemporary Australia.

BIBLIOGRAPHY

Chambers, Ross. "Deed of Agreement." North Parramatta, NSW: United Theological College, 2020.
Uniting Church in Australia. *Basis of Union*. Sydney: Uniting Church in Australia, 1992.
———. *Standards for Theological Education and Formation: Phase 2 for Ordained Ministries*. Sydney: Uniting Church in Australia, 2016.

2

A Quarter Century of Systematic Theology

BEN MYERS

IN THIS CHAPTER I investigate the discipline of systematic theology as it was taught and practiced at United Theological College (UTC) for the first twenty-five years of this millennium. The account that follows will show that systematic theology at UTC has been marked by profound tensions during the past twenty-five years: between European theological traditions and a colonial context; between confessional identity and contextual specificity; between the constructive and the prophetic; and between learning a tradition and embodying that tradition in new ways. On top of that are theological tensions arising from the diverse student and faculty demographic at UTC: domestic and international, progressive and conservative, denominational and postdenominational, and so on. Such tensions are not resolvable and have not been fully resolved during the period under consideration here. They are tensions that reflect the complex culture of the wider church, and the wider Australian society, during this period. At their best, such tensions can be generative of new theological insights and new possibilities of Christian witness. At their worst, they can pose risks to Christian identity and can undermine the church's confidence in the gospel. Tensions of this kind have been particularly pronounced at UTC, perhaps more than at any other theological institution in Australia. The history of systematic theology at UTC during the past twenty-five years is, in many ways, a microcosm of larger changes in the church and the academy during this period.

The account that follows is structured around three successive scholars who held the responsibility for systematic theology at the college during the past quarter century: Clive Pearson, lecturer in systematic theology from 1997 to 2009; Ben Myers (the author of this chapter), lecturer in systematic theology from 2009 to 2017; and Michael Mawson, lecturer in systematic theology and ethics from 2019 to 2022. My analysis draws mainly on teaching documents from these three scholars, including subject outlines, assessments, lecture notes, and other learning materials.

Given my own personal involvement in the history narrated here, this chapter will inevitably reveal something of my own bias. My interpretation of the past twenty-five years at UTC is shaped by my own theological priorities and my own perception of the place of doctrine in the culture of a theological seminary. I make no apology for this. I am aware that this story might have been told quite differently if either Clive Pearson or Michael Mawson had written it. I can only add that I have tried to mitigate my bias by consulting both Pearson and Mawson and by soliciting their feedback on earlier versions of this chapter. I have also profited from the insights and perspectives of other former UTC colleagues and students.

My aim in this chapter is to tell the story of how systematic theology has been taught at UTC across the past twenty-five years while also posing the question of whether this discipline can still be regarded as one of the "things that matter" at UTC and in the wider culture of the Uniting Church.

CLIVE PEARSON (LECTURER IN THEOLOGY 1997–2009)

Before Clive Pearson's appointment to UTC, the role of lecturer in theology had been held for a decade (1986–1995) by Christiaan Mostert, partly overlapping with the role of lecturer in theology and evangelism held by Stephen Pickard (1990–1998). Mostert's doctoral dissertation was on Pannenberg, and his approach to theology was deeply shaped by European Protestant traditions. He was critical of the growing influence of contextual theology and pointed out that new theologies aspire to "trans-contextual" relevance even though they inevitably arise from specific contexts.[1] Pickard, for his part, was interested in the interface between theology and ministry practice, as well as the way theology is embedded institutionally. His approach represented a shift towards contextual engagement that mediated between

---

1. Mostert, "Non-Contextual Theology," 130–31.

Mostert's more traditional style and the kind of thoroughgoing contextualization for which UTC would later become known.

Clive Pearson came to UTC in 1997 after teaching theology at Knox College in the University of Otago. His Cambridge doctoral dissertation, supervised by Don Cupitt, was on the Anglican modernist churchman Henry Major. Pearson was intrigued by the way Major tried to balance tradition and modernity, as well as by his attempt to reformulate the faith for a secular society in the context of a new awareness of religious pluralism. Major had spent part of his life in New Zealand, and that local connection was clearly important to Pearson. In his theological work at UTC, he would become increasingly committed to elucidating the local context as an integral part of the theological task. Especially important to him were the contexts of migrant communities living in Sydney and Pacific communities whose island homelands were threatened by the impacts of climate change. In his research he tried to develop a distinctively Australian contextual theology, with an emphasis on locating Australia as one neighbor among others in the wider Asia-Pacific region. He was particularly interested in what he called the "hyphenated" or hybrid identities of migrant communities in Australia.[2] And he argued for a granular approach to local contextualization, even down to the level of what he sometimes called a "postcode theology."[3]

The doctrinal tradition was an important resource to Pearson, but only to the extent that it helped to facilitate such contextual thinking. In a journal article published in 2007, he took his UTC predecessor Gordon Dicker to task for representing Reformed doctrine as a timeless "heritage" of "riches" that ought to be preserved, appreciated with gratitude, and handed on. In contrast, Pearson argued that the doctrinal tradition ought to be understood as a sensibility, "an open system of dispositions" that makes possible a critical engagement with the issues of our day.[4]

Notwithstanding his dissatisfaction with a "heritage" view of doctrine, Pearson's teaching at UTC combined traditional doctrinal material with new critical questions about culture, gender, and politics. The first core subject in the systematic theology curriculum, titled Critical Theology, exemplified this synthesis of old and new. The first six weeks laid the foundations for understanding the discipline of systematic theology. After that, the weekly topics became more contemporary and contextual, including a class on "The Context of our God Talk." The reading list featured the kinds

---

2. See for example Pearson and Havea, *Faith in a Hyphen*; and Pearson, "Telling Tales."

3. See Burns and Pearson, *Home and Away*.

4. Pearson, "How Shy." His criticisms are directed at Dicker's 2003 article, "Reformed Heritage."

of assigned texts that would be expected in any majority-world theological seminary. Here and there, non-Western voices appeared too: notably a journal article by UTC colleague Jione Havea, an autobiographical essay by Vietnamese American theologian Peter Phan, and several publications by Uniting Church scholars. If any voice in the reading list was privileged, it was the Canadian theologian Douglas John Hall. He was a disciple of Paul Tillich whose contextual approach to systematic theology had a large influence on Pearson's own thinking. Students sampled several works by Hall, mostly from *The Cross in Our Context* and from his autobiography *Bound and Free: A Theologian's Journey*. The first assessment task was to write a short paper discussing Hall's view of why the church needs theology. Pearson also provided a weekly worksheet to give students more options to consider on each topic and to help them contextualize what they were learning in the class. The worksheets provided a host of additional recommended readings with questions for reflection including:

- How is the word "theology" understood in your local church or culture?
- Why does Jung Young Lee argue that all theology is autobiographical?
- How does Seforosa Carroll organise her theology around metaphors of weaving and hospitality?
- How helpful has the Christian tradition been for the construction of an ecological theology?

The second core subject in the systematics curriculum was Christ and Creation. Pearson's approach to the design of this subject was similar to his approach in Critical Theology. The topics and readings were largely oriented around traditional topics. The subject aimed to lay foundations for understanding the doctrinal tradition, while also encouraging students to take some steps in a contextualizing direction. As the name suggests, the subject Christ and Creation explored two doctrines. First, the doctrine of creation was explored using entirely traditional concepts such as creation, providence, sin, the problem of evil, and theological anthropology. The second half of the semester, on Christology, was less traditional. Some of the expected topics were included, such as the two natures of Jesus Christ and the atonement (both of these were covered in a single week!). But most of the weekly classes were devoted to less conventional questions, such as the following:

- How is Jesus portrayed in film?
- How does belief in Christ relate to other religions?

- Why is gender a problem for Christology?
- How do we understand Jesus' identity from the perspective of our own culture?

The subject's assessment tasks gave students a wide range of options, with traditional doctrinal questions set alongside options such as "What are the distinctive features of the doctrine of God viewed through the experience of being a migrant?" and "Construct a two-week study on the topic of . . . the finality of Christ and the Cronulla riots." The weekly worksheets included numerous options for student reflection and were once more peppered with readings and quotations from Douglas John Hall.

In a subject called The Spirit of the Christian Life, the arrangement of the content was largely traditional with only three topics, "the emerging church," "the cross-cultural church," and "the diasporic Christian," standing out as explicitly contemporary and contextual. Yet even the apparently traditional topics were taught in a way that decentered western voices and brought contemporary voices—including theologians from Australia and the majority world—into the classroom. When Pearson taught a subject on Bonhoeffer, it was with the aim of showing how this classic German theologian provided resources for the kind of contextualized thinking that was needed in a pluralistic society like Australia. Pearson also added new subjects to the curriculum that were entirely contextual in nature. He designed and taught, for the first time anywhere in Australia, a subject on ecotheology. This later evolved into a subject on theology and climate change—a topic that would also be taken up, in different ways, by a number of Pearson's doctoral students.

One of the hallmarks of Pearson's approach to theology can be seen by counting the number of assigned and recommended readings in each of his subjects. In Christ and Creation, for example, some fifty readings were assigned, recommended, or tied to an assessment question. In Critical Theology, more than one hundred and twenty readings were listed. In both these subjects, essentially all the readings were from contemporary authors. The vast majority had been published within the preceding decade, and many had been published within just two or three years. Jürgen Moltmann (1926–2024) was the "oldest" theologian whom students would have read in most of Pearson's classes. When faced with this abundance of contemporary literature, students were not of course expected to read it all. The aim was to peruse the work of different authors, to make selections, and eventually to find a couple of key theological voices—Pearson liked to call them "allies and aliens"—that were especially helpful for the student's own thinking. One brief assessment task invited students to compare the tables of contents in several different works of systematic theology. Wherever one looks in the class materials from this period, one finds examples of Pearson's love of theological diversity and his preference for a plurality of (contemporary) theological voices. Each subject outline included the following statement to help students orient themselves to this abundance of viewpoints:

> This course is constructed on the assumption that the future of the Christian faith requires people to be at home in their own theological persuasion and also to be able to engage with those who think quite differently. Many courses seek to put forward only one option. This is not so here. You will find a diversity of denominational points of view, insights arising out of gender, age, ethnicity, sexual orientation. The authors cited come from evangelical, liberal, postmodern, feminist and charismatic perspectives. Welcome to the banquet!

Pearson was instrumental in encouraging many students, especially from migrant backgrounds, to continue through to postgraduate research at UTC. His selfless mentoring of Pasifika research students took place on a scale never seen before in any theological institution in Australia. At the time of writing, he has supervised twenty-seven research students to completion—more, as far as I can ascertain, than any other theologian in the history of Australian universities.[5] Of all Pearson's research students, roughly half have been Pasifika students with projects relating to Pasifika theology and ministry: a remarkable legacy and a remarkable contribution to the field of contextual theology.

BEN MYERS (LECTURER IN SYSTEMATIC THEOLOGY 2009–2017)

I met Clive Pearson not at UTC but in the United States. It was 2008, and we both happened to be research fellows at the Center of Theological Inquiry in Princeton. Pearson was working on a project on public theology, and I was working on Karl Barth. By this time, Pearson had become principal of UTC. With his growing burden of leadership responsibilities, he was in the process of stepping back from the day-to-day duties of teaching theology. Shortly after we met, I saw that UTC had advertised the role of lecturer in systematic theology, and I flew back to Australia for an interview. I was

---

5. At the time of writing, Australian Catholic theologian Neil Ormerod has supervised twenty research students to completion. I have not been able to find anyone in Australia, apart from Clive Pearson, with more than twenty successful supervisions in theology.

offered the position and moved directly from Princeton to Sydney at the start of 2009.

With my academic background, it seemed unlikely that I would ever become responsible for teaching systematic theology. My undergraduate and postgraduate studies were not in theology but in literature. By the time I started my doctoral studies, I was interested in the history of Protestant theology, and so I opted to write a dissertation about Milton's seventeenth-century poem *Paradise Lost* in the context of Puritan theological debates. This gave me a way of learning about the history of Christian thought. But whatever I knew about Christian doctrine was self-taught, and my first experience in a theology classroom was as a lecturer at UTC. By this time, I had published research on Milton as well as on a handful of modern British and European theologians: Barth, Bultmann, Pannenberg, T. F. Torrance, and Rowan Williams. My theological formation, such as it was, could hardly have been more different from Clive Pearson's. Yet it was an example of his characteristic epistemological pluralism that, upon my arrival at UTC, he explained to me why he thought a contextual approach was so important and assured me that I was free to follow my own path and to take the theology curriculum in a different direction.

In my first year at UTC, I tried teaching the systematic theology subjects more or less as Pearson had designed them. With my background in literature, I was particularly eager to discuss the assigned readings with students. But I felt that the sheer volume of recommended readings was an obstacle. When students were able to pick and choose from so many different texts, it was hard to facilitate class discussion around any particular text or author. I also grew dissatisfied with the contemporary outlook of the readings. In a class on the atonement, I noticed that all the assigned texts included critical discussions of Anselm, Calvin, and Gustaf Aulén. But the students had never read those authors for themselves and so couldn't really make their own informed judgments. They had to rely on secondhand information about some of the most formative ideas in Christian history. In addition, I noticed the difficulty that many UTC students faced—especially students whose first language was not English, who at that time comprised roughly half of all theology classes—when they tried reading technical theological material for the first time. Any undergraduate student with a good working knowledge of English can read Athanasius or Bonhoeffer in a modern translation; reading an academic journal article about Athanasius or Bonhoeffer is a different matter entirely. Coming from a background in literary studies, I felt that it would be more rewarding, as well as easier and more achievable, to go back to the primary sources instead of getting students to read secondary studies.

Within my first few years at UTC, I had implemented a total change to the way texts were assigned and used in theology classes. Following the method I had learned as a student of literature, I divided each weekly class into a two-hour lecture/discussion and a one-hour tutorial. The purpose of the tutorial was to have a detailed and directed conversation about an assigned text. Each class would read through only one or two (occasionally three) texts in the course of a semester. The weekly readings were kept as short as possible—sometimes only a few pages—to increase the chance that everyone would come to class fully prepared. In the first-year introduction to theology class, the tutorial discussions were devoted to select chapters from Calvin's *Institutes* (using the shorter and more accessible 1541 French edition, translated by Elsie McKee). In the first-year class Being the Church, students read the whole of Bonhoeffer's *Life Together* and discussed it in small weekly chunks. The assigned texts for Christology were Athanasius's *On the Incarnation* and selections from Irenaeus's *Against Heresies*. In other classes, students worked through Augustine's *Confessions*, Gregory of Nazianzus's *Five Theological Orations*, Julian of Norwich's *Revelation of Divine Love*, Bonhoeffer's *Discipleship*, Barth's christological chapter on "The Way of the Son of God into the Far Country" (from *Church Dogmatics* IV/1), James Cone's *Black Theology and Black Power*, Moltmann's *Spirit of Life*, Elizabeth Johnson's *Consider Jesus*, and James Evans's *We Have Been Believers: An African American Systematic Theology*. In most of my advanced postgraduate classes, students had to focus intensively for a whole semester on the work of a single author. For example, there were postgraduate classes on the works of Origen, on Barth's *Epistle to the Romans*, and on the essays of Sarah Coakley.

This text-centric approach had obvious limitations. Most notably, it sacrificed the plurality of voices and perspectives that Pearson had cultivated. But the payoff was that students could become relatively fluent in their capacity to discuss some of the formative thinkers and ideas from Christian history. I came to think that Christian doctrines could not really be contextualized effectively unless this kind of fluency had first been acquired. And although my preference was for classic works of theology, I felt that works from earlier centuries had a distinct advantage over contemporary texts. Nobody reading Irenaeus or Julian of Norwich, for example, would ever suppose that these authors belonged to our own tribe or shared our own worldview. Such voices from the past are even more different from us than we are from one another. In our pluralistic classes at UTC, where students came from such a wide range of cultural, linguistic, denominational, and theological backgrounds, it was an advantage to engage with authors who did not belong to anyone's group or share any of our prejudices. They were not familiar voices; and it was precisely this lack of familiarity that challenged students to widen their theological horizons and to think critically about their own cultural and theological blind spots.

Assessment tasks in my classes were designed to help students gain confidence in handling classic Christian texts and ideas. Even where students opted to address a contemporary question, they would typically be asked to engage in dialogue with at least one classic text. The following essay questions are examples:

- Is Jesus the savior of the whole cosmos? Compare and contrast the views of Athanasius (*On the Incarnation*) and Elizabeth Johnson (*Consider Jesus*, chapter 9).
- Discuss the theology of the church in Bonhoeffer's *Discipleship* in relation to the Uniting Church's *Basis of Union*. How is the church understood in each of these two texts? How does the historical context shape each of these visions of the church?
- With reference to Calvin's *Institutes* (chapter 17), the *Basis of Union*, and at least three other texts, answer the following question: What does it mean to say that the church is "a pilgrim people"?

Research in systematic theology was thriving at UTC during this period, thanks largely to the institutional structures and incentives that had been put in place with the CSU agreement.[6] As part of a university school, UTC attracted doctoral students from all kinds of denominational, theological, and cultural backgrounds. While Clive Pearson continued to supervise research students in contextual theology, I was guiding students towards more traditional theological thinkers and problems. I supervised dissertations in areas such as theological aesthetics, theological anthropology, trinitarian theology, and ecclesiology. In nearly every instance, the student's dissertation centered on the work of one theologian (sometimes two or three): Origen, Augustine, Barth, Calvin, Amyraut, Edward Schillebeeckx, Paul Ricoeur, Robert Jenson, Sarah Coakley, Rowan Williams, Katherine Sonderegger. This was all very different from the kind of work being produced by Pearson's doctoral students.

Taken together, the burgeoning research in both contextual theology and systematic theology fostered an uncommonly vibrant and diverse research culture during the decade in question. It is noteworthy how many of these doctoral researchers came from our own undergraduate student body. Eight of my research students during this period, and seventeen of

---

6. I have written elsewhere about the CSU agreement and the advantage of such institutional structures and incentives: see Myers, "Does Theology Belong."

Pearson's research students, had done prior undergraduate studies at UTC. I recall some cases where a student went on to write a doctoral dissertation about an idea they had first formulated in an undergraduate paper: an example of how a strong research culture can trickle down to the level of the undergraduate classroom.

MICHAEL MAWSON (LECTURER IN SYSTEMATIC THEOLOGY AND ETHICS 2019–2022)

Michael Mawson came to UTC in 2019. Originally from New Zealand, he wrote his doctoral dissertation on Bonhoeffer's ethics at the University of Notre Dame in the United States before joining the divinity faculty at the University of Aberdeen. Upon arriving at UTC, he began reading the work of Christian indigenous scholars like Anne Pattel-Gray, Gary Deverell, and Naomi Wolfe. Meanwhile, discussions with students led him to give more attention to marginalized contextual voices, especially from the Pacific. In his first year at UTC, he taught a postgraduate seminar on Bonhoeffer's theology and explored with students the way Bonhoeffer's thought had been appropriated in liberation and resistance theologies in Latin America, South Africa, and Hong Kong. In a recently published reflection, Mawson describes how his study of Bonhoeffer's late theology had already "inculcated an openness to diverse and surprising forms of Christ's presence" and to "expressions of faith that speak in a worldly way about God"—an openness that naturally led him to ask questions about the way theology related to his new context in Sydney.[7]

Mawson's distinctive contextual yet confessional approach to theology was clearly stamped on the systematic theology curriculum during his years at UTC. In the first-year Introduction to Theology class, standard textbooks still appeared—McGrath's *Christian Theology Reader* and Migliore's *Faith Seeking Understanding*—but they were relegated to a list of recommended background reading. The assigned reading for the class was more diverse, more local, and more contemporary. For the first assignment, students had to write a brief reflection on one of four prescribed books: James Cone's *Cross and the Lynching Tree*, Kwok Pui-Lan's *Introducing Asian Feminist Theology*, Gary Deverell's *Gondwana Theology*, or Winston Halapua's *Waves of God's Embrace: Sacred Perspectives from the Ocean*. The assignment was designed in a conventional way to help students acquire foundational theological skills: students were required to provide a definition of theology and to describe the sources of theological reasoning, while also demonstrating a

---

7. See the autobiographical account in Mawson, *Standing Under the Cross*, 6–7.

capacity to analyze theological texts. But the material for analysis was drawn from contemporary voices from Australian indigenous, Pacific, Southeast Asian, and Black American perspectives. The final essay for the class included a mix of traditional doctrinal topics as well as contemporary issues such as racism, colonialism, and climate change. The weekly class topics followed a traditional pattern of systematic theology while mixing classic and contemporary readings. In the first week, for example, students read excerpts from Augustine on the relation between theology and philosophy, alongside Sione Amanaki Havea on Christianity in the Pacific. In the second week, on the topic of the doctrine of Scripture, students read Bonhoeffer alongside a paper by Jione Havea on "Reading Islandly." Where earlier iterations of this subject had ended with two weeks on the topic of "Types of Christian Theology," Mawson introduced two final contemporary topics: climate change (with a reading from Mark Brett) and colonialism (with a reading from Willie James Jennings).

In Mawson's third-year undergraduate subject on theological ethics, contextual concerns came more to the foreground. The class began with a traditional Protestant grounding in a theology of the cross. Students read Mawson's own essay, "Studying Theology in a Time of Crisis: A Manifesto," a short paper written in 2020 that defined the current theological moment in the context of the recent catastrophic NSW (New South Wales) bushfires, the global COVID-19 pandemic and lockdowns, and the Black Lives Matter protest movement sparked by the murder of George Floyd.[8] Following this powerful reflection on the contemporary context, students turned to excerpts from Luther's *Heidelberg Disputation* and Bonhoeffer's *Ethics*. With these theological foundations in place, the rest of the semester was devoted to a survey of contemporary approaches to theology, including topics such as theology and trauma, ecotheology, postcolonialism, and the critique of whiteness. The assessment tasks tried to balance theological foundations with contemporary contextualization. In the first assignment, students had to answer the question (presumably using Luther and Bonhoeffer as points of reference): What is the significance of the cross for Christian thinking and action? The second assignment allowed students to choose between liberation theology, Black theology, or Minjung theology, while the final assignment involved a short research paper on a chosen contextual issue or, for a more theoretical topic, on the way the concept of "context" functions in Christian ethics.

At postgraduate level, Mawson's classes leaned still more heavily toward contemporary contextual issues. In a postgraduate class on theological

---

8. Mawson, "Studying Theology."

hermeneutics, students again received an early grounding in Bonhoeffer and Luther before turning to a host of contemporary Australian, Pacific, and Asian theological voices. A small but telling detail is the number of times the work of Jione Havea, UTC's former Hebrew Bible lecturer, appeared in the class reading lists—an example of how carefully and deliberately Mawson was attuning himself to his new local context.

Students of theology during this period were exposed not only to a variety of textual resources but to a wide range of voices in the classroom as well. Di Rayson taught ecotheology, Ockert Meyer taught the doctrine of the Trinity, Jione Havea taught Classic Texts in Christian Theology, and Sathianathan Clarke taught Contemporary Theology in a Global Context. The collaborative and multiperspectival approach to theology at UTC during this period can be illustrated by the first-year undergraduate class called Being the Church. Mawson invited Peter Walker, principal of UTC, to design and teach the class. Walker himself taught six of the eleven topics, with other weekly topics taught by Matagi Vilitama, Kyounghee Cho, and Liam Miller. The weekly readings from Veli-Matti Kärkkäinen's *Introduction to Ecclesiology: Ecumenical, Historical and Global* must have added to the impression that a study of the church in our time necessarily entails an attentiveness to diverse voices from global perspectives.

Alongside his teaching responsibilities, Mawson introduced new research emphases at UTC. Under his inclusive and inquisitive oversight, the college research colloquium became more outward looking and more diverse than it had previously been. Taking advantage of the COVID-era move of academic gatherings to Zoom, Mawson turned UTC's monthly colloquium into a forum that showcased a rich mix of voices from across Australia, the Pacific, Asia, and further abroad. Visiting speakers in 2021 included George Zachariah on "Moana Ecotheology," Garry Deverell on "The Unmaking of the White Jesus," Hirini Kaa on "Decolonising Our Faith Story," and Vicky Balabanski and Emily Colgan on ecological readings of the Bible. The following year, visiting speakers included Naomi Wolfe on colonialism and theological institutions, Te Aroha Rountree on Jesus and stolen spaces, Liz Boase on embodied trauma, Louise Gosbell on weakness and the body, and Muslim scholar Mahsheed Ansari on Islamic prophetology. Such visiting experts were scheduled alongside the customary mix of UTC faculty and research students.

Mawson left UTC after a relatively short period, returning to New Zealand in 2022 to take up the Maclaurin Goodfellow Chair of Theological and Religious Studies at the University of Auckland. There has been no systematic theology position at UTC since his departure.

THINGS THAT MATTER?

For the past quarter century at UTC, theology has been both a mirror and a lamp, reflecting the culture of its ecclesial context while also seeking to critique and lead that culture in different ways.

Although global and contextual theologies had been firmly embedded in the systematic theology curriculum during Pearson's tenure at the college, Mawson introduced a subtle yet perceptible change of emphasis. He tended to prioritize politicized approaches to contemporary theology. A commitment to postcolonial criticism runs through his teaching materials from this period, as well as an emphasis on theologies of class struggle. With a background in Bonhoeffer studies, it is understandable that Mawson's perception of the contemporary context would include a heightened sensitivity to political struggle, structural evils, and their implications for faithful Christian witness. In his paper mentioned earlier, "Studying Theology in a Time of Crisis," Mawson invokes Bonhoeffer's 1933 call for discerning a *status confessionis* in a time of crisis[9]—a call which, for Bonhoeffer, specifically referred to the Aryanization of the Reich Church and its concomitant distortion of the gospel. Reading our own time through this lens, Mawson was drawn to contemporary theologies of protest, disruption, and critique. Under the influence of such contemporary voices, he was more ready than either Pearson or I—or any previous theologian at UTC—to challenge the foundations of the discipline of systematic theology, a discipline that is, after all, a product of the nineteenth-century German university system. During his time at UTC, for example, Mawson helped to organise and edit (with Brian Fiu Kolia) a volume of essays under the title *Unsettling Theologies*, with the aim of decolonizing theological language, methods, and institutions.[10]

Pearson was also influenced by the late Bonhoeffer, but his theological style was shaped more by the method of correlation in Paul Tillich and Douglas John Hall. Prophetic criticism still occupies an honored place in this tradition, but it stands alongside what might be called a wisdom sensibility that cultivates openness to signs of God's activity in culture and in the contingencies of one's own time and place. Pearson taught and promoted varieties of liberation theology—notably Minjung theology—but his characteristic mode was not prophetic but interpretive. He wanted students to think about their specific location in place and time and to give an account of the gospel that spoke from and to the contingencies of that unique location. In the volume *Home and Away*, edited with UTC colleague Stephen

---

9. Mawson, "Studying Theology."
10. Kolia and Mawson, *Unsettling Theologies*.

Burns, Pearson had advocated for the ad hoc interpretation of local contexts which he described as "postcode theology."[11] An approach like this isn't really aspiring to overturn unjust social structures or to revolutionize theological language and institutions. It is an extension of Tillich's method of correlation, in which the gospel and the cultural context each becomes increasingly intelligible as they are thrown together in dialogue.

When I taught the subject Being the Church at UTC, one of the assigned readings was the 1946 essay by H. Richard Niebuhr—another disciple of Tillich—on the church's responsibility for society.[12] Using that essay, I asked students to discuss the question of whether a posture of prophetic criticism ought to be used sparingly in some historical contexts, especially in societies that have been profoundly shaped, for good and ill, by the Christian faith. I assigned the same essay in several classes over the years because I thought it was a helpful challenge to the Uniting Church's tendency to slip too easily into the prophetic mode when considering contemporary social causes. When I assigned James Cone's early book, *Black Theology and Black Power* (1969), in a postgraduate class on Theology in Global Context, I was impressed by the moral clarity of its analysis of 1960s American culture but also disturbed by its frank acceptance of the logic of violence and racial segregation. The students might have reached other conclusions, but at the time I made a case that a prophetic or, perhaps better, apocalyptic theology of this kind cannot easily be translated into other social contexts and historical periods. Like Pearson, I found it more helpful to foreground a conception of the common good and to invite students to consider the positive (if modest) role that Christian communities can play in the cultivation of a flourishing society. The accent was not on the political so much as on the practical, the local, and the provisional.

It seems to me that the differences between the approaches to systematic theology at UTC over the past quarter century have rested partly on differing answers to the questions: What is our context? In what situation are we currently trying to talk about God? The way any theologian answers these questions will have an enormous bearing on the way they envisage the theological task and the points of emphasis they think are necessary. There is, of course, no single correct answer to the question "what is our context?" Pearson answered this question with reference to migration, climate change, and the Australian church's special relationship to the cultures and peoples of the Pacific. I thought of the context more in terms of the Uniting Church's complicated theological makeup, in which a shared confessional identity

---

11. Burns and Pearson, *Home and Away*.
12. Niebuhr, "Responsibility of the Church."

tenuously holds together evangelicalism and progressivism, piety and activism, a practical Methodist sensibility and a Reformed intellectual sensibility. Mawson, for his part, understood the context in terms of colonial and other historic injustices, interpreted through the prism of 1930s Germany.

It is perhaps a measure of how convincing Mawson was in his decolonizing approach that, upon his departure from UTC in 2022, the college decided to dissolve the traditional position of lecturer in systematic theology. Instead, theology would be brought under the wider umbrella of a new position of lecturer in cross cultural ministry and theology. Seforosa Carroll, one of Clive Pearson's former doctoral students,[13] took up this position in 2023 after several years of service in UnitingWorld and the World Council of Churches. Theological subjects at UTC are, at the time of writing, taught by a variety of scholars with diverse areas of expertise, including Sathianathan Clarke, Ockert Meyer, and Carroll herself. But no member of faculty carries the responsibility for the study and teaching of Christian doctrine. The number of research students at the college has dwindled. It has been some years since UTC attracted new doctoral students in systematic theology.

This was not the first time one of the classic theological disciplines has disappeared from UTC's faculty structure. After William Emilsen's retirement in 2014, the position of lecturer in church history was discontinued, and a new faculty position in evangelism was created instead. The decision at that time was largely political. The college wanted to position itself favorably in relation to the priorities of the synod and the perceived theological sensibilities of the wider church. The study of the past was assumed to have little direct value for the church and its ministries; the present was all that mattered. It is hard not to interpret the disappearance of systematic theology from UTC's faculty structure in a similar light. The study of the past plays a central role in both these disciplines. Systematic theology, like church history, is deeply invested in questions about the present, but it answers those questions (at least in part) with reference to texts, traditions, and other resources from the past. This historical orientation can seem superfluous to a church culture dominated by an absorbing anxiety about the future and by a corresponding array of missional and ecclesiastical fads.

It is too soon to say how the church's identity and how formation for ministry might be affected by the decentering of history and the decentering of doctrine from the culture of the college. In the absence of a faculty structure in which scholars are appointed to teach, represent, and advocate for these things, it is too soon to say whether the college will find ways to

---

13. For her PhD diss., see Carroll, "Making Room."

embrace the church's past, together with the larger inheritance of Christian thought and practice, as "things that matter" for the church and its ministries today.

BIBLIOGRAPHY

Burns, Stephen, and Clive Pearson, eds. *Home and Away: Contextual Theology and Local Practice*. Eugene, OR: Pickwick, 2013.

Carroll, Seforosa. "Making Room for the Religious Other: Reading Interfaith Dialogue and Encounters in the Australian Context from a Feminist Diasporic Perspective." PhD diss., Charles Sturt University, 2015.

Dicker, Gordon. "The Reformed Heritage and the Uniting Church." *Uniting Church Studies* 9.2 (2003) 11–23.

Kolia, Brian Fiu, and Michael Mawson, eds. *Unsettling Theologies: Memory, Identity, and Place*. London: Palgrave Macmillan, 2024.

Mawson, Michael. *Standing Under the Cross: Essays on Bonhoeffer's Theology*. London: Bloomsbury, 2023.

———. "Studying Theology in a Time of Crisis." In *Letters to a Young Theologian*, edited by Henco van der Westhuizen, 234–44. Minneapolis: Fortress, 2022.

Mostert, Christiaan. "Is a Non-Contextual Theology Viable?" In *Mapping the Landscape: Essays in Australian and New Zealand Christianity*, edited by Susan Emilsen and William W. Emilsen, 118–33. New York: Lang, 2000.

Myers, Ben. "Does Theology Belong in the University? Schleiermacherian Reflections from an Australian Context." *International Journal of Public Theology* 15.4 (2021) 484–95.

Niebuhr, H. Richard. "The Responsibility of the Church for Society." In *The Gospel, the Church, and the World*, edited by Kenneth Scott Latourette, 126–33. New York: Harper, 1946.

Pearson, Clive. "How Shy Can a Reformed Theology Be?" *International Journal of Public Theology* 1.3 (2007) 340–57.

———. "Telling Tales: Following the Hyphenated Jesus-Christ." *Studies in World Christianity* 10.1 (2004) 6–24.

Pearson, Clive, and Jione Havea, eds. *Faith in a Hyphen: Cross-Cultural Theologies Down Under*. Adelaide, SA: Openbook, 2004.

3

Formation for Ordained Ministry at UTC

PETER WALKER AND NICOLE FLEMING

UNITED THEOLOGICAL COLLEGE (UTC) has played a central role in the formation of people selected as candidates for ordained ministry, early on by the Congregational, Methodist, and Presbyterian churches and then, from 1977, the Uniting Church in Australia. And so, throughout its history, the formation of ministers, especially ordained ministers, has been near the heart of the college's life. Rather than a history of its formation activities, this chapter will bring the college's responsibility for the formation of ministers to the surface of our awareness as a reminder that formation has always mattered at UTC. The centrality of ministry formation to the college will be highlighted by naming, from some of the Uniting Church's key documents about ordination and formation, the scope of the task entrusted to UTC by the church, and by giving an overview of the way the college has fulfilled those responsibilities. We will also name a key theme of the last twenty-five years, or what might be called a formative tension in the life of the college, which is the diversity of the ministry candidate community, and place its centrality to UTC within the current global conversation about education and formation for ministry. As we have both been at various times students, ordination candidates, and faculty members at UTC during the last twenty-five years, there will also be some personal observations along the way. Overall, we hope to recognize here, at its fiftieth anniversary, the significance to UTC of the church's processes of ministry formation and, reciprocally, the significance of UTC to the church's task of forming ordained ministers.

ORDINATION IN THE UNITING CHURCH IN AUSTRALIA

The Uniting Church in Australia believes that some of its members are called by God to be set apart for ordained ministry. Those so identified are recognized through a service of ordination to one of two offices: the ministry of the word or the ministry of deacon. The National Assembly of the Uniting Church's *Brief Statement on Ordination* indicates that ordained ministers are thereby "set apart," normally for life, into a new relationship with the whole church[1] and are to hold particular responsibilities as outlined in its *Basis of Union*:

> [They] will preach the Gospel, administer the sacraments and exercise pastoral care so that all may be equipped for their particular ministries, thus maintaining the apostolic witness to Christ in the Church. Such members will be called Ministers and their setting apart will be known as Ordination.[2]

To be set apart by ordination is, for the Uniting Church, to enter a new relationship with God, the church, and all other members of the body of Christ. Ordained ministry is a representative ministry exercised on behalf of the church and so ordained ministers offer leadership across the whole church, not just in their own community.[3] Those ordained by the Uniting Church are called to a ministry of "focussing, modelling, supervising, shepherding, enabling, and empowering the general ministry of the Church."[4] It is the formation of ordination candidates for these activities that has been entrusted to UTC by its denominational governors since classes commenced and, indeed, not only for these ministry activities but also the formation of their sacramental identities within the church.

---

1. Uniting Church in Australia, *Brief Statement*.
2. Uniting Church in Australia, *Basis of Union*, para. 14.
3. Uniting Church in Australia, "Worksheet 5."
4. Uniting Church in Australia, *Brief Statement*, 2.

FORMATION FOR ORDAINED MINISTRY

Many Christians speak of formation, of being formed as disciples of Jesus Christ, and various organizations offer formation programs focused on identifying and developing the spiritual lives and practices of Christian disciples.[5] However, formation for ordination, often called Core Phase Formation within the Uniting Church, is an intentional formation process focused on developing the attributes, knowledge, and skills expected of those who have been selected as ordination candidates. Formation for ordination requires candidates to undertake a three- to four-year program under the oversight of their presbytery (regional council) and one of the Uniting Church's theological colleges. Those years are dedicated to developing the character, identity, spirituality, theological maturity, and practical skills required for ordained ministry. UTC has been recognized since 1977 by the Synod of New South Wales and the Australian Capital Territory of the Uniting Church as the college holding oversight on behalf of the synod for candidate formation.[6] Forming ministers has always mattered at UTC, and that task, carried for and with the church, has been substantial.

The Uniting Church's *Assembly Guidelines for Theological Education and Formation* offers the following directions to those appointed by the church to teach, supervise, and mentor candidates, and to the colleges organizing and supervising these formation activities. They are a sign of the weight of the formation burden that has been placed upon UTC:

> All aspects and elements of the education and formation of candidates for ordination as Ministers of the Word or Deacons shall be oriented towards the provision of Ministers who have made appropriate progress—as part of a life-long journey—in exhibiting the following attributes:
>
> i. An understanding of God, a personal faith in Jesus Christ as Saviour and Lord, and the capacity to articulate this contextually;
>
> ii. The practice of Christian spiritual disciplines and embodying faith in Jesus Christ in their own lives;
>
> iii. Acknowledging a call by God through the Church to give themselves to the Ministry for which they are ordained, following Jesus' pattern of love and service;

---

5. United Theological College, *UTC Formation Handbook*, 5.
6. Task Group, "Ministry," 274.

iv. A mature knowledge of Christian tradition and the biblical witness, and the ability to help the Church shape its future in the light of that tradition;

v. A capacity to articulate Christian faith in contextually appropriate ways;

vi. Adherence to the *Basis of Union*;

vii. Being equipped to help the Church be faithful to its identity and lead the Church in mission in a rapidly changing and diverse cultural and social context;

viii. Commitment to the Covenant with the Uniting Aboriginal and Islander Christian Congress (1994) and working within the understandings expressed in the *Preamble to the Constitution* (2009);

ix. Embodying the Church's declarations that *We Are a Multicultural Church* (1985), *Living with the Neighbour Who Is Different* (2000), and *One Body, Many Members: Living Faith and Life Cross Culturally* (2012)

x. A well-developed and reflective understanding of their identity as an ordained Minister within the Uniting Church;

xi. Ability to engage the tasks of Ministry with critical imagination, courage, emotional maturity, theological judgment and self-reflection; and to exercise this Ministry within the ministry of the whole people of God;

xii. Readiness for the practice of day-to-day Ministry, and the quality of being and awareness which gives integrity to the exercise of this practice;

xiii. The capacity for and commitment to intentional lifelong learning; the commitment to comply with the *Code of Ethics and Ministry Practice*.[7]

Lest quoting those directions at length may seem out of place, take a moment to ponder the challenge of forming and assessing people in these fourteen attributes. Just to pluck three from the list, what do (iv), (vii), and (xi) look like in a candidate? How would you shape class and field experiences that will form these attributes in candidates? And, how would you confidently assess that a candidate has achieved these attributes? Taking seriously the church's expectation that ordination programs will form these attributes in its candidates has required of UTC constant focus, planning, supervision, and resourcing. It has also required of UTC faculty and staff

---

7. Uniting Church in Australia, *Standards*, para. 3.

that they work with candidates, and work *on* candidates, as they develop a deeper understanding of and appreciation for what being set apart for a life in ordained ministry means. The college and its faculty have for decades been exploring with candidates these questions, or variations on them: What does entering this new relationship with the church involve? What is required of you in order that the church may confidently ordain you among those called to safeguard the apostolic faith? What program is needed that the college may form in you "a mature knowledge of Christian tradition and the biblical witness, and the ability to help the church shape its future in the light of that tradition?" What must be formed, reformed, or transformed in you in order that you may "engage the tasks of Ministry with critical imagination, courage, emotional maturity, theological judgment and self-reflection?"

And so, United Theological College has held responsibility not only for the academic theological education of the Uniting Church's ordination candidates, who have always provided a significant percentage of students in the classrooms of the college, but also the formation of their spiritual life, gifts, ministry skills, and for encouraging in them practices that will integrate their theological study and ministry experience into a mature ordained identity. Formation, thus understood, is a formidable responsibility and a multifaceted challenge for the church to place at the door of a theological college. Engagement with that challenge, in the endeavor of fulfilling that responsibility, holds a significant place in the UTC story.

FORMATION AT UNITED THEOLOGICAL COLLEGE

We have gleaned from the Uniting Church's guidance to its colleges about ordained formation that classroom-based theological education for candidates, their learning and assessment in biblical studies, church history, theology, liturgy, homiletics, pastoral care, mission, and so on, is not an end in itself. Rather, that education sits within a wider process that is known by the church as formation. At UTC, the formation of ordination candidates has therefore typically included a threefold program.

Candidates have always engaged in the disciplines of formal theological study summarized above, usually in pursuit of an academic award such as a diploma or bachelor of theology. Secondly, they have also been required to participate in field-based learning in the manner, normally, of a series of year-long placements alongside an experienced minister in a congregation, in a chaplaincy, or (in the case of deacon candidates who often have a special sense of call to ministries of service beyond the church) in a school, prison, hospital, or faith community emerging outside ecclesial structures. Given these field placements typically endure for one year, and the candidate program has historically been a three-year commitment, it has been the custom at UTC for candidates to have three field placement experiences during their time at the college.

The third component of the formation program, "Integration," has been given greater time and structure in recent decades, and its significance at UTC owes much to the work of former Principal Sarah Mitchell and faculty member Rhonda White. A bridge is an inadequate yet meaningful analogy. This integrative component of formation has been the bridge between what candidates have learned in the classroom, on the one hand, and experienced in their field-placement, on the other. Many former candidates will recall, for example, what were known as Faculty Groups, Pastoral Groups, or Friday Groups; five or six candidates meeting during or after lunch on Friday of each week for a conversation, led by a faculty member, during which their experiences in the classroom and field placement were shared. The aim was to allow those experiences to inform each other and thereby, with varying degrees of success, be integrated.

From the mid-2000s, integration took a more structured form than those Friday conversations and took up more time in the candidate program. Wednesday of each teaching week became "Formation Day." Academic classes were no longer timetabled on Wednesdays, and instead the full candidate cohort, typically somewhere between fifteen and twenty students, would engage in workshops on themes of importance to their future in ministry. Integration conversations were still held in small groups as well, now led not only by faculty members but also by experienced ministers and field educators, along with worship and a shared meal. The content of the Formation Day has been reshaped from year to year and sometimes more substantially reformed when changes to key staff have occurred, such as a new dean of candidates arriving with fresh ideas. Nevertheless, this full-day format for the integration component of formation for ordination has been the norm for much of the last twenty years and remains in place at UTC today.

One consequence for ordination candidates of their involvement in the UTC formation program may already be evident from this description, yet it is worth naming more clearly. Candidates have become, increasingly over the last generation, very busy people. The three components of their formation—theological study, field placements, and the integration program—are taken altogether. So, a typical week for a candidate has included lectures or tutorials for the two or three subjects they are currently enrolled in, a full day of integration on Wednesdays, a day of activity in their field placement, meetings with their field placement supervisor, perhaps a visit to the library, preparation for chapel worship led by their group, and then reading and assessment work at home. Outside this weekly routine, occasional retreats and formation intensives, such as a week-long rural ministry immersion, have also become a staple part of the formation program at UTC.

A thoughtful reader will note we have not yet named any time for family and other personal commitments. Yet perhaps the most significant factor not yet named is the time required to earn an income. Especially since the Synod of NSW (New South Wales) and ACT (Australian Capital Territory) determined in 2010 to stop providing a living allowance for candidates, other than for those in a narrow band of serious need,[8] people involved in formation at UTC have been holding down jobs. The stress of meeting all the candidate formation commitments as well as holding secular employment has been evident to, and commented upon regularly by, those involved in the oversight of UTC formation, from faculty and staff through to presbytery advisors and mentors. Sometimes the stress is alleviated when a candidate has the church as their employer. For example, they might be a lay ministry worker in a congregation or agency. Yet even a seemingly sympathetic employer has not always guaranteed sufficient time for classes, field placements, and integration days. At the time of writing, the reintroduction of financial support for candidates engaged in UTC formation is being considered, so help might be on the way. Nevertheless for the last fifteen years, and still today, it has been ever necessary for UTC faculty to provide candidates with flexibility around program requirements in order to ensure that stress does not become an impediment to good formation.

HOLDING A FORMATIVE TENSION: DIVERSITY AT UNITED THEOLOGICAL COLLEGE

Points of tension have emerged for UTC over the years in leading formation programs for the Uniting Church. Tension is frequently encountered, of course, when the work at hand is forming and reforming people's lives. "I'm being deconstructed" has been a familiar phrase at the college. The challenge for UTC has been to turn those moments into a constructive tension, even a formative tension. One point of formative tension always evident in the candidate program, yet in growing proportions over the last twenty-five years, is captured by a word frequently heard in the Uniting Church—diversity. The challenge of finding and holding "unity in diversity" is prominent

---

8. In each year from 2018 to 2024, less than 10 percent of candidates have qualified for financial assistance.

in Uniting Church discourse. The website of the National Assembly, for example, speaks of the Uniting Church as "Empowered in Diversity. Our unity is not about sameness, but unity in diversity."[9] The Uniting Church has authorized and approved many documents since 1977 that highlight the importance of diversity to its identity.[10] Those statements have often focused on inclusion of the "other," people from cultures other than the dominant Anglo-Australian community. Yet difference is a concept that defines all humans not just those who do not originate in the dominant culture.

Former UTC faculty member Ben Myers, in *Christ the Stranger: The Theology of Rowan Williams*, explains that, for Williams, difference is *the* human attribute that draws people into the never-ending task of understanding one another and the mystery of God present in each other and that a continual striving to understand difference in others also forms awareness of our own (different) identity.[11] Robert Vosloo of Stellenbosch University, and a keynote speaker at UTC's 2024 International Bonhoeffer Congress, draws on Dietrich Bonhoeffer to affirm the need for difference in forming identity. People need each other as individuals in community to enrich each other and make God visible.[12]

Formation for ordained ministry is all about the development of identity—a ministry identity. It develops through field placements and theological study, and through relationships with those who are involved in that process: faculty, field educators, mentors, and other candidates. Relationships provide opportunities for candidates to form an understanding of their ministry identity in dialogue with those who are doing the same.

Diversity within the candidate community at UTC has become more pronounced over the last twenty-five years: in gender, culture, language, ecclesial background, theology, prior study, ministry experience, and age. One example is changing cultural composition. During the 1990s, between 8 and 20 percent of candidates were from culturally and linguistically diverse backgrounds. From 2015 to 2019, that statistic increased to between 30 and 48 percent. From 2020 to 2024, it increased again, and there were between 46 and 63 percent of candidates preparing for ordained ministry who were not from the church's dominant Anglo-culture. Given the organic

9. Uniting Church in Australia, "Our Faith."

10. The Uniting Church in Australia has published several statements on diversity, including *We Are a Multicultural Church* (1985); *A Church for All God's People* (2006); *One Body, Many Members: Living Faith and Life Cross-Culturally* (2012); and *Space for Grace: Living in the "Grace Margin" in Respectful, Empowering and Inclusive Decision-Making* (2015).

11. Myers, *Christ the Stranger*, 18, 52–55.

12. Vosloo, "Mystery of the Other," 15.

relationship between culture and theology, this growing cultural diversity has also been a marker of significant theological diversity. Naïve distinctions between "evangelical" and "liberal" theology do not even begin to map the theological diversity of the college community, which included in 2024, for example, at least nine cultural groups.

Similarly, it is interesting to note the changing map of gender diversity among UTC's ordination candidates. While the preponderance of candidates in the first twenty years of the college's operation was male, the representation of women has grown significantly in the last thirty years. Women comprised between 40 and 81 percent of candidates between 1996 and 2024. In 2024, for the first time in the college's history, every new candidate commencing formation was a woman: six in total. Furthermore, and following the Uniting Church's affirmation at its Tenth National Assembly in 2003 that sexual orientation is not a barrier to ordination, the number of candidates at UTC who openly identify as lesbian, gay, or bisexual has increased.[13] From 2015 and 2024, it is estimated that between 5 and 30 percent of candidates identified as lesbian, gay, or bisexual.[14] Applications to become an ordination candidate from people who identify as transgender or non-binary will, in all likelihood, increase in coming years and broaden the gender diversity of the formation cohort at the college even further.

Unfolding these statistics about difference in culture, theology, and gender begins to reveal this space of formative tension—diversity—that is part of UTC's story. It has historically given rise to another challenge. How can the college provide an effective formation program that meets the diverse formation needs of individual candidates yet which is still coordinated across the whole candidate group and retains the coherence necessary for consistent and fair assessment of candidates by the church against common criteria?

FIXED OR FLEXIBLE?

Just as cultural, theological, and gender diversity have been a feature of the candidate community at UTC, so has the need to respond to diversity. Expanding diversity has brought what might be called the "fixed or flexible" tension into formation planning. Moving away from a fixed program for completion by all candidates toward a flexible program that can be tailored to individuals has been a key feature of the college's response. The

---

13. Uniting Church in Australia, "Sexuality and Leadership."

14. United Theological College, "Candidates Contact List"; United Theological College, "Candidate Statistics 0611."

one-size-fits-all formation program never worked well for some, and it has proved increasingly incapable of serving a diverse church in the formation of its increasingly diverse ordination candidates. Consequently, UTC has developed over the past decade a culture of "flexible formation pathways," a phrase borrowed from the Uniting Church National Assembly's *Standards*.[15] In that 2016 revision of the *Standards*, the church asked all its colleges to provide greater flexibility in formation, so UTC has not been alone in addressing the fixed or flexible question.

While there are commonalities across the candidate group, it is now increasingly the case that each candidate entering UTC is given a program designed specifically for them, which takes account of prior study, ministry work, and ecclesial and sociocultural experience. For example, candidates with completed degrees in theology or ministry are not required to repeat that work and, instead, are given a light classroom load. Some have been asked to complete integration projects that call for structured reflection on how their prior study informs their field placement experiences. Similarly, candidates with significant prior ministry experience are asked to complete less field education.

Regional formation is another development arising from this culture of flexible pathways. With the provision of regional formation, it is no longer necessary for those accepted by the Uniting Church as ordination candidates who live outside Sydney to relocate to the city to join the program. Instead, with the support of their presbytery, they remain in their regional or rural location and participate in the UTC formation program in distance mode. The same components are required of them—theological study, field placements, and integration—however, the mode of engagement has been through online classes, along with individual or small group integration sessions in their presbytery.

The college has also been responding to candidate diversity by including subjects, assessment tasks, integration experiences, and field education placements that seek to engage the cultural diversity of the candidate group. Historically, the form and content of theological study, and of the ordination formation program, has been oriented toward the Anglo-church. This cultural bias, mostly unconscious, embedded methods of teaching and learning, as well as subject and program content, born of and biased toward the dominant Anglo-culture of the Congregational, Methodist, and Presbyterian churches, and then Uniting Church. For example, there has been has an expectation that candidates from migrant backgrounds will be "re-formed" out of their home language and cultural habits to ensure they are able to

---

15. Uniting Church in Australia, *Standards*, para. 3.

minister within the language and cultural habits of the Anglo-church. Yet the reverse has not been expected of candidates raised in the language and habits of the English-speaking church. Despite various documented commitments to be a multicultural Uniting Church, Anglo candidates have not historically been re-formed at the college to ensure they are able to minister in languages and cultural habits other than English. These cultural biases and inconsistencies have perpetuated the formation of ministers for the dominant Anglo-church even when it has been evident that its dominance, at least numerically, is waning.

Rev. Dr. Paul Goh, president-elect of the Uniting Church and a minister of Korean-Australian heritage, suggests that formation programs must continue to diversify, placing in proper perspective the historical hold of dominant cultural models of ministry and leadership that have arisen from ethnocentrism within the Uniting Church. Goh recently urged the church to be intentionally and deeply "aware of other ways of doing theology" and to become "cultural learners." He wrote of the need to move toward a theological culture of belonging:

> To be a truly multicultural, cross-cultural, and intercultural church—a culturally and linguistically diverse church at its core, there is a pressing need to cultivate a culture of belonging and cultural humility. It is a way to engage people and groups across cultural differences while understanding and acknowledging systems of whiteness, a commitment to self-evaluation and self-critique, and seeking partnerships with people and groups working to eradicate power differentials at the systemic level. Paying particular attention to the asymmetries of power in the "intercultural relationships" can go a long way in helping the Uniting Church cultivate a theological culture of belonging.[16]

These discussions about diversity that are impacting the formation program at UTC from within the Uniting Church are part of a global conversation about decolonizing ministry formation. A leading voice in that conversation is Willie James Jennings who, in *After Whiteness: An Education in Belonging*, urges colleges to address what he calls the "self-sufficient masculinity" model that dominates ecclesial leadership and informs so many programs and processes of Christian formation.[17] The self-sufficient masculinity Jennings speaks of is not about race or gender, per se. It is about ways of seeing and being in the world, and the structures and systems that emerge from them. Wrestling with self-sufficient masculinity, Jennings suggests,

---

16. Goh, "CALDing the Theological Culture."
17. Jennings, *After Whiteness*, 8–9.

will help colleges shift from colonized models of education and formation that seek to form ministry and leadership that aspires to mastery, consistency, and conformity.[18] Put another way, Jennings explains that self-sufficient masculinity, born of the colonial master's dream, is about cultivating and aspiring to achieve success through "control, possession, and mastery."[19]

Jennings calls instead for theological education and ministry formation that cultivates belonging and community in Christ, provokes imagination, values deep attention to others, and forms healthy and well-rounded ministry.[20] Rather than arriving at the destination of control, possession, and mastery, the international conversation about formation has seen many advocates like Jennings emerge in recent years to argue for the value of diversity and programs that do not privilege any culture over another, which cultivate a collective belonging in Christ.[21] As Jennings writes, these alternative ways of ministry formation look beyond models that focus on individual self-sufficiency and move toward a communion model where individuals are formed in their unique way but as part of a diverse whole, which values the fullness of humanity.[22] Diversity enhances the whole community's well-being and points toward a minister's identity in Christ.

Over the past twenty-five years, the energy and insight to embrace cultural diversity and open UTC's formation program to these currents of change, and to stay attentive to the often-unconscious ways that cultural bias manifests itself in systems of education, has come from many in the faculty and beyond, not least the significant leadership of Clive Pearson during his term as principal and Jione Havea while he was lecturer in Old Testament / Hebrew Bible. The appointment in 2023 of UTC's first full time lecturer in cross-cultural ministry and theology, Seforosa Carroll, is another manifestation of the college's desire to ensure its programs and people reflect the diversity of the church. And while there may be a stronger emphasis today on the formative tension of diversity, and the need for flexibility in the formation of ministers, a college culture that is capable of creatively reshaping education programs to meet these needs does not arrive in the mail overnight. UTC's culture of faithfully attending to its ecclesial and social context established, long ago, the ground from which today's innovations in ministry formation can emerge. One need only offer a small number of names from the past to alert the reader to that tradition of faithful and creative

18. Jennings, *After Whiteness*, 8. See also Jennings, "Against the Finished Man."
19. Jennings, "Against the Finished Man," 1054–55.
20. Jennings, *After Whiteness*, 7–9, 44, 51–52.
21. Jennings, "Against the Finished Man," 1056.
22. Faith and Leadership, "Willie James Jennings."

ministry formation: Geoff Peterson, Milton Coleman, Meg Herbert, Doug Purnell, Christine Gapes, Rhonda White, Carolyn Thornley, and Christine Sorenson.

The formation of ordained ministers on behalf of the church has always mattered at United Theological College. Especially in recent years, UTC has sought to meet the growing diversity of its candidate cohort by increasing the diversity of its own people, programs, and processes. The future is likely to see UTC continue addressing the dominant place of Anglo-culture within the church, and within its own life as a leading institution within the church, by reviewing what and how it teaches, who is doing the teaching, who is being selected by the church for formation, and how those candidates will best be formed. Among the many responsibilities the college and its staff have held in formation, the embrace and nurture of diverse cultures, theologies, and genders in ministry candidates has been demanding work for faculty, formation leaders, and indeed for the candidates themselves. Past and present candidates often speak of the challenge of being required to shine a light on their theological and cultural biases, to look at their habits in leadership and the pattern of their relationships and to ask, "What must be formed, reformed, or transformed in me if I am to minister to the fullness of the church?" UTC has held that and other spaces of formative tension with and for the church for fifty years. Given how central this tradition has become to UTC and how central UTC has been to ordained ministry in the church, it is hard to imagine a future in which formation would not matter, and deeply matter, to the college community.

BIBLIOGRAPHY

Bos, Rob, and Geoff Thompson, eds. *Theology for Pilgrims: Selected Theological Documents of the Uniting Church in Australia*. Sydney: Uniting Church, 2008.
Faith and Leadership. "Willie James Jennings: By Naming the Foundational Problems of Theological Education, We Can Aspire to an Alternative Vision." Leadership Education at Duke Divinity. Nov. 24, 2020. https://faithandleadership.com/willie-james-jennings-naming-the-foundational-problems-theological-education-we-can-aspire.
Goh, Paul. "CALDing the Theological Culture in the Uniting Church in Australia." Act2, Nov. 1, 2023. https://act2uca.com/theological-culture/calding-theological-culture/.
Jennings, Willie James. *After Whiteness: An Education in Belonging*. Grand Rapids: Eerdmans, 2020.
———. "Against the Finished Man." *Modern Theology* 37.4 (2021) 1054–64.
Myers, Benjamin. *Christ the Stranger: The Theology of Rowan Williams*. London: T&T Clark, 2012.

Task Group on the Ministry of the Church. "Ministry in the Uniting Church (1991)." In *Theology For Pilgrims: Selected Theological Documents of the Uniting Church in Australia*, edited by Rob Bos and Geoff Thompson, 230–321. Sydney: Uniting Church, 2008.

United Theological College. "Candidates Contact List by Phase—2015–2023." North Parramatta, NSW: United Theological College, 2023.

———. "Candidate Statistics 0611." North Parramatta, NSW: United Theological College, 2007.

———. *UTC Formation Handbook: Education and Formation for Ordained Ministry in the Uniting Church in Australia Synod of NSW and the ACT*. North Parramatta, NSW: United Theological College, 2023.

Uniting Church in Australia. *Basis of Union*. Sydney: Uniting Church in Australia, 1992.

———. *A Brief Statement on Ordination*. Sydney: Uniting Church in Australia, 2008.

———. "Our Faith." https://uniting.church/empoweredbythespirit/#:~:text=Empowered%20in%20Diversity,faith%20(Basis%20Par%204.

———. "Sexuality and Leadership: Documenting the History." Illuminate. Released 2009. https://illuminate.recollect.net.au/nodes/view/20331.

———. *Standards for Theological Education and Formation: Phase 2 for Ordained Ministries*. Sydney: Uniting Church in Australia, 2016.

———. "Worksheet 5: Ordination." Illuminate. Released 2009. https://illuminate.recollect.net.au/nodes/view/20708.

Vosloo, Robert. "The Mystery of the Other: Bonhoeffer and the Recognition of Difference." In *Proceedings of the XIV International Bonhoeffer Congress, Sydney, 2024*, edited by Michael Mawson, 14–18. Sydney: United Theological College, 2024.

4

Community of the Heart

REBECCA LINDSAY

WHEN I CONTEMPLATE MY associations with United Theological College (UTC), many things matter. This is where I was formed in theological study and ministry practice and widened my understanding of and engagement with the Uniting Church of Australia (UCA). It is a place connected to worship, study, teaching, conferences, workshops, accommodation, and retreat space. In all this, UTC stands as connected to a *community*, or rather *communities*, of discipleship and faith formation. The many, varied communities I have encountered include student community, candidate community, ministry formation community, and local neighborhood (of those living on-site), as well as connection with place through, for example, learning in the bush chapel or watching trees out of the windows during classes. In this chapter I tell stories of my time as part of the UTC learning community. I reflect on an unexpected—precious—peer supported "community of the heart" that formed during my studies and continues to shape me. I celebrate the rich communities of difference I experienced at UTC and the ways these continue to enrich my theological thinking. Drawing on this autoethnographic mode of engaging with "history," I weave these stories together with reflections on the importance of community in and for theological education.

So, let me tell you a story...

Many years ago, in a time before Zoom, a younger me embarked on a formal theological education. I was only going to take one subject, as part of the Period of Discernment,[1] but was so excited by all that was on offer that I left the enrollment process with three subjects to juggle alongside the rest of life. I felt exhilarated, filled up with a joyful kind of anticipation. However, at this time I could not drive and soon realized that the last bus to Parramatta station departed Masons Drive prior to the finishing time of the class. A panic set in of wondering how to make the practicalities of study work. It was a disappointment of perhaps not being able to take these classes after all. At the subsequent orientation morning, I got talking to another young woman who was beginning a similar learning adventure. By the end of the day was the beginning of friendship and the offer of lifts to the train station for late-ending classes. Over time, in classrooms and hallway encounters, two other young women joined our conversations and life-upending questionings. Many years and diverse circumstances later, we four students of theology, faith, and life still meet, with intention, to hold each other's hearts, to accompany each other, to bear witness to each other's joy and pain, and to encourage each other in faith. This community of the heart was forged at United Theological College.

The "history" within this chapter draws upon the self-reflexive methodologies of autoethnography and ego-histoire. Autoethnography is writing and method that connects the personal and autobiographical with the cultural and political.[2] Influenced by feminism, its approach to research is to begin from where one is, consciously reflecting on the place of the writer within what they write.[3] Ego-histoire draws on autoethnography to make explicit connections between a scholar's autobiography, their scholarly writing, and the wider sociopolitical context in which both living and writing take place.[4] This melding of "personal history, a broader social history and historiographical reflection" draws out the relationship between these elements.[5] In ego-histoire, at times, "the object and the subject conflate."[6] This conflation is seen in the deeply personal character of this chapter, as I seek to understand the conditions that enabled my community of the heart to develop and which influenced its shape. In adapting this approach to the things that matter at UTC, I retell elements of my own lived experience at

1. The Period of Discernment in the UCA is a time of intentional reflection about how a person's gifts and graces might be used, accompanied by a mentor. It is also the first stage in the process moving towards ordination within the UCA.
2. Ellis, *Ethnographic I*, 37.
3. Ellis, *Ethnographic I*, 47.
4. Cole, "History," 528.
5. Castejon et al., "Introduction," 5–6.
6. Passerine and Goepert cited in Cole, "History," 527.

the college alongside the story of UTC from within its own publications.[7] I consider the time period from 2008 when I first began studying my bachelor of theology at UTC until I completed my ministry formation in 2012, with some reflection on the wider time frame examined within this book. I cannot write this history in any other way because the community of the heart matters to me: there is no objective path into this reflection.

FORMATION IN COMMUNITY

Within the program of formation for ordination, ministry candidates and faculty gather weekly. The program includes faculty members sharing resources that they find helpful for ministry. This particular week something holds my attention. One member of the faculty introduces a book. Over time the book and the faculty member's presentation fade, except for one detail. The faculty member names a concept: community of the heart. I remember the moment he speaks this phrase. Immediately, I am brought to attention. Immediately, my heart jumps. This is us! This term describes the small gathering of my friends. When we next meet to tell and hear the stories of each other's lives, I offer this name to them. With it comes the practice we already embody of accompanying each other. The new name, however, carries with it a further commitment to be intentional, now and in what we hope will be long years ahead.

The term "community of the heart" comes from theologian David Ford, who uses the heart as a metaphor to describe the "home for all the concerns of our lives."[8] He reflects on how layers of relationships, with their associated memories, feelings, identities, and hopes, impact the patterns of peoples' lives.[9] Ford argues that this relationality shapes people as "our hearts are filled with the faces and voices of those before whom we live. These are the members of our 'community of the heart.'"[10] Noting that these relationships may not all be positive but also include relationships that discourage or undermine, Ford wonders how hearts, and so lives, are formed and shaped in the midst of all the "overwhelmings" people experience. He argues that this shape is recognized by examining, firstly, which people dwell within this formative community and, secondly, the boundaries of hospitality that people set.[11]

---

7. For example, in editions of *Out & About: Magazine of the United Theological College* and in various editions of the *UTC Formation Handbook*.

8. Ford, *Shape of Living*, 33.

9. Ford, *Shape of Living*, 33.

10. Ford, *Shape of Living*, 33.

11. Ford, *Shape of Living*, 35.

Ford identifies multiple overwhelmings in the stories that recount Jesus' experiences from his baptism, which led him to the wilderness, to storytelling and eating among disciples and crowds, to the anguish before his death and the strangeness of resurrection, experienced by his followers as "the most disorienting and transformative overwhelming of all."[12] For those who follow after Christ, it is this person who centers the community of their heart. Within communities where Christ is held close, questions open up about identity, hospitality, vocation, and wisdom in intentionally seeking to shape the "joyful responsibility" of discipleship. In seeking to be formed by Christ, Ford contends that the "ultimate privilege" is to be held by a wise community who sees and is seen by each other.[13]

It is important to note that I did not read Ford's book until many years after its key term was introduced to me. It was not with the book itself that I forged a connection but with the term "community of the heart" and the faculty member's elucidation of this. I also note that when I did read the book, it did not live up to my imaginings, and I will return to this later. However, I see the threads of responsibility, joy, and mutual attention, which are named by Ford, woven through the organic ways that my community of the heart developed, a development that was grounded in the learning community of the college. I am aware of other communities like mine that have emerged among particular cohorts of candidates for ordained ministry, some of which have continued over many years. I am not, however, aware of other communities of the heart that have begun when all members were *not* candidates for ordination. This does not mean that these communities do not exist, but given how much it matters, it does cause me to wonder about the conditions that have enabled a sustained intentional commitment to community.

When I began a bachelor of theology in 2008, the student cohort was small but diverse. I studied alongside members of the UCA, the Anglican church, Pentecostal denominations, the Metropolitan Community Church, the Community of Christ (a Mormon denomination), and a vast array of theological frameworks. There were people who identified as Aboriginal, American, English, Fijian, Indonesian, Korean, Papua New Guinean, Tongan, and as connected to other places. There were students straight from high school, mature aged first-timers, and others returning to study after a break. There was a sharp divide between candidates for specified ministry and everybody else. I was designated as a "private student," which carried a sense of being outside the core community of the college. I began my formal

---

12. Ford, *Shape of Living*, 50.
13. Ford, *Shape of Living*, 99.

period as a candidate for ordination in 2010, crossing to the "inside" of this student body boundary.

In 2008 the campus felt quite isolated.[14] There was one irregular bus between Parramatta and Epping stations that stopped at Masons Drive (and when missed, it was long walk up the hill from Parramatta with a bag full of text or library books). The coffee at Burnside café was mediocre at best. There was, however, always someone in the foyer of the Centre for Ministry, sitting on green chairs, waiting for conversation. This someone might have been another student, a faculty member, or a staff person from another part of the synod operations. On the green chairs where we procrastinated from assignments, ate dinner before night classes, and where "experts" sat with "novices," there was a rich experience of theological community as dialogical meeting among difference. This diversity is on display in the 2008 editions of *Out & About*, which highlight the growing Korean-language collection in Camden Library,[15] a reflection on the diversity of the cultural diversity of the student body,[16] and a feature on the idea of Communitas as community-in-progress that would be "a safe and respectful place in which the richly diverse and rainbow people of God might encounter each other" and so encounter God.[17]

It was in this context that I met three women who now hold my heart. I described the first encounter with one above, another I already knew a little through shared connection with UCA tertiary chaplaincy groups, and the third I passed in the hallway before her connections with the other two brought us together. Each of us desired theology. We sought tools for thinking about faith and for leadership within faith communities. To study at UTC was a great adventure, but also daunting, and a challenge to the patterns and assumptions of being Christian that we already held, no matter how "good" or "well formed" these may or may not have been. It was *an overwhelming*, to use Ford's language. As Ben Myers wrote in the December 2008 edition of *Out & About*, "there's no 'safe' way of doing theology . . . theology is about making decisions, taking risks, venturing to say something about God."[18] Risk is made easier in community. Sometimes it is valuable to

---

14. A 2011 report from the Student Committee in *Out & About*'s issue titled "Ministry Matters" wrote that "UTC is a small university campus. There isn't a cafe or pub on-site. . . . There aren't lots of clubs and societies for students to join up to. . . . And many students travel significant distances to attend class." Student Association Executive, "Student Executive."

15. Bryant, "Oak Trees," 8.

16. Earl, "Final UTC Graduation," 16.

17. Tahaafe-Williams, "Vision for Communitas," 7.

18. Myers, "Venturing to Say Something," 12–13.

try out questions, doubts, and new ideas with a trusted group before naming them to a wider classroom audience. In the unmaking that can come with theological education, friends help. Having grown up in hierarchical, patriarchal church systems, that these friends were women was important to me. We were all similarly-ish aged, all connected with the UCA, and all commencing our study around the same time. Something clicked, and we met to talk about coursework, church work, gossip, and life. The adoption of the name "community of the heart" helped us to move from haphazardly supportive student peers into intentional discipleship companions.

COMMITMENT TO ACCOMPANIMENT

The community of the heart has found a rhythm that guides our gatherings. The first step is waiting. We cannot begin until all are present. This can mean holding back news or conversation until everyone has arrived. Waiting is awkward. Chitchat fills the space when I wish to rush to deeper places. Once everyone is present, we each in turn share something of our lives in their fullness—how is our work, our family, our mental and physical health. This is a time for us to attend deeply to the story and experience of our friend. At the end of each story, there may be questions that arise as someone connects this story with those told previously or asks the sharer to explain a little more about her situation. There may be words spoken to affirm that our dear heart is a child of God in her vulnerability and challenge. There may be words of reminder to our dear heart, that she would remember that she is loved and called to live following after Christ. This pattern continues until all have shared and each story has been held with tenderness and care. This process takes time; it cannot be rushed. When we were students, we could stretch out our gatherings into dinners or across weekends. In this moment of life, we experience greater limits. We may have only a Zoomed hour. We care for each other in ensuring each person has time and opportunity to share that which is experienced as abundance and not scarcity. There may be tears, there may be laughter, there may be silence. Usually, someone is celebrating. Usually, someone is experiencing brokenness. Each person is free to bring what she wishes, knowing it will be held with loving-kindness.

The community of the heart began our conversations about the subjects we studied together. We talked about early church history and the oral projects we needed to present within class. We compared which biblical critical methods from the introductions to Old and New Testament studies made sense to us and which we preferred to skip over. We navigated a Trinity class reading Augustine as best we could. We were not taking the same programs or studying for the same purpose, so we compared notes on the subjects which differed, noting our favorite readings and subjects for those who took classes in subsequent years. Each embedded in communities where we offered pastoral or liturgical leadership in some way, our conversation often sought to meld what we were learning with how, or whether, it might "fit" within our practice. We were practicing "integration," although we would not have used this term at the time.[19] We helped each other in "finding our place in the ministry of Christ which is *the mission of God the Father in and for the world in the power of the Spirit*."[20] This integration, understood as essential to the discipleship and formation of those training to be ordained, was something that was missing from the formal college experience of "private students" at this time. The "green-chair theology" of the Centre for Ministry foyer and the fledgling heart community filled this gap.

Despite its lopsided focus on candidates as those to be formed, the college did invite all its students to join in chapel worship. The pastoral community at the center of the college's life set the tone for other students and visitors to its life. Faculty members at the time modeled hospitality and vulnerability. They were pivotal in creating the circumstances that enabled our heart to form. I remember one lecturer, seeking to build community in an evening class, placing a variety of drinks and cheese on a trolley and wheeling it around to serve students during a small group discussion time within the tutorial portion of the lecture. Another, who lived on campus, celebrated the end of a semester by welcoming us to his home for a class dinner shared with his family. Looking back, having spent time both as a student and a lecturer at UTC and in other places, this posture of hospitality suggests to me a faculty who felt at home within the college, enough to entangle themselves beyond formal teaching.

There were also moments of vulnerability and radical honesty that, at times, shocked me. When I began my formal study at UTC, I was relatively new to the Uniting Church. I was not naïve enough to believe that the church is always a place of good behavior, but the Uniting Church, and the college within it, were places of respite for me—my experiences of poor behavior enacted by the institutional church and its representatives had been from other denominations. Midway through my first year of study, one faculty member took up a placement elsewhere. Two things struck me in the address she gave at her closure service. The first was her acknowledgment of her own failings in her role, a liturgical movement I subsequently

---

19. The concept of "integration" is key within the process of formation for ordained ministry, as seen in the *UTC Formation Handbook* of 2012 prepared by Carolyn Thornley, 2018 prepared by Christine Sorensen, and 2024 prepared by Nicole Fleming.

20. Thornley, *UTC Formation Handbook*, 9. Italics in original.

appreciated within the closure of placement and funeral liturgies of *Uniting in Worship 2*. The second was a statement she made acknowledging a tension in how other staff perceived her work.[21] The blunt honesty took me aback, and I have often reflected on this moment and the ways that the worship central to college life is able to shape conversation among its participants. In another moment, while a candidate for ordination, I asked faculty members a question about how they held their many roles and responsibilities within and outside of formal ministry. One responded, "I don't think I did that very well." These moments acknowledged the challenges within the college community but also modeled a form of leadership and ministry that did not have to be always "successful" or flawless.

Ultimately, it was intentionality that turned a group of fellow students into a community of the heart. Especially in the midst of busy work, geographical spread, the chaos of family, and changing nuances of theology, the commitment to keep meeting with each other continues our community of the heart. The growing time span of this community means the ability to bring past experiences to our present engagement. Intention is the glue. As one member reflected in conversation, this commitment enables an accountability within which we have ceded the choice to hide our lives away. This accountability is not to an institution. Rather, she identifies that "what matters most to me is how you three offer me accountability to my journey in formation, ministry, and life. It's intentional space to listen to my own heart and give voice to this."[22] Ford reflects similarly on the importance of accountability in shaping lives after Christ. Pointing to Jesus' time in the wilderness, he identifies Jesus' response to the temptations in this place demonstrating accountability to God and so "taking responsibility for his life and mission. The crucial thing for his vocation, and for ours, is to whom is he is accountable and to whom he is responsible: the God who loves and delights in him."[23] The accountability within the community of the heart seeks to mirror this love and delight and so remind each other of the love and call of God again and again.

TEARS AND JOYS

My dear heart is upended by an unexpected medical emergency in her family. There is nothing I can do but listen and share in her tears. Years later I am surrounded by a circle of care. I speak my story of loss. It is a story I have told

21. Monro, "Anita's Farewell Discourse."
22. Ellie Elia, Facebook direct message to author, Feb. 12, 2024.
23. Ford, *Shape of Living*, 65.

previously but always felt the need to self-edit, to worry about how others will be affected by encounters with death. But to my heart I speak without censoring my words or my tears. I trust this community. Their holding of me binds me to them.

To accompany each other has meant not only to share in academic or ecclesial questions but to bear witness to, and at times enter into, the tragedy held within each other's lives. Ford notices the importance of receiving compassionate attention amid suffering but also notes its fragile possibility, for it is not certain that such attention will find us.[24] The fragility is held in the one overwhelmed by their experience but also in the potential encounter with those who might hold them. There is vulnerability and trust in being able to speak of what is broken. There is also vulnerability and trust in holding—gently, "care-fully," responsibly—another who is broken. My whole world has been shattered more than once in the years of our accompaniment. To speak honestly of this in that first moment of not trusting myself, let alone "the church," risked a deeper breaking. I have learned to trust my external heart to see in me a story that I cannot always see myself.

The documents that demonstrate the life of the college acknowledge the challenges of living that flows from baptism into Christ. "The journey of life with God is not an easy one.... Allow yourself to lean on God and your community and receive from both the encouragement and insight about yourself that you will need to make important decisions about your life."[25] Regarding the specific work of preparing for ordination, the *UTC Formation Handbook* notes that "most candidates find that entering the formation process presents difficulties, even if they have been engaged in lay or specified ministries for many years."[26] The challenges posed by engagement in the global context of disaster and changing climate were also a regular feature of chapel and the college magazine. In the wake of the Christchurch earthquake, Dean Drayton writes that "in the mystery of God's power what we are most sure about is the compassionate presence of this God with us in the midst of the agonies and joys of life."[27] I would suggest that one gift of a community of accompaniment is that when I am *not* sure about God's compassionate presence, I have others whom I trust to hold that truth. At times, I may be the one who embodies this understanding and holds it on behalf of my friend.

---

24. Ford, *Shape of Living*, 168–69.

25. Thornley, *UTC Formation Handbook*, 12.

26. This phrase is found with slightly differing punctuation or phrasing in the *UTC Formation Handbook* of 2012 (13), 2018 (10), and 2024 (7).

27. Drayton, "On Faith and Earthquakes," 8.

I wonder, at this point, how such communities of accompaniment and vulnerability might function within a setting such as the college. The 2012 *Formation Handbook* names the expectation that formation will take place within community and that this community ought to be marked by courage, vulnerability, encouragement, and collaboration.[28] UTC, however, is an institution which is part of the Uniting Church as an institution. It has responsibilities for theological education and Phase 2 formation for specified ministry with the Uniting Church in the Synod of NSW (New South Wales) and ACT (Australian Capital Territory). This means that, despite shared discipleship symbolized in the commonality of baptism, there are multiple power dynamics at play that may impede the formation of communities of vulnerability and trust. There is a disjunction between being vulnerable and being assessed for essays or ministry competency, naming brokenness and being aware of power and roles which may impact future ministry opportunities. This raises the question of what heart communities might look like within a space of imbalanced power.

Alongside sharing in difficulty has been the intentional practice of naming joy. A common question during our meetings, usually in the space after one heart has shared her story, is where are you finding joy? The sense of being overwhelmed by challenges is often unavoidable—the visceral interruption of grief or trauma invades life-as-normal. Joy, however, can be more elusive. Ford names joy as risk, given that it opens people up to disappointment or the experience of deceit.[29] The practice of naming joy has been a sharing of delight. This delight has been vast, including everything from meeting babies to weekly sauna visits, a medication working to the smell of salt air. Given our connection to UTC and formal education, we have celebrated essays submitted and silly hats thrown in the air. The joy we seek to practice is not averting our gaze from pain. Sometimes this joy is not even a feeling but is the relief of being held by intentional companions.

WHO IS MISSING?

I am on maternity leave. COVID-19 has been disrupting patterns of life and church. Between lockdowns, we are visiting friends for a few days. I am feeling disconnected and exhausted, uncertain of who and how to be in this context. I pick up a book from my friend's pile and begin to read. "Formation is an elusive thing to see in practice. It is the shining goal of all education, especially

---

28. Thornley, *UTC Formation Handbook*, 27–28, 30–32.
29. Ford, *Shape of Living*, 184.

*theological education."*³⁰ *I read on, noting Jennings's argument of the homogenizing process of Western (theological) education to form "a white self-sufficient man, his self-sufficiency defined by possession, control, and mastery."*³¹ *I do not want to put this book down although the need to feed small people and get them to bed means I will have to wait. I find my heart enlivened by the alternative community built out of fragments that Jennings alludes to. This, I think, is the kind of faith community I want to belong to and be a part of shaping.*

One of the things I notice about my community of the heart is our sameness as well as our difference. We come from differing education backgrounds, family systems, suburbs, theologies. When we met, our experiences of faith and denominational life were certainly not the same, although we have now all journeyed many years within the UCA, our identities connected with this embodiment of church. But we also share similarities: we are all white women who grew up in the lands now called Australia and had access to tertiary education. Ford suggests that the boundaries of hospitality, both given and received by a person, demonstrate the shape of their heart. Given the diversity within the college that I have already named, I wonder what this sameness demonstrates about our community. I noted earlier that when I finally read *The Shape of Living*, I found it disappointing. This was because I read it *after* encountering Jennings and his critique of the assumed whiteness of Christian theological education. I note that this critique has long been part of the college seen, for example, in wrestling with the commitment of the Uniting Church to be multicultural,³² with Indigenous theologies,³³ and with interfaith dialogue.³⁴

Within Australia, those formed within the dominant and dominating frameworks of settler thinking tend to assume that white bodies and Western assumptions are "normal" and "common sense." This raises questions about how communities akin to the community of the heart might be formed within institutions such as UTC, which emerge from within these assumptions, despite the college's diverse students and staff. The white members of the Mud Flower Collective, an experimental feminist collective of diverse theological educators in the United States, express this in terms of accountability. They contend that "white women must realize that we, no

---

30. Jennings, *After Whiteness*, 4.

31. Jennings, *After Whiteness*, 6.

32. For example, Carroll, "Welcoming An(Other)"; Tahaafe-Williams, "Vision for Communitas."

33. For example, Havea, "Indigenous Theologies."

34. For example, Carroll, "Education for Ministry"; Pearson, "Emerging Interfaith Relationships."

less than women of color, need to be clear about to whom, in particular, we hold ourselves accountable."[35] Asking "what might it involve to be in solidarity with one another across the lines that divide us?" they identify justice in the world as the goal for which theological education ought to strive.[36]

There is resonance here with Jennings, who argues for a *different* kind of formation within theological education: an embrace of fragments that might unmake the self-sufficient white man and form instead "a gathering that breaks boundaries and crosses borders" and moves towards "an elusive goal—life in a place of communion."[37] Speaking to members of the Uniting Church at the *Walking Together* conference, Bidjara theologian Anne Pattel-Gray identified the need for new language to express new forms of theology and new relationships that would describe and enable differently shaped, decolonized communities.[38] The community of the heart, as a community holding vulnerability, trust, honesty, and accountability, ought to be part of such movement. Even in the challenge of holding their diverse community together, the Mud Flower Collective write that "only insofar as our strongest loves and fears, hatreds and hopes are known to us and shared with others can we actually learn/teach anything worth knowing about God."[39] Again, this vision only makes sense for them when justice is named as the center and purpose of theological education and formation.[40]

GREEN-CHAIR THEOLOGY

When I was a student at UTC, I learned as much outside of the classroom as within it. The "green-chair theology" of those waiting between classes or on breaks from the library was a formative space. It was here the diversity of those involved with college life could be seen. The experience of conversation—deep and inane—held in these chairs stays with me. The chairs are now red . . . and often empty.[41] I recognize within this emptiness the inclusivity of hybrid learning communities that open the college to those who are grounded in other physical locations or life situations. This is a gift to them and to the learning communities who share in their wisdom and presence. I do wonder, however, about the challenges hybrid learning brings and I

---

35. Cannon et al., *God's Fierce Whimsy*, 5.
36. Cannon et al., *God's Fierce Whimsy*, 61, 33.
37. Jennings, *After Whiteness*, 148, 46.
38. Pattel-Gray, "Raising Our Tribal Voice."
39. Cannon et al., *God's Fierce Whimsy*, 196.
40. Cannon et al., *God's Fierce Whimsy*, 204.
41. Apart from formation days.

wonder if my community of the heart would have formed today without our embodied encounters and the need for a lift home after an in-person class. How do we attend to (disembodied) community as those embedded in a faith whose central markers are embodiment?[42] I hope that UTC will engage with this question to create the conditions which might enable other communities of the heart to form.

Pattel-Gray argues that the language we need for a decolonized community, the theology of who we will be, is not yet created. It is in places such as UTC that this work must take place, creating new communities of the heart that are more full and less othering. My experience of learning, of being formed, of friendships and accompaniments at UTC is one for which I am deeply appreciative. In the "green-chair theology" that takes place now, I hope that the discipleship and faith formation is worked out in communities of truth-telling, truth acceptance, compassionate accompaniment, and prayer. One member of my community of the heart suggested that the intentional attention which is integral to the community of the heart might be understood as a blessing to the wider church. Through practicing vulnerability with and for others, "we try to help the church to be more shaped like a heart."[43] This is the substance of what matters.

BIBLIOGRAPHY

Bryant, Moira. "Oak Trees Grow from Acorns." *Out & About* 14 (2008) 8.
Cannon, Katie G., et al. *God's Fierce Whimsy: Christian Feminism and Theological Education*. New York: Pilgrim, 1985.
Carroll, Seforosa. "Education for Ministry and Mission in Multifaith and Multicultural Australia." *Out & About* 23 (2011) 20–22.
———. "Welcoming An(Other): Exploring an Ecclesiology of Hospital*eity* in Multicultural Australia." *Out & About* 7 (2006) 11–13.
Castejon, Vanessa, et al. "Introduction: 'Ngapartji Ngapartji: In Turn, in Turn'—Ego-Histoire and Australian Indigenous Studies." In *Ngapartji Ngapartji: In Turn, in Turn: Ego-Histoire, Europe and Indigenous Australia*, edited by Vanessa Castejon et al., 3–20. Canberra, ACT: Australian National University Press, 2014. https://doi.org/10.22459/nn.11.2014.01.
Cole, Anna. "'The History That Has Made You': Ego-Histoire, Autobiography and Postcolonial History." *Life Writing* 16.4 (2019) 527–38. https://doi.org/10.1080/14484528.2019.1633249.
Drayton, Dean. "On Faith and Earthquakes." *Out & About* 24 (2011) 8.
Earl, Michael. "Final UTC Graduation with SCD." *Out & About* 15 (2008) 16.

---

42. This work is already happening, and has been for many years, within the UCA and in other places.

43. Ellie Elia, Facebook direct message to author, Apr. 12, 2024.

Ellis, Carolyn. *The Ethnographic I: A Methodological Novel About Autoethnography*. Walnut Creek, CA: AltaMira, 2004.
Ford, David F. *The Shape of Living: Spiritual Directions for Everyday Life*. Grand Rapids: Baker, 2004.
Havea, Jione. "Indigenous Theologies: First People, Second Citizens, and Restless Stories . . ." *Out & About* 13 (2007) 17–18.
Jennings, Willie James. *After Whiteness: An Education in Belonging*. Grand Rapids: Eerdmans, 2020.
Monro, Anita. "Anita's Farewell Discourse." *Out & About* 17 (2008) 4–5.
Myers, Ben. "Venturing to Say Something About God." *Out & About* 17 (2008) 12–13.
Pattel-Gray, Anne. "Raising Our Tribal Voice." Paper presented at the Walking Together conference, Sydney, Oct. 22, 2022.
Pearson, Mary. "Emerging Interfaith Relationships." *Out & About* 13 (2007) 8.
Student Association Executive. "Student Executive." *Out & About* 24 (May 2011) 21.
Tahaafe-Williams, Katalina. "A Vision for Communitas." *Out & About* 16 (2008) 4–7.
United Theological College. *UTC Formation Handbook*. Edited by Carolyn Thornley. North Parramatta, NSW: United Theological College, 2012.
———. *UTC Formation Handbook*. Edited by Christine Sorensen. North Parramatta, NSW: United Theological College, 2018.
———. *UTC Formation Handbook*. Edited by Nicole Fleming. North Parramatta, NSW: United Theological College, 2024.

5

Multiculturalism, Theological Learning, and Community at UTC

SEFOROSA CARROLL AND CAROLYN CRAIG-EMILSEN

THIS CHAPTER SEEKS TO explore the changing cultural diversity of the United Theological College (UTC) community between 1999 and 2024, focusing on the changing Australian cultural and religious landscape and how theological education at UTC has reflected this.

In Australia, migration has brought diverse cultures, religions, and forms of church worship. As early as 1985, the Uniting Church boldly declared itself to be a "multicultural church." In making this declaration, the UCA (Uniting Church of Australia) recognized the importance of relevant theological education for preparing people for ministry and discipleship in this emerging Australian cultural context. Paragraph 8 of the 1985 statement asserts, "The Assembly recognizes the need for special ministerial education programs to prepare people for ministry in multicultural parishes and ethnic congregations."[1] Furthermore, resolution 85.95 of the Eighth Assembly requested

> the Ministerial Education Commission, in consultation with the Commission for Mission, to encourage theological colleges to explore alternative forms of theological education by which

---

1. Uniting Church in Australia, *Uniting Church*.

candidates from ethnic backgrounds, for whom English is a second language, can be prepared for Ministry of the Word and Ministry of Deaconess within the Uniting Church.[2]

Maintaining a high standard of theological education and a vibrant community of learning have been core values of UTC since its inception in 1974. Considering its first twenty-five years, historian Geoffrey Barnes noted UTC strived to keep the balance between "life situations from which students come and . . . the constituency its graduates will serve."[3] Barnes also noted that "the increasing multiculturalism of Australian society was only gradually reflected in the College" and that "only in the 1990s did Australian students begin to appreciate the deeper enrichment of cross-cultural faith stories."[4]

By the early 2000s there had been considerable changes in the way multiculturalism was reflected in the Australian religious landscape. Writing in 2006, Helen Richmond and Myong Duk Yang observed,

> The Australian Christian landscape has been . . . dramatically changing. As Australia has become increasingly multicultural, so issues of identity, belonging, racism and living with diversity have come onto the agenda of churches. Today, many congregations sense the need to engage in ministry and mission in a multicultural and multifaith context, taking up the opportunities and challenges of living with diversity in the Body of Christ. For the churches in Australia, living with diversity requires a willingness to learn and change.[5]

Within this broader context of a changing societal landscape and the challenges of "living with diversity in the Body of Christ,"[6] as Richmond and Yang eloquently expressed, our chapter seeks to explore UTC in light of three key ideas. The first is as a gathering place for many cultures. The second is as a community which embraces the intersections between learning, culture, and faith. The third is an ethos which has encouraged deep spiritual growth and lifelong learning.

In light of these three key ideas, we have chosen to do oral history interviews with seven students from different cultural backgrounds who attended UTC at various times between 1999 and 2024. Oral history is a

---

2. Uniting Church in Australia, *Multicultural Policies*, 5.
3. Barnes, *Doing Theology*, 100.
4. Barnes, *Doing Theology*, 106.
5. Richmond and Yang, *Crossing Borders*, 7.
6. Richmond and Yang, *Crossing Borders*, 7.

recollection of lived experience in the person's own voice. Oral history is practiced, taught, and written about both inside and outside tertiary contexts.[7] The English historian Paul Thompson, in the first edition of his classic text, *The Voice of the Past* wrote: "Oral history thrusts life into history itself and widens its scope."[8] The North American oral historian Michael Frisch has argued that memory should be seen "as the object, not merely the method of oral history" and that used in this way, oral history could be a

> powerful tool for discovering, exploring, and evaluating the nature of historical memory—how people make sense of their past, how they connect individual experience and its social context, how the past becomes part of the present, and how people use it to interpret their lives and the world around them.[9]

The oral history interviews are not to be considered as a sociological sample. The interviewees are from seven different cultural backgrounds. All are permanent Australian residents. They include an Anglo-Australian, Tongan, Korean, Indonesian, Indian, Rotuman, and an Aboriginal Gudang elder from Cape York. Their experiences and decisions involved in studying theology and their cultural and faith journeys have involved complexity, sacrifice, courage, and determination.

We believe the answers to the questions used in the interviews reflect the three key ideas we are interested in. The questions were firstly: In what ways were your theological studies (and, where applicable, ministry formation) shaped by your experience as a student as part of a multicultural community at UTC in terms of learning, culture, and faith? The second question was: How were you enriched, encouraged, and stimulated by this experience? The third question was: From your perspective now, what value do you see as having been a student in this community? And finally, what memories and influences have stayed with you? How have these shaped your endeavors since leaving UTC in either ministry, other professional contexts, or your own life? A great deal of thoughtful reflection was embodied in these oral history interviews. It is the elements of personality, affect, personal observation, positive and negative nature of experience, strong emotion, humor, remembered significance, the strength of conviction, attributed and lasting values, and surprise that makes the oral record a human record. Some of the nuances of the human voice cannot be captured in the

---

7. Oral history was included in the subject "Uniting Church Studies" at UTC in the 1990s taught by William and Susan Emilsen.

8. Thompson, *Voice of the Past*, 18.

9. Frisch, *Shared Authority*, 188.

written account. But the words themselves reveal many primary human emotions, which express the human dimension of these stories.

Our chapter is written by two people who were (one still is) a part of the community at UTC from 2000 to 2024. Each of us has had a period of time of close involvement with UTC and a time apart. The first five students in the oral history interview cohort studied at UTC between 2005 and 2014. This was a time when there was a growth in the number of students from different cultural backgrounds. This period coincided with Craig-Emilsen's involvement at UTC, where she was the Study Skills tutor and also taught a course called Critical Thinking. The course had been initiated several years earlier, with great foresight by Susan Emilsen. Critical Thinking subsequently became Reasoning, Values, and Writing when UTC became part of Charles Sturt University.

In 2007, Carroll returned to the UTC community to do her PhD, after eight years in ministry. While studying, Carroll worked part-time at Camden Theological Library, during which time she experienced firsthand the challenges students faced, particularly those from non-Anglo-Australian backgrounds. From 2012 to 2014, Carroll was the First Year Mentor at UTC, where she and Craig-Emilsen worked together as part of the Student Support Team. The ethos of the team was to academically and pastorally support students, particularly those from non-English-speaking backgrounds. The remaining two students who were interviewed studied at UTC between 2020 and 2024. Carroll returned to UTC in January 2023 as the lecturer in cross-cultural ministry and theology and is now the academic dean.

As a possible overall approach to our exploration of these oral history narratives, we have embraced concepts of space and place. The spaces we occupy, invite others into, or are welcomed into have histories. The recognition that "there is no such thing as a physical geography divorced from its human geography" has entailed the phenomenological approach to space.[10] At a basic level, space is the place we occupy, dwell, or inhabit. A space is always linked to land, a country, a place, and a body/bodies. But as John Inge points out, "what begins as undifferentiated space becomes place as we get to know it better and endow it with value. It is from the security and stability of place we are aware of the openness and freedom and threat of space, and vice versa."[11]

A space becomes a place when it is storied by human experience and meaning. According to Edward Relph, "it is through particular encounters and experiences that space is richly differentiated into places, or centers of

---

10. Inge, *Christian Theology*, 16.
11. Inge, *Christian Theology*, 1.

specific personal experience. A place is a location of experience."[12] Relph further states that "places are constructed in our memory and affections through repeated encounters and complex associations and place experiences are necessarily time deepened and memory qualified."[13] A space becomes a place when it has been lived, given meaning, and "storied" with meaning. Inge proposes that space becomes a place when it is endowed with value.[14] Spaces acquire meaning and value through memory, inhabitation and encounters, which in turn transform a space into a place of meaning.

A GATHERING PLACE FOR MANY CULTURES

Although it may not have been an explicit original intention that UTC would be a gathering place for many cultures, this gradually emerged out of the mission for the Centre for Ministry (CFM), which opened in 1987. The intention was that CFM be a place of meeting, gathering, and interchange between four educational ministries: Education for Lay Ministries (ELM), Continuing Education, Institute for Mission, and UTC. Over time this vision, the place, space, and location of CFM would play a critical role in shaping the community.

The CFM "was designed to give expression to the doctrine that every gift has its corresponding service."[15] The architecture of the Centre was inspired by the *Basis of Union*, which "encouraged ministers and laity to develop their individual gifts to enhance the life of the whole and bear witness to the one ministry of Christ."[16] As Barnes observed, "The pastoral and intellectual needs of the church were constantly being challenged by the need to express the faith of the gospel in cooperative human institutions without quenching the Spirit."[17] The architects Bert Hely and Associates "created a complex remarkable for its flexibility for all sorts of functions."[18] Careful consideration was given to the location of the chapel within CFM and its design. A guiding principle was that "there needed to be a sense of community and intimacy."[19]

12. Cited in Inge, *Christian Theology*, 79.
13. Cited in Inge, *Christian Theology*, 83–84.
14. Inge, *Christian Theology*, 2.
15. Barnes, *Doing Theology*, 83.
16. Barnes, *Doing Theology*, 83.
17. Barnes, *Doing Theology*, 89.
18. Barnes, *Doing Theology*, 88.
19. Barnes, *Doing Theology*, 89.

The design of the CFM was intended to create community and facilitate enriching relationships. The intent for a space that promoted gathering, meeting, and interchange has continued to the present day. From the mid-1990s to the present, UTC has hosted students from Africa, the Middle East, Europe, Asia, the Pacific, and Australia. UTC has reflected the broader multicultural society of Australia and striven, in a modest way, to create a positive model of what might be achieved in the wider community, be it church, society, or the world.

At the time of writing in 2024, UTC's student body comprised a majority of students from a Pasifika background. At the UTC retreat in February 2024, eight of the sixteen candidates were from non-Anglo-Australian cultural backgrounds. Of those eight candidates, one was Asian and seven were Pacific Islanders. Out of the seven Pacific Islanders, there was one man and six women. Six of the islanders were Tongan. The cultural diversity of the college in 2024 is different from that of the early 2000s, when there seemed to be a more even spread of cultures. In the early to mid-2000s, Korean students had a strong visible presence. There have been attempts at Indigenous curricula and partnership in teaching at UTC, but unfortunately, these have not materialized into a permanent relationship. The number of Aboriginal students at UTC has been minimal. In 2019, as part of CSU policy, Indigenous Australian Cultures and Spiritualities became a core subject of the BTh program. In addition, UTC offered Reconciliation (a compulsory subject for all candidates) and, years prior, offered the subject Doing Theology on Indigenous Land.

UTC was to become known, however, as a gathering place for many cultures, for making new connections and forming lasting relationships. As Christine Gapes asserts, "UTC has tried to be a culturally resonant space where people see, hear, and experience parts of their culture so that they have a little bit of 'home' in this strange place."[20] Pearl Wymarra, who studied at UTC from 2019 to 2024, insightfully speaks of the embodiment of space, place, and people, stating, "I realized just as with people coming from overseas that as an Aboriginal person, I have a diaspora within. Here at UTC, you are in an academic tradition, yet within the learning you're able to bring together the journeys of faith and culture while holding the diaspora within you."[21] Steve Lee, who studied from 2008 to 2012, described his experience of place and space in this way: "The formation of the Atrium area and the library, the design of the building itself is really about welcome.

20. Gapes, "Braiding Learning," §21.
21. Wymarra, interview, June 12, 2024. Pearl Wymarra, a Gudang Cape York elder and community liaison officer for Penrith City Council, studied at UTC from 2019 to 2024 (BTh).

As soon as I entered the front entrance, I could see the chapel, the library, and the little café area. I felt comfortable to be in this space, welcomed. The chapel was always open. You could sit there."²² Linda Turton, who studied from 2005 to 2010, spoke of her experience in a similar way: "In the Atrium, there were student lunches, people mixed with different cultures, hosted by different groups. It was a small community. The placement of the Atrium in the Centre worked well for gathering. It worked well to allow us to get to know each other."²³

Xavier Lakshmanan, a postgraduate student at UTC from 2009 to 2013, spoke of the welcome and support he received on arrival: "Initially, I didn't have family with me. Both academic and administrative staff supported me. I attended morning teas, chapel, and everything the community offered. It was not boring, not lonely, and so enriching."²⁴ Hani Ieli, who studied from 2015 to 2024 and at the time of writing was Senior Student comments, "One of the things I loved was the sharing of food and learning how to experience and to respect other cultures."²⁵ Wymarra described her experience in this way: "Students weren't just relating in class but sharing more like a family with lots of different cultures. I was learning a lot from interacting, but I still felt I had to try harder. I tried to concentrate on the positives. As Aboriginal people, we have a way of picking up very quickly. Are they getting who we are? It made me concentrate more on my spiritual life. Culturally, more and more, I came to focus on the similarities. You can accept the differences. You can stand among it. I became spiritually stronger here."²⁶

The spiritual writer Henri Nouwen writes of what "creating a free and friendly space" means:

> The paradox of hospitality is that it wants to create emptiness, not a fearful emptiness, but a friendly emptiness where strangers can enter and discover themselves as created free; free to sing their own songs, speak their own languages, dance their own dances; free also to leave and follow their own vocations.

---

22. Lee, interview, Feb. 2024. Steve Lee, Uniting Church chaplain, studied at UTC from 2008 to 2012 (BTh).

23. Turton, interview. Nov. 22, 2023. Linda Turton, library assistant at Blue Mountains Library, studied at UTC 2005–2010 (BTh).

24. Lakshmanan, interview, May 15, 2024. Xavier Lakshmanan, Principal, Australian College of Christian Studies, studied at UTC 2009–2013 (PhD).

25. Ieli, interview, May 24, 2024. Hani Ieli, a Minister of the Word candidate 2022–2024, studied at UTC 2015–2017 (BTh), 2018–2024 (MTh).

26. Wymarra, interview, June 12, 2024.

> Hospitality is not a subtle invitation to adopt the lifestyle of the host, but a gift of a chance for the guest to find his own.[27]

INTERSECTIONS BETWEEN LEARNING, CULTURE, AND FAITH

As spaces become meaningful places, storied through the encounters and interactions of all who inhabit that space, a foundation for formative theological education is developed. Colleen Griffith and Hosffman Ospino define formative education as that which

> keeps the whole person in view, cares about the development of character, values appropriation of one's learning, fosters inclusive communities, cultivates a relational sense of the human, is interested in meaning and purpose, raises hopes, attends to content intellectually and affectively, encourages openness and dialogue, welcomes contextual standpoints, expands the self, advances creativity, and connects learning and the world.[28]

Expanding this notion further, Ospino and Griffith argue that this vision is at its core spiritual in its threefold concern for the integration of whole persons (recognizing that the task is unique to each), the practical relevance of learning in relation to the world, and the active desire for inclusive communities.[29]

UTC was and continues to be a place where learning, culture, and faith intersect. Supporting a diverse community of learning was sustained through the intentional creation of hospitality (in theory and practice) through community and relationship building. Faculty, library, academic support, and administrative support staff at UTC all value the importance of relationships, the empowerment of individual student learning, and the traditions and cultures each student brings. All encouraged students to integrate these with the broader Christian tradition through ongoing theological reflection. As Lakshmanan put it, "The UCA has a theological heritage of being open to all kinds of people—you are respected, listened to and accepted."[30] Ieli reflected on her experience of learning this way: "My learning was helped by being welcomed into the learning space and the support of the faculty. The faculty would help us along. Communication

---

27. Nouwen, *Reaching Out*, 69.
28. Griffith and Ospino, *Formative Theological Education*, 4.
29. Griffith and Ospino, *Formative Theological Education*, 4.
30. Lakshmanan, interview, May 15, 2024.

was something important I learnt and asking questions about what I didn't understand."[31]

As a space where learning, culture, and faith intersected, UTC deepened student, faculty, and staff learning experiences in mutually enriching and challenging ways. A noteworthy lasting impression on students was that of their lecturers. Adi Mariana Waqa, a former student at UTC in 2013, described it this way:

> UTC is fantastic as it offers an environment that encourages academic and spiritual exploration, as well as having a culture of community and respect. The lecturers are both learned and passionate about theology; they do not merely teach theology; they engage with it and inspire students to continually dig and press into the depths of its richness. It is evident that they love God, love what they do and that they want their students to excel at whatever level they may be at. The best thing about being a student at UTC is the opportunity to be in an environment where community and academic explorations go hand in hand.[32]

Lee also spoke of this positive engagement of staff with students: "The other really positive experience I had was with the lecturers. They encouraged me to be who I am. You were allowed to share your church life so far and the ways you are being challenged. Otherwise, you can't expand or go deeper into your theological understanding of the Bible or the church. So, I had great encouragement from the lecturers."[33] Raymond Joso's recollection was, "We had great solid theologians and biblical scholars in our faculty. What we received from the lecturers was not just what was in the textbook. They really researched their subjects. We were encouraged to learn from books and journals, but we also wanted to know what the thinking is around this today, and lecturers engaged with that too."[34] Joso also commented on the cultural sensitivity he experienced from lecturers, "I have to say the lecturers were very aware of the challenges many of us were facing. The lecturers were also aware of how to deliver content that was sensitive to students from different cultural backgrounds. This helped me to learn in a way that was open and deep."[35]

---

31. Ieli, interview, May 24, 2024.
32. Waqa, cited in Insights Magazine, "Community of Learning."
33. Lee, interview, Feb. 2, 2024.
34. Joso, interview, Feb. 2, 2024. Raymond Joso, minister at Blacktown Uniting Church, studied at UTC 2009–2011 (BTh).
35. Joso, interview, Feb. 2, 2024.

Turton expressed a similar view: "The modelling from lecturers was outstanding, especially from those who were from a non-Anglo-Australian background. Representation from three broad cultures was strong."[36] Current UCA President Rev Charissa Suli, while deeply appreciative of UTC's "openness in recognizing cultural diversity within the church," nevertheless asserted, "I don't think formation really was structured interculturally," although "there was a message of collaboration from the College, despite a Western framework."[37] Joso, speaking of the Western legacy of theological education and its implications, said,

> Because everything is done in English, sometimes there is a legacy of Western thinking which assumes it's the same theology as, say, in Indonesia or Hong Kong or Thailand. We have a lot of candidates from other parts of the world. Studying in English shaped me, but it is missing that part of us. We should be proud of where we come from and be able to express our theology in our own way. I would like to see more teaching and conversation in other people's languages. Language is a matter of the heart."[38]

Joso's concern about language is significant. This concern is not new. In the earlier years of UTC, college policy originally stated that undergraduate theological study ought to be done in one's first language.[39] The rationale for this premise was that candidates from other cultures, mostly from overseas, were preparing for ministry in their own ethnic cultures at the time. However, in the last twenty years, the cultural landscape in the Uniting Church has been changing. Although there has been an influx of students from different cultural backgrounds entering UTC, the assumption that they are preparing specifically for ministry in their ethnic communities can no longer be held. Living in the diaspora now brings with it a different optic and experience that needs to be engaged for the sake of present and future generations for whom Australia will become home. However, the concern for language remains an important one.

Encounters and interactions deepened faith and spirituality, sharpened questions on identity, and facilitated personal growth in confidence, awareness, and knowledge. In this sense, UTC was a community intent on learning how to be diverse and hold together that diversity without the erasure of

---

36. Turton, interview, Nov. 22, 2023.

37. Suli, interview, Jan 24, 2024. Charissa Suli, president of UCA 2024–present, studied at UTC 2012–2014 (BTh).

38. Joso, interview, Feb. 2, 2024.

39. Barnes, *Doing Theology*, 106.

difference or tokenistic inclusion. This continues to be an ongoing challenge for theological education and formation for ministry in terms of curriculum content, delivery, faculty representation, and academic support for students.

The appointment of UTC's third principal, Sarah Mitchell, in 1996 signaled change in various ways. Sarah Mitchell, a Presbyterian and New Zealander, was UTC's first female principal. She brought a vision for transforming theological education that was contextually aware and relevant and, with it, a commitment to the ongoing struggle of UTC "to keep a balance between the pursuit of scholarly excellence for its own sake and the practical formation of disciplines."[40] Christine Gapes described Mitchell's term:

> With energy and vision, Sarah, like her biblical counterpart, took UTC on a journey, often through the wilderness, certainly through the complexities of living in a multicultural society. A new vision was established which would take account of the ever-increasing changes that were challenging theological education. In particular the college saw itself more clearly to be part of the Asia Pacific region and began to focus on the cultural diversity, which makes up the Uniting Church in Australia.[41]

During Mitchell's term, she appointed several teaching staff whose teaching emphasis was contextuality. Jione Havea, a Tongan and member of the Free Wesleyan Church in Tonga, was the first non-white full teaching member at UTC. He was appointed lecturer in Old Testament/Hebrew Bible in 2000. Havea's approach to biblical studies was not only contextual; it was also provocative and always seeking to push normative boundaries of biblical interpretation. Clive Pearson was another. His teaching approach was contextualizing the systematic theological agenda, making Western theology accessible and relevant to the contemporary time, and bringing non-Anglo-Australian and Indigenous cultures into conversation with traditional theology. Pearson encouraged students "to consider theological concepts from within their own traditions" and "engage with the doctrines of the church from within their own culture, contextualizing them for their current situation."[42] During Pearson's term as a lecturer in theology and later as principal of UTC, he introduced several new subjects. Among these were the Cross Cultural and Interfaith Dialogue intensives, which continue to be a core part of the candidate formation program. Pearson invited, encouraged, and mentored non-Anglo-Australian lecturers to teach. A third appointment was Stephen Burns, whose teaching contribution was

---

40. Barnes, *Doing Theology*, 62.
41. Gapes, "Braiding Learning," §4.
42. Gapes, "Braiding Learning," §16.

in practical theology and liturgy.[43] Burn's approach was contextual, creative, welcoming, and enabling, allowing students to explore different approaches to worship. Havea, Pearson, and Burns were enablers in their own unique ways, opening different teaching and subject content pathways. They articulated traditional theological concepts differently and explored fresh ways of teaching.

Another key shift in the college occurred in 2022, under the leadership of Peter Walker, when an opening for a lectureship in cross-cultural ministry and theology was advertised, a promise of a new horizon of change that signaled an intentional commitment by the Synod of NSW (New South Wales) and ACT (Australian Capital Territory) to respond to the changing cultural landscape of the UCA and its implications for theological education and formation. Seforosa Carroll, a Rotuman and a UTC graduate, was appointed to the role in January 2023. In September 2023, the Synod of NSW and ACT adopted a sixth strategic direction—"To live cross-culturally as a multicultural and intercultural Church," a hopeful indication that the recommendations pertaining to theological education and formation in the UCA's 1985 declaration and the subsequent statements that followed in 2006 and 2012 could finally be realized.[44]

Richmond and Yang argue, "One of the main challenges we face living in a multicultural and multi-faith Australia is learning to live together peacefully and creatively, in ways that enrich our common life and reflect mutual respect."[45] This is an ideal for which UTC strives. Looking back on his key learnings at UTC, Joso averred, "I have been able to take with me the practices and skills that I've learnt here at UTC. Not everything learnt at UTC will prepare you for the placement or context you will be in. But just as was taught and encouraged here at UTC, what matters most is mutual respect."[46] Wymarra shared that mutual respect comes from "observing and looking for the best, and a real pastoral challenge is trying to understand and encourage."[47] Reflecting on this theme, Lakshmanan revealed,

> I was a very reserved person, but this atmosphere helped me to become more open. My PhD supervisor, Dr. Ben Myers, was both patient and encouraging, always looking for the positives (English is my third language). Ben wrote comments that were

---

43. Stephen Burns was appointed in 2007.

44. Uniting Church in Australia, *Church for All*; Uniting Church in Australia, *One Body*.

45. Richmond and Yang, *Crossing Borders*, 7.

46. Joso, interview, Feb. 2, 2024.

47. Wymarra, interview, June 12, 2024.

always constructive and affirming. He would look at what was not working and suggest alternative approaches. The property manager, David Holden, helped me understand what it meant to relate to people in different roles, and it is a memory I carry with me in my current role.[48]

Turton revealed how her time working at Camden Theological Library continues to have a lasting influence:

> I have an admiration for the UCA being so inclusive. In the Camden Theological Library used by UTC students, where I worked part-time for many years, I had some challenging students. I learnt under Moira Bryant how to relate. In the Blue Mountains Library where I now work, although a very different environment, there are people from different socio-economic backgrounds and some with mental illness and my experience at CTL has helped me.[49]

Joso shared this: "My memories of studying at UTC were great. Finding identity in a safe, multicultural, cross-cultural environment I remember thinking I was part of something bigger. I was able to learn about values and beliefs that I had never encountered before."[50] Lee reflected,

> My interactions with other cultures were limited before I came to UTC. When I engaged with class conversations at Wednesday worship, it was enriching in the sense I didn't know much about Tongan, Fijian or Indonesian culture, but the way they engaged with other cultures and gave themselves to God, to church and to ministry was really an eye-opening moment for me.[51]

A common theme among the interviewees was that UTC was a place where assumptions could be tested and challenged. Suli stated: "There was no question you could not ask. The message from lecturers was to lean into theological study and what will help you."[52] Joso shared that "there were never closed questions or answers. There was never a discussion where there were right or wrong answers. It was always that journey of learning, exploring, how we bring our faith to this in order for us to be a better person, better society and a word that has God's vision in it."[53] For Lee, "The way

---

48. Lakshmanan, interview, May 15, 2025.
49. Turton, interview, Nov. 22, 2023.
50. Joso, interview, Feb. 2, 2024.
51. Lee, interview, Feb. 2, 2024.
52. Suli, interview, Jan. 24, 2024.
53. Joso, interview, Feb. 2, 2024.

students engaged with other students and lecturers was quite challenging for me. The way UTC teaches was completely different. I got to know that I can challenge myself and learn from others by asking questions and sharing why I don't know what I know."[54]

A special space and place for learning and deepening faith was the chapel's weekly worship and communion services, a long-standing tradition of UTC. Lee avowed, "Sharing worship was another example of learning. I was really touched by the Tongan perspective when they brought some of their communal cultural practice into worship. There is also a theological perspective behind it and there is the opportunity to learn through that culture into the theological differences."[55] Suli named the chapel services as space where collaboration was visible, expressed, and implemented. She affirmed, "The college did their best to create spaces for collaboration among the students, like the way we had to do worship. There was a mix between the diverse year groups. We were all travelling together. I felt enriched by the community."[56]

Students come to UTC for a variety of reasons as part of their commitment to studying theology and discerning the path of ministry. For those of other cultures, especially whose second or third language is English, the challenge of rigorous academic study in a Western institution, studying in another language, and the Western cultural assumptions often embodied in theological education can make theological study a challenge and can often be alienating for some. Joso recalls, "In my first year at UTC, I found writing essays a challenge. I didn't grow up writing essays. My university degree in Indonesia was from a science background. So, writing a 2,000-word essay in English, which is my second language, was not an easy task."[57] Wymarra articulated the experience this way: "At times, I'd feel uncomfortable that I'd say something back that meant I didn't really understand the question. I was nearly not going to stay on, but I reminded myself I had done this as a call to develop my theological understanding."[58]

Even those of Anglo-Australian background found the experience of studying alongside those of other cultures a gift and challenge. Turton reflected,

> It was a good experience, a challenge communicating with non-English students, which sharpened my experience of how to

---

54. Lee, interview, Feb. 2, 2024.
55. Lee, interview, Feb. 2, 2024.
56. Suli, interview, Jan. 24, 2024.
57. Joso, interview, Feb.2, 2024.
58. Wymarra, interview, June 12, 2024.

communicate authentically and sincerely. It was also a positive experience of being in a multicultural community and sharing Christian faith with other cultures. I had studied anthropology at an earlier stage in my life. At UTC, there was an expansion of my knowledge studying alongside students from the Pacific in particular, and I began to have an increased understanding of what it might be like to be in a Christian family.[59]

As the number of students from other cultures grew, there became a need for academic support for students whose first language was not English. The support systems were not solely set up for language or academic support. At heart, they were pastorally focused. In the earlier years UTC set up a buddy system where students of Anglo-Australian background were paired with a student from another culture. The role of the Anglo-Australian student was to support the non-Anglo-Australian student in their study by meeting regularly to unpack or talk through theological terminology, concepts, or ideas, as well as working through assignments.

The Overseas Students Committee was reestablished in the early 2000s to support and facilitate overseas students' transition into college life and adjusting to Australian culture. At a practical level, the committee members ensured overseas students had the necessities, such as household items, information about where to shop for groceries in their local area, medical care when needed, and meeting pastoral needs when they arose. Academic and financial support and hospitality (hosting students for meals at committee members' homes) were also a function of the Overseas Students Committee.

The First Year Mentoring Program (FYM), established in 2012 with funding support from Charles Sturt University as part of the Higher Education Participation and Partnerships Program (HEPPP), made a significant contribution to academic support for students in the college. The objective of the FYM program was student retention and support for students. Most students in this category were those of other cultures and low socio-economic backgrounds, and many were the first in their families pursuing a university education. However, the underlying pastoral work was mainly to foster belonging in order to begin to build confidence and competence in their academic work.

Contextualized for UTC, the FYM program was implemented through a team of committed people.[60] Commitment, collaboration, communication, and respect were key to effective teamwork with faculty and students. The Student Support Team (SST) comprised the first-year mentor (Seforosa

---

59. Turton, interview, Nov. 22, 2023.
60. See Insights Magazine, "Community of Learning."

Carroll), study skills tutor (Carolyn Craig-Emilsen), and Camden Theological Library staff (Moira Bryant and Adele Smith) with student administrative staff (Jenny Stockton, Renee Kelly, and Joanne Stokes). The SST worked alongside and in collaboration with teaching faculty to support all students in their diverse learning needs. The SST shared one common objective: the understanding that, for many, the study of theology is a faith journey and not just purely an academic one. Therefore, the imperative was to provide pastoral support and care for students throughout their time of study. The SST team strongly believed that each student should feel a genuine sense of belonging and engagement with their peers, in addition to the different learning support services the university offers. The FYM program was again an indication of a shift toward recognizing that students of different cultures are not simply individuals but embodied within their communities, bringing with them a web of relationships. The ongoing development of theological education and formation needs to take account of that.

GROWTH AND LIFELONG LEARNING

UTC is a community that values the principles of formative theological education. Former students reflected on their time at UTC as deepening their spiritual maturity and fostering a desire for lifelong learning. Their collective responses reflected eloquently theologian John Inge's words noted earlier: "What begins as undifferentiated space becomes place as we get to know it better and endow it with value."[61]

Students travel on individual learning journeys. But learning at UTC was not simply an individual or isolated experience. Learning took place within a community. Several key factors enabled spiritual growth and emboldened a keenness for lifelong learning. At UTC, students learned from each other and their lecturers. Multiple perspectives and sharing were encouraged. This generated energy, creativity, and synergy, which in turn cultivated a sense of belonging and solidarity, leading to lasting friendships. Suli recalled, "In the cohort I was in, there were about seven of us. On the first day, we had an exercise to create an artwork. We were diverse. We came up with a cup and beverage as an image. By working on the artwork, we created hope and trust. We were called 'the Brewers of Hope.'"[62] Joso articulated his journey this way:

---

61. Inge, *Christian Theology*, 1.
62. Suli, interview, Jan. 24, 2024.

Looking back to my time of learning at UTC, I most benefitted from the confidence I have that we are all made in the image of God. UTC gave us an open space, meaning I have been able to listen to leaders from our First Peoples, different church leaders and different perspectives, which have enriched me so that I am able to understand diversity and not just "Oh, they're different to us."[63]

Parker Palmer observes, "Solitude and community, rightly understood, go together as both-and."[64] He continues, "When we split solitude and community into an either-or and act as if we can get along with only one or the other, we put ourselves in spiritual peril." Following Bonhoeffer's warning in *Life Together*, "let the person who cannot be alone beware of community. Let the person who is not in community be aware of being alone."[65] Palmer concludes, "We need solitude and community simultaneously; what we learn in one mode can check and balance what we learn in the other. Together they make us whole, like breathing in and breathing out."[66] Ieli's experiences encapsulate Palmer's notions of the "both-and" experience of community, its challenges, its necessary risks, and the courage needed: "My first year was a bit scary. I'd been away from study for almost 30 years. Would I fail? What were the expectations? Also, I couldn't mingle well. Maybe it is being an introvert. I tended to keep to myself. Gradually, I was able to find myself in the community. . . . I began to feel included, and in some cases, I made friends for life."[67] Joso also acknowledged the importance of his identification with other students: "I embraced the challenge because I knew I was in a community where I was not the only one having difficulty. I think suffering alone is not good, but when we suffer together, things can change and get better."[68] Similarly Suli was frank about both the challenges and the rewards of being a student: "College was so hard because of the expectations—like doing your theory and practice all at the same time. If I were to go back, I think I would encourage people to work intentionally. I would encourage students to find ways of applying what they were learning at college. I was enriched by the community. I loved my years at college even if it was hard."[69]

63. Joso, interview, Feb. 2, 2024.
64. Palmer, *Hidden Wholeness*, 54.
65. Bonhoeffer, *Life Together*, 78.
66. Palmer, *Hidden Wholeness*, 55.
67. Ieli, interview, May 25, 2024.
68. Joso, interview, Feb. 2, 2024.
69. Suli, interview, Jan. 24, 2024.

It seems that UTC has been, to use Inge's proposition, a space which has indeed become a place that has been "endowed with value."[70] UTC has enabled and empowered students to expand their understanding of faith, themselves, and others. They have been encouraged to grow in confidence on their theological journey. Students have many reflections looking back: seeing connections with the present, identifying pathways to meaningful involvement with other communities, and embracing the value and belief in lifelong learning. Lee spoke of the connections between his learning then and his sense of vocation now:

> Even though I experienced things in a different way at college, I have come to realize that, in fact, I already had a capacity in terms of understanding or engaging in meaningful conversation with new ideas and perspectives. That realization has helped me a lot. Now, as a Uniting Church chaplain working in Aged Care, I understand people's lives are different; their stories and perspectives, beliefs, and stages in life are all different. So, because of those cultural differences and the learning I had in classroom discussions and engagement with students and lecturers at UTC, I think I have developed a capacity to engage in meaningful conversation.[71]

Ieli spoke of her desire to apply her learning about building relationships in UTC to relationship building in the broader community: "If I learn to build relationships here this helps to build relationships outside, to get to know the people's stories, needs, culture, community, and aspirations. My hope is I want to leave this place better than when I came, discover my weaknesses and strengths, and also how my gifts can benefit the whole community I am sent to. Learning doesn't stop here. It carries out from here."[72]

Finally, UTC was and continues to be a place and community that encourages spiritual and faith growth and lifelong learning. Suli revealed,

> I do go back to the memories and how they have sustained me. I have grown in my spirituality and theology. The college helped me articulate my theology. They set the foundation. I began to recognize how important continuing education is. I have a Graduate Diploma from the Adelaide College of Divinity and am now enrolled in a Master of Theology at Melbourne School

---

70. Inge, *Christian Theology*, 2.
71. Lee, interview, Feb. 2, 2024.
72. Ieli, interview, May 24, 2024.

of Divinity. . . . I think it is so important for ministry agents to continue in education.[73]

Lakshmanan captured this sentiment by relating it to the trajectory of his academic career and faith journey:

> Coming to UTC to do my doctorate was a game-changer for me, for my academic career, my life and future ministry. There are three main values I take away from my time at UTC. The first is academic discipline and especially how you deal with students. The second is respect for people no matter what culture, taking the opportunity to listen to and learn from each other. The third is to encourage a desire for lifelong learning, to keep on writing and, in terms of belief, to hold on to our convictions; we can expect others to be different, and sometimes working, studying and living with them may be difficult, but people *are* different, you are different, I am different, yet we can always be welcoming.[74]

Ieli, who began as a private student in the BTh program, acquired a thirst for ongoing learning and its significance to her spiritual growth and understanding of the intersections between faith and culture:

> I have gone on to do a Masters. I'm a believer that learning can help us to understand other cultures and help us change how we see God. I have learnt you can't take the Bible in its literal interpretation. I am so blessed to be part of this learning community. I wanted to deepen my understanding of the way I think about God. What caught my attention is the mystery of it all. It is like a magnet that draws me. The hope is that my learning doesn't stop in this community.[75]

Wymarra articulated a vision of identity and its connection to lifelong learning and community arising out of her experience as a student at UTC:

> It has given me a wide perspective of what I, as an Aboriginal person, am here for. It's a place I can call home that's teaching me to go back into my community. The penny dropped when I did Practical Theology with Dr. Ockert Meyer. I was meant to be here. I come now from the background of a practical theologian. I am just observing and looking for the best in people, a real pastoral challenge trying to understand and encourage. Mutual

---

73. Suli, interview, Jan. 24, 2024.
74. Lakshmanan, interview, May 15, 2024.
75. Ieli, interview, May 24, 2024.

respect is so important. For as long as I can, I want to be able to be there for the young people; we've got to help grow that seed.[76]

FUTURE DIRECTIONS

The journey has not ended. It continues, influenced and shaped by the cultural changes in the Australian landscape and their implications for the church and ministry. Although 1985 marked a symbolic moment for the UCA, the journey and struggle to articulate that vision began several years before and has continued since 1985 with two further statements—in 2006, *A Church for All God's People*, and in 2012, *One Body, Many Members: Living Faith and Life Cross-Culturally*.[77] The 2012 statement embodied many frustrating years of culturally diverse communities feeling that they still existed on the peripheries of the UCA and were still not being considered full members of the church despite their many years of membership. The statement sought to move the UCA into action by "giving shape and intent to content," by explicitly naming how and what it means to be "a multicultural church, living its faith and life cross-culturally."[78]

Each document called for an investment in culturally sensitive theological education and leadership formation for lay and ordained people that would lead to building and strengthening cross-cultural and intercultural competencies. The fortieth meeting of the Synod of NSW and ACT in September 2023 resolved to adopt a sixth direction: "Living cross-culturally as a multicultural, intercultural church."[79] The implications of this phrase need deeper theological exploration. This work presents an exciting opportunity for ongoing theological exploration and is well within the bounds of giving "shape, content and *praxis* to intent" as named in the 2012 statement.[80] This has implications for theological education and formation and for shaping leaders for, and ministries of, the church. But the theological foundation had been laid by the dedicated and intentional work of cross-cultural theologians in the UCA many years prior, several of whom have been cited in this chapter.

76. Wymarra, interview, June 12, 2024.

77. Uniting Church in Australia, *Church for All*; Uniting Church in Australia, *One Body*.

78. Uniting Church in Australia, *One Body*.

79. Uniting Church in Australia, "Intercultural Ministry."

80. Uniting Church in Australia, *One Body*.

As a result of ongoing conversation within the councils of the UCA, relevant committees, and several replications of the shape and form of theological education in a culturally and religiously diverse Australia, the document on *Standards for Theological Education and Formation: Phase 2 for Ordained Ministries* (2016) lists under its educational philosophy the following:

> It is essential that there is an active interaction between culturally shaped insights, experiences of Ministry, and the academic disciplines. Candidates will study in an open learning environment where they are encouraged to question, to think creatively, to try new forms of Ministry and then to evaluate and reflect upon them theologically. Given the nature of contemporary Australian society, a significant portion of this study will take place in a multicultural and ecumenical context, where life in a multifaith society is in view.[81]

UTC is a space lived in, and given meaning with and by, the shared experiences of the people who inhabited it from 1999 to 2024. What was a space for those who entered initially as strangers, became a storied place, a place of value through memory, inhabitation, and encounters. It has been a gathering place for many cultures. This community has embraced the intersections between theological learning, culture, and faith and has worked consistently at sustaining an ethos that has encouraged deep spiritual growth and lifelong learning.

BIBLIOGRAPHY

Barnes, Geoffrey. *Doing Theology in Sydney: A History of United Theological College, 1974–1999*. Adelaide, SA: Openbook, 2000.
Bonhoeffer, Dietrich. *Life Together*. New York: HarperCollins, 1954.
Frisch, Michael. *A Shared Authority: Essays on the Craft and Meaning of Oral and Public History*. Albany, NY: State University of New York, 1990.
Gapes, Christine. "Braiding Learning: Weaving Mats and Eating Kim-Chee Pie." Religious Education Association. https://old.religiouseducation.net/member/04_papers/Gapes.pdf.
Griffith, Colleen M., and Hosffman Ospino. *Formative Theological Education*. New York: Paulist, 2023.
Inge, John. *A Christian Theology of Place*. Aldershot, UK: Ashgate, 2003.
Insights Magazine. "A Community of Learning." *Insights*, Feb. 2014. https://www.insights.uca.org.au/a-community-of-learning/.
Nouwen, Henri. *Reaching Out: The Three Movements of Spiritual Life*. Glasgow: Collins, 1976.

---

81. Uniting Church in Australia, *Standards*.

Palmer, Parker J. *A Hidden Wholeness: The Journey Toward an Undivided Life.* San Francisco: Wiley, 2004.

Richmond, Helen, and Myong Duk Yang, eds. *Crossing Borders: Shaping Faith, Ministry and Identity in Multicultural Australia.* Sydney: UCA Assembly and NSW Board of Mission, 2006.

Thompson, Paul Richard. *The Voice of the Past: Oral History.* New York: Oxford University Press, 1978.

Uniting Church in Australia. *A Church for All God's People: Vision Statement.* Illuminate. Released 2006. https://ucaassembly.recollect.net.au/nodes/view/198.

———. "Intercultural Ministry." https://www.nswact.uca.org.au/mission/intercultural-ministry/.

———. *Multicultural Policies 1985–2004.* Illuminate. Released 2004. https://ucaassembly.recollect.net.au/nodes/view/407.

———. *One Body, Many Members: Living Faith and Life Cross-Culturally.* Illuminate. Released 2012. https://ucaassembly.recollect.net.au/nodes/view/416.

———. *Standards for Theological Education and Formation: Phase 2 for Ordained Ministries.* Illuminate. Released 2016. https://ucaassembly.recollect.net.au/nodes/view/465.

———. *The Uniting Church Is a Multicultural Church.* Illuminate. Released 1985. https://ucaassembly.recollect.net.au/nodes/view/162.

6

Pasifika Voices Flourishing in the Presence of Others

Clive Pearson

THE PRESENT HIGH PROFILE

The present bears witness to the high profile of a number of former graduates of United Theological College in the life of the church and academy. Charissa Suli has become the first Tongan president of the Assembly; Faaimata Havea Hiliau is the current moderator of the Synod of New South Wales and ACT (Australian Capital Territory). Salesi Faupula is moderator-elect of the Synod of Victoria and Tasmania while, until recently, Haloti Kailahi was the general secretary of the Northern Synod. In the academy Seforosa Carroll now lectures in theology and cross-cultural studies, having returned to Australia after several years working with the World Council of churches as program executive for mission from the margins/ecumenical indigenous peoples' network. Carroll had also held a fellowship at the Center of Theological Inquiry in Princeton. Matagi Vilitama served for several years as the advocate for the Assembly circle overseeing what it means to be a multicultural church. Both Faupula and Kailahi had been senior students during their times of ministry formation in the college.

It is an impressive list that marks a number of firsts that sit alongside a growing number of Pasifika candidates placed in positions of ministry. It is more than well matched by the number of former students (alumni) who have taken up responsible positions back in their home islands. Zebedee Padokana became a bishop in the Solomon Islands after studying public theology; others have been appointed to lectureships at Sia'atoutai College (Tonga), Davuilevu and Pacific Theological Colleges (Fiji), Tangintebu Theological College (Kiribati), Seghe Theological Seminary (Solomon Islands) as well the National University, and Malua and Piula Theological Colleges in Samoa. On his return to Tuvalu, Maina Talia was elected to parliament by the peoples of Vaitupu; having once been the cochair of the United Nations' Global Indigenous Forum on Climate Change and regular attender at COP (Conference of Parties) climate conferences, he became Minister for Home Affairs, Climate Change, and the Environment (and waste).

Their vocations are but one face of the college's participation in the South Pacific Association of Theological Colleges (SPATS). The reception of the college into this body came into being during the principalship of Sarah Mitchell. Through her work on the Council for World Mission, Mitchell envisaged a college that was open to diverse cultures, creating a Communitas program for that purpose.[1] It was as if she harbored a vision of a regional equivalent to Bossey in Geneva.

The appointment of Jione Havea to the lectureship of the Hebrew Bible during her time enhanced greatly the Pasifika presence and profile of the college. Havea would build upon his international standing as a postcolonial scholar seeking out "[alter]native" interpretations, "a sea of readings," and an island hermeneutic.[2] In terms of a methodology, Havea introduced the way of *talanoa*—"storytelling"—and its inclusion of oral "texts." In making use of this native way of sharing and reflecting, Havea situated Pasifika studies inside an emerging body of scholarship that assumed the employment of talanoa across many disciplines. Through his initiative, United Theological College hosted the first Talanoa Oceania conference in 2008 (it would do so again in 2024). It was seen as a means of "disrupt[ing] or subvert[ing] essentialist thinking," which was inclined to regard Pasifika peoples as excelling only in sport, entertainment, and hospitality.[3] It sought to reveal, share, and unpack longings and memories through conversations in a "sacred space" that was "safe." It offered an alternative to the "business" of Western biblical interpretation, the history retold from the perspective of the colonizing missionary and the doctrinal constructs of a systematic theology. These talanoa conversations remained unfinished and held out the

1. Mitchell, "*Communitas* of Christ."
2. Havea, *Losing Ground*, 27–42; Havea, "Islander Criticism."
3. See Havea, *Losing Ground*, 21–23.

possibility of "work[ing] together to find practical expression in the world in new, creative, imaginative and life-sustaining ways."[4]

Havea's energy and insights would lead to an outstanding list of published anthologies, which he edited beyond the time of his tenure at United Theological College. Through his membership in the Centre for Public and Contextual Theologies of Charles Sturt University, a link with the college remained. Havea effectively created opportunities for Pasifika students, past and present, to be published. Inise Foiakau, for example, was able to make known a Fijian feminist reading of the character of Zipporah in Exodus.[5] Havea's influence has been far reaching. It is no accident that he was invited to deliver the first of the public Havea Lectures; these were named in honor of his father, Sione 'Amanaki Havea, described by one critic—Ma'afu Palu—as the "architect of a Pacific theology" and "father" of the "Pasifikans."[6]

Some care needs to be exercised, though. The Pasifika label has the potential for masking an homogenizing effect. At the most basic of levels, the term represented a further variation of naming rights, like Oceanic and *moana*, to be found throughout the "liquid continent." The Pasifika label sits within the rapidly evolving fields of a majority world theology, both of which are likely to be decolonial and impatient with received "white" theologies that had dismissed indigenous understandings of the interrelationship of humanity with sea, land, air, and other creatures—a "whole way of life."[7] For all its appeal, it nevertheless possesses its own politics. There have been instances, at times, of pushback and resistance—and ambiguities.

The recourse to a talanoa methodology was not universally shared across cultures. That was despite the intention behind the talanoa conference being one of "gather[ing] Pasifika peoples from the diaspora and the homeland to share, exchange, challenge, celebrate and provide space for new knowledge to emerge." It was "open to all Pasifika people from all walks of life and disciplines."[8] The communal and relational nature of a talanoa was indeed put to constructive use by Kamaloni Tu'iono in his model of a *pikipikihama* or "outrigger" understanding of supervision in which others come to the assistance of those in need.[9] It offered an alternative to the standard one-on-one sessions of oversight. It could also be deployed in

---

4. Carroll, "*Talanoa*."
5. Foi'akau, "Sipora"; for further work by Foi'akau, see "Silent Voice."
6. Palu, *Pacific Theology*.
7. For further research into this topic, see Vaai and Casimira, "*Whole of Life*" *Way*.
8. Carroll, "*Talanoa*."
9. Tu'iono, "Seeking to Create." Also see Tu'iono, "Reflections."

association with other cultural customs, themes, and means of sharing insights into the life of faith and the well-being of the church.

In this regard Vilitama expressed a preference for gathering around the *umu*—that is, the preparation of an "earth oven" (in diaspora, around a feast)—in other words, around a specific task where there are roles that need to be fulfilled and carried out for the sake of the whole. Furthermore, he drew upon ethnomusicology in order to mediate Niuean songs, chants, and dances at risk of being lost through migration and depopulation.[10]

Writing on threats posed by climate change to life on the islands of Tuvalu, Talia overtly rejected the option of talanoa in favor of the *muna o te fale*—"the wisdom of the household"—through which traditional knowledge and skills were handed on from one generation to another.[11] The difficulty some saw in the talanoa method lay in the last syllable where *noa* can mean "nothing." Now it is true that Havea and other Pasifika scholars like Winston Halapua are able to define this "nothing" along the lines of "com[ing] together, detached from preconceived ideas or commitments and without a predetermined agenda," without concealment.[12] Talia was not convinced, being particularly wary of the risk of a talanoa becoming a site littered with gossip and jokes as well as less-than-serious talk. It was not necessarily the sacred space others might experience elsewhere in other settings.

The urgency, the *kairos* nature of rising sea levels, the prospects of low-lying home islands becoming uninhabitable, further focused attention on the prospective audience of a talanoa. Clearly it enabled the desirable effect of including "normal" readers of Scripture—but here lies a potential proviso. What happens if and when the subject matter under consideration must necessarily engage with those who lie beyond the immediate region and whose worldviews are of an altogether different order? Carroll noted that talanoa is "regionally specific." It is "practised mainly by those who are Christian and who share the Pacific culture."[13]

Talia made use of indigenous wisdom in his inclusion of *muna o te fale*, but the category of neighbor—*tuakoi*—was designed to be used in addressing the geopolitics of climate change. Here there was a careful recognition that the people he represents are "weak actors" on the global stage: the way in which the ethics of being a good neighbor were permeated with insights from other

---

10. Vilitama, "Singing the Niuean '*Fetuiaga Kerisiano*.'" See also Vilitama, "*Fetuiaga Kerisiano*: On Becoming a Liquid Church."
11. Talia, "Am I Not Your *Tū/akoi*?"
12. Carroll, "*Talanoa*."
13. Carroll, "*Talanoa*."

disciplines—climate and Earth system sciences—was designed to furnish a moral and theological challenge to neighbors both nearby and far away. The method and context of a talanoa was too limited for such: his dissertation is to be published by Routledge (London) under the title of *Tuvalu, Theology and the Geopolitics of Climate Change*, which illustrates the point.

Further, Talia was wanting to privilege *fatele*—a customary form of song and dance—for the purposes of communicating ideas. Given the vulnerability of islands like Tuvalu and Kiribati, Talia was clearly deeply resistant to larger island groups, like Fiji, Samoa, and Tonga, employing a label like Pasifika in a way that combined all cultures into the same predicament. There is no "inland" or "high land" in the particular context of Tuvalu to which people can move. Talia is not alone. Sulufaiga Uota from Niutao sought to address the question, "Who is Jesus Christ in a time of climate change?" Rather than proceed with a talanoa, she elected to make use of metaphor of indigenous survival values—*pule fakalaga*—and place them in conversation with Celia Deane-Drummond's ecotheology.[14]

One further dilemma lay in the composition of the student body: it included some students who were "overseas" students from their home islands while others were, or were becoming, Australian citizens. These contexts were clearly not the same. That this should be the case was reflected in the doctoral dissertation of Peletisala Lima dedicated to a remigrant Christology. In the background to this research lay the parable of the prodigal son and Albert Wendt's novel on *Sons for the Return Home* and his play *The Songmaker's Chair*. It differed from the conventional diasporic theology insofar as Lima was born in Samoa, emigrated as a child to Aotearoa–New Zealand, and returned to work in the country of birth—then migrated back to Australia where this dissertation was done. The pivotal point upon which this Christology turns is the return to the homeland which proves to be more demanding and untenable on account of no longer being able to fit so easily in with the traditional expectations of *fa'aSamoa*. The remigrant is no longer the same person due to the mixing of influences on life lived. S/he is now a *tagata mai fafo*—that is, "a person raised from the outside." In order to "perform" received cultural-life ways, there becomes a need to "improvise" and reinvent, with the ever-present fear of rejection. Lima explored various understandings of home, *oikos*, and patterns of family, kin, *aiga*. The point of adhesion with the person and work of Christ lay in how the one who had been rejected became the cornerstone of a new community.[15]

14. Uota, "Who Is Jesus Christ?"

15. Lima, "Remigrant Theology." See also Lima and Pearson, "Becoming *Tagata Mai Fafo*."

The sheer ambiguity of living in diaspora, of living in between two cultures, was vividly captured in Sisilia Tupou-Thomas's "Telling Tales," which sought to explore "Who am I?" and "Where am I now?"[16] Writing in the prologue to *Faith in a Hyphen*, she described how she was a "drifting seed." Her placenta is buried outside her paternal grandparents' house. "A tree was planted on the spot to mark my earliest source of life before birth. There is a part of me, my birthing, buried there, connecting me to my ancestors on my island home."[17] Tupou-Thomas has now lived in Sydney longer than she has lived in Tonga. She is embodied in its suburban way of life. The language she first babbled in, Tongan, remains the language of her heart; even though she comes from an oral culture, Tupou-Thomas is more confident in writing than she is in speaking in this country. "Writing does not often reveal my foreignness; it does not have an accent. If the grammar is right, I am not caught out."[18]

Tupou-Thomas understood herself to be a hyphenated being. She came to like this hyphen (-), signifying her life in between Tonga and Australia. It established a connection between past and present. "This grammatical sign is like a little island" that connects her to the liquid continent, "whispering still to me of an oceanic hermeneutic, but it does so in the down-to-earth existence in a dry, often parched continent."[19] Her life and theology is not the same as it would have been had she remained in the Pasifika home into which she had been born.

Tupou-Thomas's life has become mixed in a way and to a degree that differs from the impulses that lie behind the case Sioeli Vaipulu made for a Tongan *'otualogy*. Here the hybridity was expressed in a neologism (rather than a hyphen) where the Tongan word for God, *'otua*, was bound to the logos of study and talk. In this instance Vaipulu's focus was on how the doctrine of God permeated a Tongan society that was deemed to be patriarchal and hierarchical. Vaipulu found it difficult to imagine how such a culture could consider itself to have fully received the gospel of Jesus Christ. Through a rereading of missionary history, he concluded that the gospel itself had been miss-given, miss-heard and miss-taken.[20]

What Tupou-Thomas's telling tale of living inside a hyphen that she "quite liked" reflected, in an autobiographical fashion, was a variation on

---

16. Tupou-Thomas, "Telling Tales," 1–2.
17. Tupou-Thomas, "Telling Tales," 1.
18. Tupou-Thomas, "Telling Tales," 3.
19. Tupou-Thomas, "Telling Tales," 3.
20. Vaipulu, "Towards an *'Otualogy*."

issues of belonging, home, and identity.²¹ This theme was more fully explored by Carroll in her doctoral dissertation that deployed a theory of homemaking—*oikeiosis*—for the sake of interfaith relationships. It was thus, not strictly speaking, the conventional quest to discern what is and where is home that most migrants set out to explore in seeking to come to terms with their liminality. Carroll applied a diasporic feminist hermeneutic partly on the basis that migrant women know well the challenge of what it means to put into practice the habits that create a home in a new land: it is one where it is a "movement" rather than being merely a fixed space of dwelling.²²

Tupou-Thomas had written as a first-generation migrant. The argument she mounted on behalf of a theology of respect is unique; it is the only one that has ever addressed how families negotiate living in a city of many cultures from the perspective of this particular generational lens. She wrote as a mother and a grandmother where many of the received traditions of *faka'apa'apa*, respect, and the accompanying attributes of honor and shame have been compromised.²³

IN THE PRESENCE OF OTHERS

The emergence of these Pasifika voices, among others, has been a significant achievement effected through United Theological College. It is misleading, though, to separate the role of Pasifika students from the presence and research of students from other cultural backgrounds. It is not simply because the present profile and concentration of Pasifika students and graduates is a relative anomaly in the cultural makeup of the college. It was not always so. In its origins the theological formation that lay behind this narrative was common to those whose ethnicity was Korean, Sri Lankan, Indian, Middle Eastern, and African. In a manner that may not always be realized, the principles that lie behind the college's turn to contextuality, diaspora, the practice of communitas, and a cross-cultural theology was not due to any one set of related cultures. There is a complementary story to be told here.

Its most recent iteration begins back in November 1997. Aeryun Lee submitted a piece of course work she had done into a competition run by the publisher Openbook for the best theological essay for that year. She had done so through her own initiative. She won the award for the undergraduate section. The title of her essay, which was subsequently published in the

---

21. Tupou-Thomas, "Telling Tales," 3.
22. Carroll, "Making Room."
23. Tupou-Thomas, "*Teolosia 'o e Faka'apa'apa*."

anthology *Faith in a Hyphen*, was "Who Is Jesus Christ for Us Today?"[24] The essay was commended by the judges because of its perceived originality. In seeking to address this question that was becoming core to a contextual Christology, Lee's "us" were those, like herself, who were Korean migrant women to Australia. In terms of any theological category, this theme was unchartered territory.

As has been the case for many who have sought to construct a diasporic theology in Australia, Lee was a pioneer. No one had preceded her and mapped out the terrain of the journey. She depended upon a set of potential theological allies, including those with whom she shared classes, Pasifika students included. In class Lee referred to the insights of Risatisone Ete, a second-generation Samoan student raised in Aotearoa–New Zealand. Ete had assisted in one subject and explored a theology for those whose cultural confusion had been expressed in a parody of the well-known children's story of the ugly duckling. He had been made to feel like a "quacking swan" in the ways of *fa'aSamoa*, a *pakeka* (a potato, brown on the outside and white on the inside). In the dominant *palagi* (white) culture he had grown up being told he was a "coconut."[25] Ete would compose a Christology that exchanged the more conventional title of *matai* for Jesus to one of being the *vale* (a fool).[26] Lee suggested that "we" (the class, both Asian and Pasifika) shared the "same virus" of confusion and the need to explore questions of cultural identity in their quest for a refreshed theological understanding. The imperative was to be innovative, creative.

Without the bonus of winning an essay competition, several Pasifika students thus began to explore a more contextualized form of theology. Samata Elia drew upon themes of navigation; Salesi Finau laid the foundations for his subsequent dissertation and publication on Jesus the *Haua*. In a manner that showed affinity with Ete's *vale*, Finau's *haua* referred to a "wanderer," to one who stands outside the Tongan hierarchical social order, an outsider.[27] Carroll drew upon the imagery of a frangipani *lei* for the sake of a Christology of hospital*eity*.[28]

This mixing of Asian and Pasifika cultures marked a crucial difference in what was beginning to unfold in Sydney at this time compared with was taking place across the Tasman. The more diverse range of island cultures and resident population in Aotearoa–New Zealand had meant that distinct

24. Lee, "In Search."
25. Ete, "Bridge," 2–5.
26. Ete, "Ugly Duckling."
27. Finau, "Jesus the *Haua*." See also Finau, "Diaspora Theology."
28. Carroll, "Strangers and Frangipani *Lei*."

Pasifika theologies were evolving in conversation with another, unlike what was the case in Sydney where Asian and Pasifika seemingly shared the "same virus." Across the Tasman, Ete's research into Jesus the *vale* had followed hard upon Matagi Vilitama's theology of Christ and the *umu* (earth oven), based upon village life in Niue. Vilitama would subsequently do his doctoral dissertation on a "liquid church"—the *fetuiaga Kerisiano*—through United Theological College. The theological cultural context in which he did this latter work was very different from the one in which he had broken new ground with his *umu* Christology.

These fresh forms of theological imagining did not arise out of disciplinary vacuum. It is one of the givens of a formal systematic theology that the turn to principle of contextuality arises for good reason. Daniel Migliore believes that these causes include the inability of a given, well-established theology to address specific life experiences in particular situations.[29] Such a reading does not do away with the importance of what Chris Mostert, a former lecturer at United Theological College, described as a transcontextual theology.[30] Lee and others read Mostert's counternarrative in conversation with the systematic theology of the Black African American theologian James Evans, Jr. The core systematic agenda, that which is transcontextual, is preserved but interpreted through the experience of slavery, liberation, discrimination—hence cultural and contextual experience.[31]

For those in Lee's cohort—and for those who followed them—the pressing need was to establish a connection between experience and theology. One of the texts that lay behind this call to find one's theological voice was Fumitaka Matsuoka's *Out of Silence*. Matsuoka was the director of the Pacific and Asian North American (PANA) Institute in the Pacific School of Religion, Berkeley. On two occasions Matsuoka came to assist in the teaching of cross-cultural and contextual theologies at United Theological College. Through his scholarship he mediated considerations to do with race and sociology that were theologically relevant. He captured that sense of living in between cultures through his notion of "holy insecurity."[32] Indeed one Tongan student, Filimone Olivetti, was ordained in a service where the sermon bade him to go forth and explore what it meant to be insecure in this way. Matsuoka realized how vulnerable diasporic students can be—at times intimidated by the dominant majority and subject to critique from the

---

29. Migliore, *Faith Seeking Understanding*, ch. 9.
30. Mostert, "Non-Contextual Theology."
31. Evans, *We Have Been Believers*.
32. Matsuoka, *Out of Silence*.

birth culture. Over the ensuing years Matsuoka would often be an examiner for postgraduate work.

The organizing question for Lee and others was, of course, a variation on Dietrich Bonhoeffers's seminal concern expressed in his *Letters and Papers from Prison*: "Who is Jesus Christ really for us today in a world come of age?"[33] The "world" for which Bonhoeffer was writing was far removed in time, in place, and in context from the situation in which Lee began her inquiry. She had been a student in a class of twenty-seven students; they came from nineteen different ethnic backgrounds. Some, like a student whose original home was Vietnam, had lived in refugee camps and would have been regarded in the terminology of the 1990s as one of "the boat people." Others had migrated in a quest for a better life, however that was to be understood. Now they were facing their equivalent of the psalmist's cry of nostalgia: "How shall we sing the Lord's song in a foreign land?" (Ps 137:4 RSV). That was the topic of an essay by Sitiveni Rogoimuri. Where was "home" was a heavily laden, not easily answered, question. Jo Mar, then a candidate for ministry living in suburban Sydney for some years, had said "Suva"—and then became a little perplexed as the class probed further.

The level of pluralism in the class provoked a set of interrelated considerations all lining up for future work. At that moment in time, the Uniting Church had only passed one set of resolutions at an Assembly level to do with cultural diversity. Back in 1985 the Uniting Church had declared itself to be a "multicultural church"; this statement was followed in due course with two others—*A Church for All God's People* (2006) and *One Body, Many Members* (2012).[34] In the actual performance of faith, these statements were essentially aspirational. There were no supporting processes put into place to oversee and monitor how the various clauses of these declarations were then enacted in the fields of theological education and ministry formation. The spirit in which these documents were crafted and approved was probably no more evident than in the cross-cultural praxis of United Theological College.

Lee was writing in the wake of the 1985 declaration *We Are a Multicultural Church*. In this confession the Uniting Church was evidently coming to terms with the changes to the laws overseeing immigration that were passed in 1973; it represented a step as such that went beyond the implicit ecclesiology to be found in the church's foundational document, *The Basis of Union*. This later declaration made explicit reference to indigenous peoples

---

33. Bonhoeffer, *Letters*, 279.

34. Uniting Church in Australia, *Multicultural Church*; Uniting Church in Australia, *Church for All*; Uniting Church in Australia, *One Body*.

alongside the reception of peoples from diverse migrant cultures. This student cohort was thus exploring dimensions of theology within a framework that had already been established by the national church.

The focus of these first intimations into a diasporic and cross-cultural theology were inclined to be centered on how to profess Christ in the light of other core questions to do with identity, home, gender, and generation. The declaration itself had not specified any of these things—and had, as such, mirrored the critique Mark Lopez had made of the legislation of the 1970s. The capacity for migration had not been initially matched by a sufficiently thought-through understanding of what might be the consequences of multiculturalism.[35] In the case of the Uniting Church, the bold proclamation that "We Are a Multicultural Church" comprised of "people of many races, cultures and languages" did not envisage the prospect of alternative expressions of theology and ethical differences.[36]

Its emphasis had fallen instead in three areas. The first had set out to establish the foundation upon which these many cultures came together in one church. The basis was laid in how "Jesus Christ has made peace between people of every race, culture and class." This peace was deemed to be "a gift of God, a foretaste of the reconciliation of all things in Christ."[37] From the missional perspective of bearing witness, this "gift" was reckoned to be a "sign of hope" to the Australian nation.[38] The subsequent preference that emerged in college classes for the naming of a cross-cultural, rather than a multi- or intercultural, flow from these convictions.

Writing (as an Anglo-Australian) in *Faith in a Hyphen*, Jon Humphries captured the organizing ideas that had arisen out of conversations in which Pasifika students had played a key part.[39] The Word of the cross lay at the heart of why these students from such diverse cultures were gathered together in the first place: reference was made to how Jesus has called those who follow him (irrespective of the particularity of their culture) to take up their cross. The underlying assumption here is that there are times when it is both politic and a matter of discipleship to let go of a custom or habit that is culturally determined for the sake of the other "in Christ." Humphries had also drawn attention to how this imagery of the cross marked Jesus' own public ministry and did so in a way that is not so scripturally established in the rival terminology of multi- and intercultural. Jesus himself often

---

35. Lopez, *Origins of Multiculturalism*, 446–52.
36. Uniting Church in Australia, *Multicultural Church*, para. 5.
37. Uniting Church in Australia, *Multicultural Church*, para. 3.
38. Uniting Church in Australia, *Multicultural Church*, para. 5.
39. Humphries, "Crossing into the Unknown."

crossed boundaries that were sometimes physical, political, and sometimes intracultural.

The inevitable discussions that surround this praxis envisaged the complexity of a cross-cultural hermeneutic where many in the student body felt compelled by dint of circumstance to use English, which may be their second or third language. In other theological classes a persistent attempt would be made to explore linguistic variations on key theological terms. The urgency behind this concern was ever present. In her prizewinning essay Lee would make a distinction between the "language of the heart" (through which piety and devotion was expressed—in this case, in Korean) and "the language one gets by in" (English).[40]

This wrestling with language and a cross-cultural hermeneutic necessarily raised matters of meaning and competency. With regards the former, where is meaning to be found? Is it in what is said? What is heard? Or, is meaning to be negotiated in the liminal space in between saying and hearing, as it crosses over from one to the other? This tension was negotiated against the background of a spectrum of cross-cultural competency. One Armenian student, Levon Kardashian, was first to make use of Mark DeYmaz's five stages of a continuum that progressed from destruction through blindness, awareness, and sensitivity to competence.[41] Subsequently, Tu'iono employed this spectrum in his dissertation on more appropriate cultural models of supervision for those in ordained ministry—as allowed for in paragraph 1.8 of the Code of Ethics.[42]

The recognition of this need to address the issue of competency presumed differences in worldview and the capacity to communicate intention. Of particular assistance here has been the work of Lydia Johnson on *Drinking from the Same Well*. Johnson's particular subject area had been pastoral care in Pasifika contexts. It had included reference to how important it was to be familiar with the range of observances to be found in rituals surrounding funerals and other passages of life. These kinds of concern would subsequently feature in modules of relevant subjects alongside the cross-cultural orientations that candidates for ministry would need to fulfill. Johnson allowed students to capture what lay behind differences in customary practice. She posed the dilemma of how "easy" (or otherwise) it is to understand the worldview of another culture and proposed a model of interpathy as best practice.[43] This way of thinking assumed that no matter how determined

40. Lee, "In Search," 89–90.
41. Kardashian, *Leadership and Culture*.
42. Tu'iono, "Seeking to Create," 41–44.
43. Johnson, *Drinking*, 59–62.

one might be, the empathetic hope behind the understanding of another culture, true competency requires the realization that there must be a point at which this attempt breaks down.

That reality was tested in class when students were invited to participate in theological and ethical discussions as if their birth culture was other than their own. Levon the Armenian got to play a Tongan while a Tongan student might be Korean or Filipino or Tamil for an hour. In the light of this interaction (and switches of identity), the class proposed a cross-cultural lens through which to read Scripture. For that purpose they decided upon a set of themes familiar to those migrating or living in diaspora—like journey, hospitality, language, margins, expressions of power.

There was a clear purpose to this acting out. Under Tony Floyd the Assembly's multi/cross-cultural reference group had set out as one of its goals the desire for a multicultural leadership. What was meant by this aim was the prospect of a Fijian minister, for instance, not serving in a Fijian or Anglo-dominant congregation but learning the skills of how to minister to a congregation made up of other or many cultures.

The failure to attend adequately to this knot of concerns to do with language, differing worldviews, and competency was identified in yet another use of the word *cross*. Humphries reported on how the class could become rather aware of how there might be a lack of justice in the relationships between and among cultures. There was likely to be an imbalance of power between the dominant culture and minority cultures. In more recent times that scenario was increasingly likely to lead to complaints of aversive or "nice" racism—then a turn to decolonialism and an impatience with a not sufficiently nuanced "white" theology. In this earlier period, though, the word *cross* was able to stand for being *angry*, hence a prophetic concern for justice. It did so in a way that neither the labels of intercultural or multicultural can do. With respect to the declaration of being a multicultural church, it was consistent with the ethical imperative lying behind the commitment to be "one fellowship [seeking] to achieve justice, affirm one another's cultures, and care for any who are the victims of racial discrimination, fear and economic exploitation."[44]

The preference for a cross-cultural mode of understanding the life together of diverse cultures was confirmed in a discussion on why students were finding themselves in one another's company—and forming friendships across culture. It was not for the sake of establishing a "boutique multicultural" experience where food and hospitality was shared, though that might happen. Through an illustration, Humphries had demonstrated

---

44. Uniting Church in Australia, *Multicultural Church*, para. 2.

how in a multicultural model of a culturally diverse society, the ever-present temptation is for cultures to assemble in their own cultures within the much larger orbit of the whole. Nor was the reasoning behind this gathering of different ethnicities due to any particular desire to enter into the experience of another through a fairly surface intercultural encounter. It was recognized that such relationships happened on the horizontal axis of one culture relating to another in Christ. They did not delve deeply enough. The vertical line was missing. The suggestion was made that those who had migrated, or were second generation, were more than hyphenated beings—Tongan-Australian, Rotuman-Australian (or, as Carroll declared, "Australienated"[45]). The Christian faith represented a third culture: such a theory might not immediately commend itself to first-generation Pasifika migrants insofar as the close relationship between culture and the Christian faith appeared to render them indistinguishable. For a second-generation growing up in a new land and needing to "invent" its place in a "globalized" rather than a traditional "integrated concept of culture," it seemed more plausible.[46] The biblical and theological foundation thus became one of baptism—and the Romans reading, 6:1–4, which described dying to the old self and rising to new life, alongside the baptismal formula in Gal 3, where all are one in Christ through baptism, through the cross.

Without necessarily realizing the connection, this setting of a theology of cultural diversity within the *locus* of the cross confirmed the earlier work of a former principal of the college, Gordon Dicker: some time before he had argued that the foundation of the multicultural church lay in the doctrine of justification by faith alone.[47] The costly nature of the cross further enabled the church to stand within a theology of the cross (rather than ones of glory) as proposed by Douglas John Hall in the wake of 9/11. The hidden transcript was effectively one of seeking to deepen the discourses of weaving multiculturalism and interculturalism into the very cornerstone of Christian belief.[48]

The declaration of being a multicultural church did not ignore the future prospects of an enriched pattern of ministry. It made reference for opportunities to be made "for bilingual worship and for fellowship across racial and cultural boundaries."[49] There should be "special ministerial education programs to prepare people for ministry in multicultural parishes

---

45. Carroll, "Making Room," 29.
46. Schreiter, *New Catholicity*, 43–61.
47. Dicker, "Theological Perspective."
48. Hall, *Cross in Our Context*.
49. Uniting Church in Australia, *Multicultural Church*, para. 7.

and ethnic congregations."⁵⁰ The declaration looked to the implementation of programs of "theological study in both countries": it was recognized that this kind of initiative would enable theological reflection on the "life situations of members of the culturally diverse congregation."⁵¹

These resolutions were not widely put into practice across the national church. They hinted at the critical role of an architecture of cross-cultural practice and knowledge. It is in this area that so much work was done prior to the emergence of a talanoa method and conference—and the higher profile of Pasifika cultures that have now become visible in key positions of the church. Some necessary foundations needed to be put into place: students were given the permission to explore cultural images and symbols and apply them to biblical interpretation and theological reasoning. Classes were dedicated to the principles of diaspora and contextuality, which allowed for the writing of assignments, research, publications, and peer critiques. Andrew Thornley taught a subject on Pacific church history. The Camden Theological Library, under the leadership of Moira Bryant, set about the task of collating relevant works and dissertations for the cultures to be found in the student body. The practice of studying in classes alongside cultures that were not Pasifika allowed for learning from others while serving as a summons to clarify one's own position. The benefit of being in the presence of the other cannot be easily dismissed. It was critical.

THE FLOURISHING

The metaphor of weaving threads has been selected by Suli for the theme of her presidency of the national church. It is the kind of root metaphor frequently used within Pasifika settings across the region. It is designed for the interlacing of stories in an embracing, inclusive manner. The remarkable proliferation of Pasifika dissertations that coincided with the number of students being formed for ministry unfolded in the presence of stories from other cultures. That this praxis should have evolved has required the employment of images and models that have gone beyond the invocations of talanoa, hospita*lei*ty, and *tagata mai fafo* (and the like) for the sake of a larger, more varied ecclesial whole. These themes have their place, but they are not acted out in a context that is only Pasifika. This proviso must always be kept in sight: United Theological College is not a college that is located in Fiji, Samoa, or Tonga, irrespective of how its life might be enriched from these institutions.

50. Uniting Church in Australia, *Multicultural Church*, para. 9.
51. Uniting Church in Australia, *Multicultural Church*, para. 8.

One of the dilemmas that then presents itself has been the failure so far of the Uniting Church to call for research that might help it determine the relationship of gospel to culture—and the gospel to cultures and the dominant culture. It is this failure which has led to the confusion surrounding the use of terms like multicultural, intercultural, and cross-cultural. In the absence of such, a number of Pasifika theologies arising out of United Theological College have been obliged to wrestle with the default position of gospel and culture being seen as rather tightly woven together. What happens if the experience of diaspora and the encounter with other cultures, faiths, and no faith leads to the unravelling of a *fa'aSamoa*, *fakatonga*, and the like?

Hawea Jackson, for instance, inquired into the relationship between Niuean cultural values and the gospel of Jesus Christ. There was a frank recognition here of the challenges that presented themselves in and through the experience of diaspora for the sake of constructing a "re-evangelized church for a re-contextualized church."[52] Vilitama was more radical in proposing a "liquid church" that was willing to sacrifice the familiar "solid" image of the church as an *ekalesia* for one of being a *fetuiaga*, a gathering, "on a distant shore." Through a thorough engagement with the known typologies of the church, Vilitama sought to address "the inner geography" of altered space;[53] being a dispersed community in a large, culturally diverse city is quite different from being the body of Christ in a village. Vilitama laid the foundations of his liquid ecclesiology within an expanded understanding of "where is Christ" to be found that embraced family and cultural events that transcended the formal service of worship.[54]

The relationship of gospel to culture was likewise the background for Isileli Jason Kioa's research into the status of the Tongan National Conference.[55] The lack of the clarification that should have followed in the wake of the 1985 declaration meant that national conferences that were subsequently established lacked authority and definition of purpose. Were they supposed to serve simply as an annual (or biannual) coming together, a celebration of congregations from the same ethnic group? Were they bridges between the Uniting Church and the sending church back in the islands? Were they advisory bodies for the Assembly to consult with on controversial matters like those to do with same-gender relationships? What was their function in

---

52. Jackson, "Niuean Cultural Values."
53. Vilitama, "Singing the Niuean '*Fetuiaga Kerisiano*,'" 137–38.
54. Vilitama, "Singing the Niuean '*Fetuiaga Kerisiano*.'"
55. Kioa, "Role of the Tongan."

the interconciliar Uniting Church? Kioa wrapped these kinds of concerns around the question: What did it actually mean to live cross-culturally?

The potential for the gospel to be involved in a dialectical relationship with culture has been most patently obvious in works of public theology. Through its ongoing work in this emerging field, the college was able to mediate insights from around the world in theologies seeking to address points of tension and urgent concern in island cultures in the region. Charles Uesile Tupu, for instance, composed a response to the disputes surrounding customary land, the formation of new political parties, and a constitutional crisis. In the process he established the case for a Christopraxis reading of where Christ is to be found in public and political issues: the cultural idiom was preserved through observing the ritual practice of a *silagtoga*.[56] In a similar way to Faala Faamatuainu (Sam) Amosa, he made the case for a need to break the "silence of the church" on matters to do with public life.[57] It was time for ordained ministers, even within the *malae* of the local village, to exercise the function of being a public *faifeau*. Amosa's more particular focus had been on how a court case, in which the church was taken to task by one of its ministers, represented the "shaking of the foundations" (the *fa'a-vae*), the way in which the compact among the pillars of society—the church, *fa'aSamoa*, the law, and government—was beginning to fracture. Amosa discerned the pressing need for the church to adapt to changing circumstances and exercise a more prophetic role.[58]

The role of Pasifika students, staff, and research has flourished over the past quarter century. It has been imaginative in the way it has initiated fresh methodologies, addressed difficult issues, wrestled with issues to do with belonging, identity, and homemaking. It has nurtured ordinands and future leaders. It has done so in the presence of the ethnic and cultural other—and with due awareness of the always evolving nature of the global discussions that attend the various disciplines taught year by year.

BIBLIOGRAPHY

Amosa, Faala Faamatuainu. "Courting a Public Theology of *Fa'a-vae* for the Church and Contemporary Samoa." PhD diss., Charles Sturt University, 2020.

Bonhoeffer, Dietrich. *Letters and Papers from Prison*. Edited by Eberhard Bethge. New York: Simon & Schuster, 2011.

---

56. Tupu, "*Fa'aola Fanua*."
57. Amosa, "Courting a Public Theology," 38, 58, 75, 82, 161, 196.
58. Amosa, "Courting a Public Theology."

Carroll, Seforosa. "Making Room for the Religious Other: Reading Interfaith Dialogue and Encounters in the Australian Context from a Feminist Diasporic Perspective." PhD diss., Charles Sturt University, 2015.

———. "Strangers and Frangipani *Lei*: Exploring a Christology of Hospita*leity*." In *Faith in a Hyphen: Cross-Cultural Theologies Down Under*, edited by Clive Pearson and Jione Havea, 145–57. Adelaide, SA: Openbook, 2004.

———. "*Talanoa* Is More Than Mere Storytelling." United Theological College, Apr. 29, 2024. https://www.utc.edu.au/blog/talanoa-is-more-than-mere-storytelling/.

———. "Weaving a Frangipani *Lei* Down Under: Theology in Diaspora. A Christological Approach." MTh diss., Sydney College of Divinity, 2004.

Dicker, Gordon. "A Theological Perspective on Multiculturalism." In *The Vision of a Multicultural Church*, edited by Seongja Yoo-Crowe, 7–13. Sydney: Uniting Church, 1998.

Ete, Risatisone. "A Bridge in My Father's House." Bachelor's thesis, University of Otago, 1996.

———. "Ugly Duckling, Quacking Swan." In *Faith in a Hyphen: Cross-Cultural Theologies Down Under*, edited by Clive Pearson and Jione Havea, 43–48. Adelaide, SA: Openbook, 2004.

Evans, James H., Jr. *We Have Been Believers: An African American Systematic Theology*. Rev. ed. Minneapolis: Fortress, 2012.

Finau, Salesi. "Jesus the *Haua*." MTh diss., Charles Sturt University, 2004.

———. "Jesus the *Haua*: Diaspora Theology of a Tongan." *Pasifika Occasional Papers* 1.2 (2008) 26–31.

Foi'akau, Inise Vakabua. "The Silent Voice of *Yalewa Bokala* in Numbers 12." *Uniting Church Studies* 23.1 (2021) 59–70.

———. "Sipora (Zipporah), Both Native and Foreigner: A *Marama I Taukei* Reading of Exodus 4:24–26." In *Sea of Readings: The Bible in the South Pacific*, edited by Jione Havea, 117–23. Atlanta: SBL, 2018.

Hall, Douglas John. *The Cross in Our Context: Jesus and the Suffering World*. Minneapolis: Fortress, 2003.

Havea, Jione. "Islander Criticism: Water, Ways, Worries." In *Sea of Readings: The Bible in the South Pacific*, 1–22. Atlanta: SBL, 2018.

———. *Losing Ground: Reading Ruth in the Pacific*. London: SCM, 2021

Humphries, Jon. "Crossing into the Unknown." In *Faith in a Hyphen: Cross-Cultural Theologies Down Under*, edited by Clive Pearson and Jione Havea, 159–74. Adelaide, SA: Openbook, 2004.

Jackson, Hawea. "Niuean Cultural Values and Their Relationship to the Gospel of Jesus Christ." DMin diss., Charles Sturt University, 2016.

Johnson, Lydia. *Drinking from the Same Well: Cross-Cultural Concerns in Pastoral Care and Counseling*. Eugene, OR: Pickwick, 2011.

Kardashian, Levon. *Leadership and Culture: Re-Imagining Cross Cultural Leadership in the Uniting Church in Australia*. London: Lambert Academic, 2014.

Kioa, Isileli Jason. "The Role of the Tongan National Conference in the Uniting Church in Australia." DMin diss., Charles Sturt University, 2020.

Lee, Aeryun. "In Search of a Christ of the Heart." In *Faith in a Hyphen: Cross-Cultural Theologies Down Under*, edited by Clive Pearson and Jione Havea, 88–94. Adelaide, SA: Openbook, 2004.

Lima, Peletisala. "Performing a Remigrant Theology: Sons and Daughters Improvising on the Return Home." PhD diss., Charles Sturt University, 2012.

Lima, Peletisala, and Clive Pearson. "Becoming *Tagata Mai Fafo*." *Uniting Church Studies* 23.1 (2021) 19–28.

Lopez, Mark. *The Origins of Multiculturalism in Australian Politics 1945–1975*. Carlton, VIC: Melbourne University Press, 2000.

Matsuoka, Fumitaka. *Out of Silence: Emerging Themes in Asian American Churches*. Cleveland, OH: United Church, 1995.

Migliore, Daniel. *Faith Seeking Understanding: Introduction to Christian Theology*. 4th ed. Grand Rapids: Eerdmans, 2023.

Mitchell, Sarah. "*Communitas* of Christ: Risking the Cross-Cultural Way." In *Faith in a Hyphen: Cross-Cultural Theologies Down Under*, edited by Clive Pearson and Jione Havea, 175–84. Adelaide, SA: Openbook, 2004.

Mostert, Christiaan. "Is a Non-Contextual Theology Viable?" In *Mapping the Landscape: Essays in Australian and New Zealand Christianity*, edited by Susan Emilsen and William W. Emilsen, 118–33. New York: Lang, 2000.

Palu, Ma'afu. *Pacific Theology: Problems and Proposals*. Nuku'alofa, Tonga: Ichthus, 2017.

Pearson, Clive, and Jione Havea, eds. *Faith in a Hyphen: Cross-Cultural Theologies Down Under*. Adelaide, SA: Openbook, 2004.

Schreiter, Robert. *The New Catholicity: Theology Between the Global and the Local*. Maryknoll, NY: Orbis, 1997.

Talia, Maina Vakafua. "Am I Not Your *Tū/akoi*? A Tuvaluan Plea for Survival in a Time of Climate Emergency." PhD diss., Charles Sturt University, 2022.

Tuiai, Aukilani. "The Congregational Christian Church of Samoa, 1962–2002: A Study of the Issues and Policies That Have Shaped the Independent Church." PhD diss., Charles Sturt University, 2012.

Tu'iono, Kamaloni. "Reflections Arising Out of Paragraph 1.8 of the Code of Ethics." *Uniting Church Studies* 23:1 (2021) 49–58.

———. "Seeking to Create '*Vā* ' Spaces as a Means of Fostering a Communal Model of Supervision in a Cross-Cultural Setting." DMin diss., Charles Sturt University, 2021.

Tupou-Thomas, Sisilia. "Telling Tales." In *Faith in a Hyphen: Cross-Cultural Theologies Down Under*, edited by Clive Pearson and Jione Havea, 1–4. Adelaide, SA: Openbook, 2004.

———. "*Teolosia 'o e Faka'apa'apa*: Being Respectful from the Perspective of a Tongan in Diaspora." *Uniting Church Studies* 23.1 (2021) 71–79.

———. "A Theology of Respect from a Tongan Perspective." MTh diss., Sydney College of Divinity, 2004.

Tupu, Charles Uesile. "*Fa'aola Fanua*: A Samoan Public Theology of Taking Care of Customary Land (*fanua faa-le-aganu'u*)." PhD diss., Charles Sturt University, 2021.

Uniting Church in Australia. *A Church for all God's People: Vision Statement*. Illuminate. Released 2006. https://ucaassembly.recollect.net.au/nodes/view/198.

———. *One Body, Many Members: Living Faith and Life Cross-Culturally*. Illuminate. Released 2012. https://ucaassembly.recollect.net.au/nodes/view/416.

———. *We Are a Multicultural Church*. Illuminate. Released 1985. https://ucaassembly.recollect.net.au/nodes/view/494.

Uota, Sulufaiga. "Who Is Jesus Christ for Us in Our Time of Climate Change? How Should Christ Be Professed in Tuvalu Today?" Unpublished essay. United Theological College, 2008.

Vaai, Upolu Lumā, and Aisake Casimira, eds. *The "Whole of Life" Way: Unburying Vakatabu Philosophies and Theologies for Pasifika Development*. Suva: PTC, 2024.

Vaipulu, Sioeli Felekoni. "Towards an '*Otua*logy: Revisiting and Rethinking the Doctrine of God in Tonga." PhD diss., Charles Sturt University, 2013.

Vilitama, Matagi. "*Fetuiaga Kerisiano*: On Becoming a Liquid Church." *Uniting Church Studies* 23.1 (2021) 39–48.

———. "On Becoming a Liquid Church: Singing the Niuean '*Fetuiaga Kerisiano*' on a Distant Shore." PhD diss., Charles Sturt University, 2015.

7

Things That Matter to Koreans

MYUNG HWA PARK

IN APRIL 1889 THE first Australian missionary to Korea, Rev. Henry Davies, died only six months after he had arrived in the country. But Henry Davies' short-lived missionary endeavor wasn't forgotten. He was followed by 106 Australian men and women between 1889 and 2025 who undertook what Henry Davies had hoped to: preach the gospel, teach young men, set up hospitals for women and children, support people in poverty, and work for human rights. One hundred years later, in 1989, two Korean students—Myong Duk Yang and Myung Hwa Park—became the first from their background to study at United Theological College (UTC). They were followed by thirty-six Koreans who became ministers in the Uniting Church in Australia (UCA) after being trained at UTC. Many more did postgraduate studies and courses like the Lay Preacher's course, as well as studying for admission to become ministers in the UCA from other churches. Those Korean ministers, formed by UTC and ordained by the UCA, ministered in congregations from Clunes-Dunoon to Canberra, from country churches to inner city churches in the Synod of New South Wales and Australian Capital Territory. Some of them worked in other synods. Most served in congregational ministry, and many played significant roles in the Presbytery, Synod, and Assembly of the UCA.

In this chapter fifteen people, including the author, reflected on "things that matter" from when they studied and worked at UTC. There were eleven

UTC-trained Korean ministers including Myung Hwa Park, Jason Chong Bok Choi, Aeryun Lee, Seung Jae Yeun, Ace Kim, Do Young Kim, HeeWon Chang, Sunny Lee, Sang Hyun Nam, DooAh Yoon, and Myong Cheol Oh; two ministers from UCA's partner churches in Korea ministering in Korean congregations, Young Min Suh and Eojin Lee, who did postgraduate study; Sang Taek Lee, who coordinated the joint postgraduate program between Charles Sturt University (CSU) and Han Nam University in Daejeon, South Korea, in 2009; and Phoebe Kim, who works at Camden Theological Library.

The author suggested some questions to prompt the fourteen contributors to ponder on their experiences at UTC. Those questions were: What matters the most as you reflect on your time at UTC, highlighting the joys, achievements, struggles, and contributions you made? Every reflection is unique, so bringing them together wasn't easy. However, the author weaved the fourteen reflections together under common themes.

A TAPESTRY OF FAITH AND TRADITIONS

As a minority group at UTC, Koreans were often seen as all looking alike, quietly spoken, shy but friendly, and formal but not rigid. This stereotypical perception of Korean characteristics can be misleading. Migration is a complex experience, but studying in a foreign context adds complexity and adversity for Korean students. However, Koreans at UTC brought an awareness of cultural differences by being Koreans and encouraged diverse expectations as Korean immigrants, thus adding to UTC's tapestry of faith and traditions. The following reflections from individual Korean students demonstrate the breadth of expectations and experiences through their involvement at UTC.

Choi, a professor of architecture from Korea, came to UTC to learn more about the UCA. He recalled,

> When I studied for a PhD at the Faculty of Architecture, Sydney University, in the early 1980s, I happened to read the "Interim Regulations of UCA." I also audited a "Christian Ethics" class at UTC in Enfield. That led me to take one year of study leave and come to UTC. One night in December 1990, I had a unique and personal experience of God. My family supported me by voting to continue my training at UTC. Thus, I submitted a resignation letter to the university and continued the ministry formation process.[1]

---

1. Jason Chong Bok Choi, email message to author, Feb. 22, 2024.

A. R. Lee, who first arrived at UTC thirty years ago as a private student, had cherished the thought of being an ordained minister since her adolescence. She often pondered "why ministers from various churches I attended had strongly encouraged me to study theology, especially when women were not allowed ordination."[2]

Like A. R. Lee, S. Lee had a similar aspiration to come to UTC. She said,

> As I immigrated to Australia, I dreamed of being ordained in a country where there would be equal opportunity for ordination without gender discrimination. In Korean churches, some of the major Presbyterian and Baptist churches do not still ordain women. And then I met the Uniting Church. On my first visit to the UTC, I chatted with Professor William Emilsen. Hearing about UTC and learning that women could be ordained just like me filled me with immense gratitude.[3]

Yoon was born a day after the Lunar New Year in the Year of the Tiger in a patriarchal society with a strong Confucian belief. A girl with the Tiger sign is hard to marry off because a tiger girl is courageous and wild, while a tiger boy would be a preferred offspring. In the strong patriarchal society, she felt invisible. So she tried to attract people's attention by working hard as a "doer" and helping to resolve others' problems. Some years later, she came to Australia with the dream of freedom and a new start. She studied at Southern Cross Bible College and went to China for a one-year mission trip. Returning from China, she started an intercultural service at Dong San Korean Uniting Church in Mays Hill. Forty people from more than ten nationalities joined the Saturday evening service. Yoon said, "I needed transitional ministry training to transition from missionary to minister. I finished the 'Period of Discernment' and joined UTC."[4]

Since UCA advocates for diversity, equality, and inclusivity of all cultural backgrounds, Suh, who ministers in a Korean congregation in Ermington, found it easier to study at UTC despite criticisms from conservative denominations. Suh, from one of the partner churches in Korea, the Presbyterian Church of Korea (PCK), joined the Uniting Church, while many other ministers from his denomination joined the Presbyterian Church of Australia because they saw the UCA as too liberal on issues of sexuality and same-sex marriage.

2. Aeryun Lee, email message to author, Apr. 30, 2024.
3. Sunny Kyung Hee Lee, email message to author, Apr. 29, 2024.
4. DooAh Yoon, email message to author, Feb. 22, 2024.

One of the most recently ordained ministers, Oh, commenced his theological study in 2016 and ministry formation in 2019. He saw a rich cultural tapestry when he immersed himself in UTC. He recalled,

> Beyond the surface allure of experiencing diverse nationalities, my encounter with cultural diversity at the College reflects deeper into the roots of faith and traditions. This profound exploration facilitated a nuanced understanding of the universal human experiences of life and death, fostering an environment of love, care, prayer, and communal living. Despite the inherent challenges of embracing such diversity, the spiritual unity forged through our shared calling and diverse gifts fostered a harmonious community life. Indeed, the cultural diversity at the Theological College manifested as a symphony of lights, tastes, and airs, enriching our collective journey of faith.[5]

Like all the others, Oh, a gifted artist before he entered UTC, added color and movement to the rich tapestry of UTC.

> I supported the College by contributing to photography and hip-hop dance workshops, which enriched my experience and fostered a sense of belonging and camaraderie within the College community.[6]

IN-YEON (인연) "FATE AND RELATIONSHIPS"

For some people, UTC was a warm and welcoming place, but for others it was an alien environment where people struggled with language, cultural, and theological differences. For some the physical environment, for others the social interactions, and for others the theological studies and academic life would make a strong impact on them.

Chang had early exposure to UTC. She recalled her childhood memory of a simple thing like the furniture and, comparing it with her adult experience, wrote,

> My journey with the United Theological College began in the 1980s when my mother studied there. Then, I studied at UTC as an international student in 2009, when the red chairs in

---

5. Myeong Cheol Oh, email message to author, Apr. 3, 2024.
6. Oh, email message to author, Apr. 3, 2024.

the foyer were once green, and the main entrance had heavy wooden doors.[7]

Suh, a minister serving a Korean Uniting Church, frequently attended gatherings and educational sessions at UTC. For him, UTC was a comfortable and convenient place that was sensitively accommodating to his physical condition. He recalled,

> Upon arrival, I immediately felt a sense of comfort. Because of my leg surgery early in my youth, I struggled with navigating numerous buildings and stairs. Still, UTC, with its single-story building structure, was a comfortable and convenient place for me to be.[8]

But the very same place made a different impression on D. Y. Kim, who recalled his first day at UTC:

> When I first stepped foot on UTC grounds in 2004, it felt like entering a small, humble, serene village church in Korea rather than a college campus. UTC seemed modest in size and stature compared to the theological school I attended and the churches I ministered in.[9]

Yoon recalled the importance of the relationship with other students she built at UTC:

> The relationship between candidates was supportive and encouraging, especially at lunchtime. Initially, once a week, we brought cultural dishes for lunch, which helped to develop a wonderful sense of community among our different cultures. Unfortunately, a year later, we were encouraged to prepare a simple lunch instead: just salads, bread, and fruits. This was quick and efficient—we didn't need to use chopsticks. However, from a Korean perspective, hospitality is very important, and I found the switch to this simple lunch to be more task-oriented than relationship-oriented.[10]

A. R. Lee, who was the winner of the undergraduate section of the 1997 Openbook Annual Theological Essay Award with her essay "Who Is Jesus for Us Today?" was the first Asian woman entrant, and the first from UTC, in the competition's history. She remembers encountering a number

---

7. HeeWon Chang, email message to author, Apr. 29, 2024.
8. Young Min Suh, email message to author, Apr. 2, 2024.
9. Do Young Kim, email message to author, May 2, 2024.
10. DooAh Yoon, email message to author, Feb. 22, 2024.

of excellent teachers like Graham Hughes, who "introduced a profound phrase, 'think prayerfully, pray thoughtfully,'" which was a guiding post throughout her ministry. Clive Pearson, also,

> played a pivotal role in steering us from the traditional Western systematic theology towards a more inclusive and diverse approach—embracing contextual, cross-cultural, women, liberation, public theology and many more. His teachings encompassed the rich tapestry of works by theologians from around the world.[11]

For some international students, UTC became a pathway to UCA, and this was the case for Nam, who studied a master of theology program in 2010. Nam recalled,

> I cannot miss mentioning my first encounter with the Uniting Church in Australia (UCA). As I attended a Korean immigrant church based in the Presbyterian Church of Korea (PCK), the existence of UCA, which is rare in Korea, appealed to me. Questions and answers about its appeal were gathered at the UTC. The easiest and most accurate way to access information about UCA—its history, its systems, its ministries—through its people and libraries was at UTC. The meeting of Uniting Church ministers and ministry agents during my M.Th. study at UTC and Uniting Church's ministerial candidate program (2018–2020) created great opportunities to see and taste the colours of the Uniting Church of Australia.[12]

E. Lee, who did a postgraduate program at UTC, reflected,

> I vividly recall instances where I stumbled over words and crafted grammatically awkward sentences. Instead of impatience, the lecturers displayed remarkable understanding. They patiently waited, enduring the linguistic hurdles I presented, and encouraged me to keep trying. Their advice echoed in my ears—the assurance that every effort, no matter how challenging, was a step toward growth. Their smile encouraged me to overcome my discomfort and continue striving to communicate clearly in English. These experiences of encouragement and acceptance profoundly shaped my outlook, instilling in me a sense of empathy and inclusion.
> In 2018, I began my current role as senior minister at a Korean immigrant church in Sydney, where the Korean language and

11. Aeryun Lee, email message to author, Apr. 30, 2024.
12. Sang Hyun Nam, email message to author, Apr. 17, 2024.

culture are dominant. Drawing from my struggles, I identified with those in my congregation who were not confident in Korean language and culture. I was able to understand how they might feel marginalised and frustrated if church proceedings were conducted in a language they didn't understand. I took it upon myself to bridge the language gap within the church community. I tried to implement translation services, ensuring that everyone could actively participate in worship and meetings, regardless of their linguistic abilities. The act of inclusion became a cornerstone of our church's ethos, fostering an environment where individuals felt seen, heard, and valued.[13]

LIKE AN AIRPORT

UTC was a place where theology and culture interacted in the classroom, the common room, the library, and the chapel. This was a two-way process. Korean students brought the gifts of their language, culture, and life experiences to the Uniting Church, and UTC allowed them to broaden their understanding of Australian life and the Uniting Church and its theology. Nam viewed his journey at UTC as giving him unexpected gifts. For him,

> UTC was like an airport due to the coexistence of Eastern and Western differences in Christianity. There were many different theologies coming and going from various people at UTC. Still, there was an understanding and consideration for the theology and spirituality that the individual pursued. This gave me a step towards understanding the Korean colour of faith, especially the Presbyterian tradition, Australia's public theology, and the many theologies shared by the South Pacific and Aboriginal communities.[14]

For Nam, UTC will always be an essential academic airport and the first stepping stone to understanding Australian theology and the UCA.

A. R. Lee reflected on theologizing from her own experience as a person of the East living in the West. "Clive Pearson's insightful teaching, coupled with the impactful statement from Karl Barth, the 'Journey of the Son of God into the Far Country,' was thought-provoking and ignited reflections, intertwining my experiences and culture in both my homeland and on foreign soil. As an Asian woman, I found resonance in this beautiful

---

13. Eojin Lee, email message to author, Mar. 28, 2024.
14. Nam, email message to author, Apr. 17, 2024.

statement, a journey that deeply reverberated with my spiritual and theological explorations."[15]

Suh, who ministers at a Korean congregation in Sydney, also experienced UTC as a place where different theological streams meet and influenced one another. He said,

> Coming from a conservative evangelical background in Korea, I felt that studying theology at UTC was quite progressive. Embracing and respecting diverse contemporary theological perspectives created a different atmosphere from what I had experienced before in Korea. When studying church history, particularly the history of the UCA, I saw that social justice was a significant issue, unlike my previous Korean church experience, where the emphasis was on the Bible, pastoral work, and Christian education.[16]

Yeun saw himself standing on the margins, which can be unstable but also promotes flexibility at the same time. He said,

> The formation process I experienced (2012–2014) gave me the opportunity to look at the other side from a micro-level of the Korean immigrant church's perspective and to be curious about how non-Korean-immigrant churches within the Uniting Church live out faith in Christ and practise their theology and its implications in the context given.[17]

Yeun described the coexistence of cultural and theological differences as an experience of "hybridity" during his time at UTC.

UTC was not only the place where West and East met. It also provided Korean students with encounters with Aboriginal People. For A. Kim, who started a unique ministry for young people called "One Heart Faith Community," UTC was a platform through which he entered into a new relationship with Aboriginal people. He said,

> UTC helped me understand the significance of the mission and relationship with Aboriginal sisters and brothers in Australia. Hearing the voices of Aboriginal people through conferences and fellowship inspired and taught me how to build a body of Jesus Christ together.[18]

---

15. Aeryun Lee, email message to author, Apr. 30, 2024.
16. Young Min Suh, email message to author, Apr. 2, 2024.
17. Seung Jae Yeun, email message to author, May 29, 2024.
18. Ace Kim, email message to author, May 1, 2024.

Chang, instead of pursuing a PhD, chose formation at UTC where she recalls,

> I had the opportunity to hear and meet world-leading theologians and biblical scholars, like Anthony Reddie and R. S. Sugirtharajah, and hear from some Indigenous voices through conferences on Myths on Whiteness and Postcolonial Engagement. At UTC, I was introduced to Talanoa and to face the texts of terror in the Bible by Jione Havea. It was a place that affirmed my identity as a Korean woman. Throughout my studies and formation, I was encouraged and invited to explore how my Korean-ness gave way to other ways of interpreting the biblical text and theology. And because of this affirmation, I was able to learn and dialogue with people from diverse backgrounds.[19]

Someone like S. Lee, who studied theology in Korea, clearly saw UTC as a place where we not only encounter differences but also where the problems that can accompany differences can be overcome. She said,

> I appreciate UTC as it explores and practices ministry and theology from a women's perspective. It aims to provide equal opportunities for women to receive ordination, serve in specified ministries, and become leaders in the Church. This ensures that women gain confidence in leadership and receive the support they need to engage in ministry proactively. With such a background, I proudly say that 11 UTC Korean female graduates have been ordained, and most of them are currently actively serving in various ministry placements.[20]

Most Korean students did their studies at UTC, but not D. Y. Kim. He wrote,

> While other candidates followed the curriculum tailored to their situations and experiences, I studied English at Hornsby TAFE for an entire semester. UTC's accommodation of my circumstances was also a gesture of kindness. It was amusing how, while other students commuted to UTC in the morning, I left the UTC student dormitories to greet them on my way to Hornsby TAFE, experiencing a peculiar sense of duality.[21]

Camden Library was another place where West and East coexisted. P. Kim, who works at Camden Library, proudly said, "There are over 4,500

---

19. HeeWon Chang, email message to author, Apr. 29, 2024.
20. Sunny Kyung Hee Lee, email message to author, Apr. 29, 2024.
21. Do Young Kim, email message to author, May 2, 2024.

Korean theological books and a small selection of fiction and children's Bible storybooks."²² She also shared about how the Korean library started:

> I learned from our manager that a suggestion from Dr. Emilsen prompted the inclusion of Korean books in our library. Dr. William Emilsen recognised the value of providing access to Korean materials to support Korean-speaking students further. The purchase of the Korean translation of the "Confessions" by Augustine marked the inception of Korean language books in our library.
>
> However, over the years, we have benefitted from and greatly appreciated various gifts from individuals within the Korean community.²³

The Korean collection at the Camden Theological Library has impacted well beyond UTC. P. Kim said,

> These resources are highly valued by pastors within the Uniting Church and students at UTC. Local church ministers also utilise them, as well as lay workers and students from neighbouring theological colleges. Camden Library assisted a Korean student pursuing a theology master's degree program in Melbourne by acquiring new resources to aid him in his studies.²⁴

P. Kim was so proud that "Camden Theological Library serves the Sydney area and is a valuable resource center for Korean researchers throughout Australia."²⁵ The library at UTC is not only a place for books and resources, but for Korean students like Oh, it was also a place of comfort and support. He remembers, "I found solace in the abundance of Korean theological references, which facilitated a deeper comprehension of complex theological concepts in both English and Korean."²⁶

UNITY IN DIVERSITY

"Unity in diversity" was a catchphrase for balancing the challenge of embracing the new concept of multiculturalism. In 1985, the UCA declared itself a multicultural church. However, multiculturalism wasn't widely observed or practised then as it is now. Since then, more people at UTC, both students

22. Phoebe Kim, email message to author, May 7, 2024.
23. Phoebe Kim, email message to author, May 7, 2024.
24. Phoebe Kim, email message to author, May 7, 2024.
25. Phoebe Kim, email message to author, May 7, 2024.
26. Myeong Cheol Oh, email message to author, Apr. 3, 2024.

and faculty members, have come from various cultural backgrounds and pushed the boundaries of the theological framework.

Choi was the only one with a culturally and linguistically diverse background (CALD) out of twenty-three candidates ordained in 1993. He was among the few Korean ordinands who took up a Korean congregation. The new Korean congregation Choi planted from scratch is still strong after thirty years. After several ministerial experiences—planting a Korean congregation, working as a mission consultant to the Synod of VIC/TAS (Victoria and Tasmania), and being a minister at Greystanes in the western suburbs of Sydney—Choi has had diverse ministerial experiences. He fondly shared that

> I supported one Ghanaian lay leader in becoming the first African-background UCA minister in the Synod of NSW. Each placement was quite different, but I tried to focus on an inclusive banquet of God, including not just me and us but also those I tend to exclude.[27]

A. R. Lee is grateful to UTC because it had provided her with "a theological and ministry home that transcends cultural, racial, gender, historical, and economic boundaries. It has invited me to rediscover myself and deeply value what I have."[28] A. R. Lee shared how this impacted her ministry in this beautiful story:

> One of the compelling testimonials from the members of other cultures in the community I have served echoes, "We have lived here in this community for over ten years, but for the first time, I have felt accepted and a part of this local community, thanks to this Uniting Church." As a ministry agent, what more could one hope to hear?[29]

D. Y. Kim's experience of studying at UTC was not easy. He encountered many hurdles and problems. However, his encounter with Professor J. "who shared his struggles during his doctoral studies abroad due to family, environment, and cultural differences, offering pastoral care and genuine prayers changed his decision to abandon the school and return to Korea."[30] D. Y. Kim believes that:

---

27. Jason Chong Bok Choi, email message to author, Feb. 22, 2024.
28. Aeryun Lee, email message to author, Apr. 30, 2024.
29. Aeryun Lee, email message to author, Apr. 30, 2024.
30. Do Young Kim, email message to author, May 2, 2024.

my presence has presented many challenges to UTC, perhaps in ways different from contributing through strengths or gifts. Through my weaknesses and unique approaches to matters, as well as my different skin colour, unique accent, and my own experiences, they would develop a more mature approach to the CALD community. This would lead to a reinterpretation of ministry in UCA.[31]

Unity in diversity is not just adding another color or flavor but allowing you to be who you are and bringing what you are to your church community. Yeun was encouraged to be who he is in this culturally diverse context of UTC. He shared,

> This is one of the recommendations I received during the final progress interview in the advanced year. Be sure to find your Korean-ness. This meant to me that it's okay if I'm Korean. I can be Korean and minister in the Uniting Church. Just as I was accepted as I am, so everyone would be accepted as they are in this church![32]

Yeun began his cross-cultural journey at UTC, a life of hybridity, where he lived in both Korean and Australian cultural and theological perspectives.

> My hybridity may have started here. At times, I was criticised or blamed by both sides, but I used it as an opportunity to mature. I was determined again and again to expand my boundaries during the formation years. I could bear it because everything was an opportunity for me to learn a lesson and gain wisdom from the follies of others. The formation programs provided me with theological frameworks and theories to reflect on everything I experienced.[33]

Chang valued her growth at UTC, reflecting on how UTC helped her become who she is while encouraging her to express herself. She recalled,

> UTC did not tell me how to think or be but created enough space for me to ponder, wonder, question, and be challenged. It offered me a space to grow and a sense of belonging. Instead of telling me who I am or how I should think, UTC allowed me to develop a language about who I am, be willing to learn from my experience and show interest in what I say.[34]

31. Do Young Kim, email message to author, May 2, 2024.
32. Seung Jae Yeun, email message to author, May 29, 2024.
33. Yeun, email message to author, May 29, 2024.
34. HeeWon Chang, email message to author, Apr. 29, 2024.

Oh pointed out the importance of linguistic diversity

> that bridged cultural divides and promoted cross-cultural dialogue and mutual understanding, fostering a spirit of inclusivity and collaboration within the College community. The formation programs at the United Theological College gave me freedom, allowed me to be my best self, and created a place to be proud of myself.[35]

FROM LITTLE ACORNS

I remember struggling at UTC as an international student from Korea, and studying in English was a formidable hurdle to overcome. Language is a channel for communication, learning, and building relationships. But it is a means to an end, not an end. But when you are not fluent in English, you can feel inadequate, less intelligent, and sometimes invisible and insignificant. Most Korean students experienced the need for more fluency in English at UTC, and most Korean ministers trained at UTC find English challenging in their ministry situations because English is not their mother tongue. However, I also learned that communication is not solely by words; sometimes, actions can speak louder than words.

Nam, who studied as an international student, expressed this:

> One day, I felt discouraged because my insufficient English skills prevented me from completing a subject. Looking back on it now, I would have completed my studies properly in that situation with the consideration and guidance of the faculty and staff of the College.[36]

E. J. Lee, who did postgraduate study at UTC, wasn't an exception in his struggle with the English language. He said,

> As a Korean immigrant, I had to fight to survive in a foreign and fearful language environment during my early days. English, the medium of learning, became a formidable barrier, and I often struggled with frustration in discussions and presentations. The early days were tough, and there were moments when I questioned my ability to communicate effectively in a language that was not my own. The classroom setting, where articulate expression was essential, became a testing ground for my linguistic

---

35. Myeong Cheol Oh, email message to author, Apr. 4, 2024.
36. Sang Hyun Nam, email message to author, Apr. 17, 2024.

abilities. I became increasingly timid and intimidated whenever I struggled to express my thoughts accurately in English. In these moments of vulnerability, I met professors and colleagues who served as beacons of encouragement. They recognised my struggles and, rather than dismissing them, offered unwavering support and guidance.³⁷

E. J. Lee saw how his experience of vulnerability at UTC changed him. He was now aware of the concept of fragile little acorns growing into mighty oak trees. He reflected on his experience:

I took it upon myself to bridge the language gap within the church community. I tried to implement translation services, ensuring that everyone could actively participate in worship and meetings, regardless of their linguistic abilities. The act of inclusion became a cornerstone of our church's ethos, fostering an environment where individuals felt seen, heard, and valued. Today, as I witness our church thriving, I am reminded that the seeds of empathy and encouragement planted in UTC have blossomed into a rich harvest of unity and spiritual abundance.³⁸

A person on the margins, Yeun developed his new nature with hybridity. He said he was determined to grow. Yeun played a pivotal role as a member of the Korean Presbytery. The presbytery had a role that they needed to fill, and he was given the opportunity to serve when the presbytery's dissolution was discussed. Furthermore, he could share what he had learned and experienced in the Uniting Church with the members and leaders of the presbytery. In living on the margins, he experienced the transformative image of "little acorns" that grew into mighty oak trees.

Yoon, the only Korean university chaplain, saw how a little acorn grew into a big oak tree in her ministry as a chaplain at Wollongong University. She said,

At UTC, public theology, eco-theology, and interdisciplinary studies through Han Nam University and Charles Sturt University shaped my theology and ministry. Since 2019, I have led a service called "Season of Creation" in September every year. It has been a great opportunity to have an outdoor service with discussion and lunch. We focus on our relationship with God, our relationship with human fellows and our relationship with nature.³⁹

---

37. Eojin Lee, email message to author, Mar. 28, 2024.
38. Eojin Lee, email message to author, Mar. 28, 2024.
39. DooAh Yoon, email message to author, Feb. 22, 2024.

A. Kim saw UTC as an incubator. "At UTC, I was allowed to be myself and was encouraged to dream about how I could serve and love God's people. I have gained new perspectives on building and leading a cross-cultural, missional, and intergenerational church."[40] Since his ordination in 2013, he has engaged in pioneering a ministry, "One Heart," witnessing where little acorns grew into mighty oak trees. S. Lee quietly observed how UTC helped many Korean women conduct excellent ministries within the UCA. She recorded, "I proudly say that eleven UTC Korean female graduates have been ordained or are in the ordination process. From 1990 to now, Korean female ministers have covered over 30 placements."[41]

S. T. Lee, whose tireless work was to bring joint initiatives between Charles Sturt University and Han Nam University, never gave up the vision for theological education that helps Korean pastors with limited access to theological education in Australia due to the language barrier. There is an ongoing necessity for theological education in over two hundred Korean churches in Sydney, where the Korean immigrant population exceeds one hundred thousand. Furthermore, there is a need for second-generation education and lay leadership.

Writing this reflection on "things that matter" has allowed fifteen Koreans to return to the time when they first entered UTC, to recount their encounters with people, fellow students who were both different and similar to them, and of lecturers who encouraged, inspired, and supported them to be who they are today. Many fondly remember UTC as a place where they found solace and comfort, with its peaceful chapel, the Camden Theological Library, and the bush setting.

What are the things that matter? Almost every one of the correspondents expressed their heart-filled gratitude to the people they knew and for the experiences they had at UTC. Oh, one newly ordained minister, sums up the feelings of many:

> With renewed conviction and purpose to embark on the next chapter of my ministry, fortified by the lessons learned and the bonds forged within the sacred confines of the chapel, where the echoes of home and divine calling reverberate in harmony.[42]

Finally, the task of collating and editing the reflections of the fourteen people who contributed to this chapter can be best concluded in prayerful thoughts Choi offered for the fiftieth anniversary of UTC:

---

40. Ace Kim, email message to author, May 1, 2024.
41. Sunny Kyung Hee Lee, email message to author, Apr. 29, 2024.
42. Myeong Cheol Oh, email message to author, Apr. 3, 2024.

The Jubilee in the Bible is related to enslaved people becoming free and all debts being forgiven. But more than that, I think it means a call from God to make a fresh start together. I pray for another fifty years as good as, or even better than, the first fifty years of UTC. I also pray that more candidates from Korean backgrounds may rise to respond to God's call to ministry through UTC.[43]

---

43. Jason Chong Bok Choi, email message to author, Feb. 22, 2024.

8

Camden Theological Library
Not Simply an Excellent Theological Library

WILLIAM W. EMILSEN

MOIRA BRYANT COULD FEEL well pleased with the progress that the library had made when she looked back on her first three years. The Camden Theological Library (CTL) at the Centre for Ministry in North Parramatta had been without a library manager for five months before she was appointed, and there was much to be done when she took control in November 1999.[1] The first matter Bryant attended to was improving the physical layout and appearance of the library, making the entrance area more inviting, installing specially designed furniture, and improving access to digital resources. She also reshelved all the items in the main collection, making sure to leave generous space on each shelf to avoid overcrowding, then placing the oversized books in one place and the audio-visual material in another. A dedicated computer room was set aside for student access. Old spine labels were replaced with clearer ones. Rarely borrowed books and older journals were relocated to Stack. Current journals were shelved in a designated journal room. The All Saints Missionary College Library, which had been housed

---

1. Jocelyn Morris, the previous library manager, left in June to fill the position of library manager of Lohe Theological Library at Luther Seminary in Adelaide. Diane Bertelsmeier, the library's cataloger, was the acting library manager in the interim. She was on the library staff from 1993 to 2008.

separately for years, together with recently donated books by the Institute for Theology and the Arts and Robert Stringer's collection on sexuality were integrated into the main collection. Returning to work in the library in 2001, after just a year away, Ann Wrightson observed many "positive changes."[2]

Bryant's next task was to address the lingering and unflattering concerns raised by the Ministerial Education Commission (MEC) visitation review in May 1999. The MEC acted as a kind of quality assurance body for theological education within the Uniting Church. Its report criticized the "ad hoc way" the collection had developed over recent years and recommended revision of the library's Collection Development Policy.[3] From the outset, Bryant recognized the legitimate concerns expressed by the MEC panel and immediately set about exploring ways to develop the collection in a more systematic way. Within six months of her appointment, Bryant, together with the principal and the faculty of United Theological College (UTC), had settled upon a revised Collection Development Policy and devised realistic strategies to implement it.[4]

The upgrading of the library's outdated computer system, or more accurately the library management system (LMS), was the other high priority concern raised by the MEC. This entailed software designed to manage most of the functions of a library, including ordering, cataloging, and circulating books, journals, and other library resources. In fact, it was not updated at all because a new and far more versatile, user-friendly system called Horizon was evaluated by Bryant as a much better option and installed within twelve months for approximately the same cost as an upgrade of the original system would have been. Besides covering the basic functions of circulation, acquisitions, and cataloging, Horizon also provided financial reports and had modules that enabled internet access to the catalog.[5]

Looking back on three years of improvements successfully completed, there could have been cause for self-congratulations and the temptation to coast along. Bryant, however, stressed to her staff and the library committee that this was "unwise and short-sighted."[6] Instead, she used her 1999 to 2002 end-of-year review of the library as an opportunity to question where it was heading and to reset the library's objectives and priorities for the next two

2. Ann Wrightson (later changed surname to Varcoe) did work experience at CTL in 1997 and then was employed as a casual library assistant from 1998 to 1999. From 2001 to 2007 she was employed primarily as a part-time library technician.

3. Bryant, "Library Manager's Report," Mar. 9, 2000, 2; for confirmation of this criticism, see Insert B in Pender, *Centering*.

4. Bryant, "Library Manager's Report," May 11, 2000, 2.

5. Bryant, "Proposal to Upgrade."

6. Bryant, "Library Manager's Report," Aug. 22, 2002, 3.

years. Armed with research into excellence in academic libraries coming out of the Association of College and Research Libraries in America, Bryant presented her vision of excellence for Camden Theological Library.

A VISION OF EXCELLENCE

How then might a small, modestly funded theological library like the Camden Theological Library aspire to be a first-rate organization? The journey towards excellence, Bryant insisted, embraced four distinguishing hallmarks. The first was offering a high level of service. It was outstanding service, she maintained, and not necessarily extensive on-site collections, capacious facilities, rare books, and bountiful resources that distinguished an excellent library. Excellent service was achievable when all the library staff were oriented towards service and committed to high quality, cost effective supporting processes. The latter included an increased emphasis on digital resources, improved access to the library's resources via the internet, timely access to research materials for senior and postgraduate students whose information needs were not able to be met by CTL, and offering appropriate reader education and library research skills for each student.[7] From this time on an extraordinary level of service became central to the mission, values, and performance of Camden Theological Library.

A strong emphasis on improving the quality and depth of the library collection in both its print and digitized formats was listed as the second hallmark of an excellent library. As already mentioned, Bryant had made great strides in realizing this mark of excellence following the MEC's stinging charge of ad hockery in the library's Collection Development Policy. Instead of ad hoc purchases, Bryant invited the college faculty to involve themselves in building up a quality collection that was sufficiently diverse, current, and relevant to the academic curriculum. The faculty did not need any encouragement. Though the college was a relatively young institution, only twenty-five years old, its faculty had already been engaged in rigorous conversation on the marks of academic excellence in theological education. Not surprisingly then, a well-resourced library was rated highly by the faculty, if not absolutely essential, to the continuation of theological education for both the mission of the college and the spiritual well-being of the Uniting Church.[8]

---

7. Bryant, "Library Manager's Report," Aug. 22, 2002, 3.

8. In December 1999, the UTC Council adopted a detailed Statement of Strategic Directions, which included a strong commitment to excellence in Academic scholarship, including postgraduate study and teaching.

Regular reviews of administrative procedures and staff activities were the third hallmark of library excellence. This practice was also close to Bryant's heart. Her small full-time staff of three[9] received in-house training, attended the Australian and New Zealand Theological Library Association (ANZTLA) conferences, and sometimes the American Theological Library Association (ATLA) conferences as part of their professional development, and participated in regular self-assessment exercises, reviews, and surveys. Bryant's own decisions were consistently based on thorough research and analysis with the aim of achieving positive outcomes for both the users of the library and attaining the most cost-effective results for the church. Always alert to appropriate technologically driven solutions and improvements, mindful of budget restraints, and careful to avoid wasteful practices, Bryant instilled in her staff a "can do, will do" attitude with often limited resources at hand.

Lastly, Bryant pointed to the central role the parent institution plays in supporting the library's journey towards excellence. In its planning and goal setting, the library needed to be willing to align its aspirations with those of the parent body and key stakeholders. She understood that a broad knowledge of changes in higher education and the economic realities bearing on the library were paramount. This included meeting the needs and expectations of the synod, the college, and to a lesser extent Charles Sturt University once UTC became part of its School of Theology in 1999. Flexibility and adaptability were also called for. The ability of the library to quickly and successfully adapt to the changing environment within the parent organization and its various stakeholders was an important measure of excellence.

Despite Bryant's best efforts, this last hallmark of library excellence would prove to be the most problematic. The relationship with the synod was especially strained. Certainly, the level of support for the library was generally lukewarm and sometimes obstructive. Few of the key people in the synod ever visited or used the library. There may not have been overt criticism of the library staff or the services it provided, but there were persistent concerns from within the synod's upper echelons ("those working in Pitt Street") about the cost of running the library. There were also perpetual and painful questions about the future and value of theological education. Regrettably the upper levels of management within the synod, especially its finance committees, seemed to neither value the library nor truly understand its processes. There was even a lack of awareness of what the library did and how it operated. Sometimes the synod's blanket legislation, as when

---

9. In 2002 the library staff consisted of the library manager, Moira Bryant, the cataloger, Diane Bertelsmeier, and the library technician, Lynette Thorn.

it insisted on surpluses being returned, undermined the library's book purchasing efficiencies. Over time even the synod's IT support for the library fell away. The library had few "champions" in the synod, and praise for Bryant's fiscal responsibility was begrudging or even nonexistent. This lack of conviction about the central role of a theological library in the life of the synod presaged some unwelcome warning signs.

NOT SIMPLY AN EXCELLENT THEOLOGICAL LIBRARY

In early 2003, John Oldmeadow, executive director of the synod's Board of Education, advised Bryant that in the future it would "not be enough for the library simply to be an excellent theological library."[10] In short, he meant that "if the Library were to maintain its funding, it need[ed] to be a resource for the whole church."[11] It was not an easy message for the executive director to convey. He was a passionate advocate for the library and a staunch supporter of the library manager. He was also a bibliophile with broad experience in the book trade and one of the few advocates for the library within the synod. Only months before he had donated a complete set (twenty volumes) of the Oxford English Dictionary to the library as "a tangible expression" of the Board of Education's desire that "the Library should continue to grow in the direction of being a quality academic library."[12] He also found funding for a part-time library technician when it was urgently needed to address the cataloging backlog caused by the arrival of the Gillespie Presbyterian Collection, formerly located at St. Andrew's College within the University of Sydney.

The executive director was proud of the library and repeatedly voiced his firm conviction that the Camden Theological Library is "the jewel in the crown of the NSW (& ACT) Synod," even publishing his view of the library, alongside many other positive responses from users, in a promotional piece within the pages of the synod's magazine, *Insights*.[13] However, despite all the encomiums the library received from its users, Bryant and her staff had little choice but to explore creative ways of offering its resources and services to a wider group of people within the church. Budgetary restrictions and increased productivity expectations were running high. The synod wanted more from its library with the same, or sometimes less, financial input.

10. Bryant, "Library Manager's Report," Mar. 13, 2003, 4.
11. John C. Oldmeadow, email message to author, Mar. 3, 2024.
12. Bryant, "Library Manager's Report," Aug. 9, 2001, 4.
13. Board of Education, "Camden Theological Library."

Moira Bryant was certainly not insensitive to the needs of the wider Uniting Church. Indeed, she was much in favor of it and keen to see more researchers, ministers, and lay people within the church take advantage of the resources and services the library had to offer. On several occasions she had received requests from members of the church to purchase books of a more general nature, often books that had been reviewed in *Insights*. Yet, she was hamstrung. There was no budget for such books, and very little discretionary funding was available to her.

Moreover, there were structural difficulties to circumvent. Ever since the opening of the Centre for Ministry in 1987, the Camden Theological Library had been envisaged as a key resource for ministry within the four schools that made up the Centre: the ELM (Education for Lay Ministries) Centre, the Institute for Mission, the School of Continuing Education, and United Theological College. Camden Theological Library was not the college's library as was often mistakenly thought (administration of the library passed from UTC to the Centre for Ministry in 1988).

The reality, however, was that books and other resources were purchased out of UTC's book budget, and the primary group of library users were the faculty and students of the college. The Institute for Mission, for its part, had little contact with the library. Only a few ELM students enrolled with Coolamon College, the Brisbane-based national Uniting Church's agency and provider of distance theological education, used the library. There was only sporadic use by students enrolled in higher degrees and Intentional Ministry courses through the School of Continuing Education. And though some individual members of the Uniting Church did borrow from the library, they did so with varying degrees of regularity.[14] It was obvious to Bryant and her staff that the "more" requested by the synod needed a complete reimagining while, at the same time, safeguarding against "mission creep," that is, the tendency to take on more and more tasks that may in fact be extraneous to the central mission of the library.

REIMAGINING MORE

Creating the Korean Collection

While the services requested by the church were never specified, other than in general terms of serving the needs of the wider church, it was left to Bryant to take the initiative and to seize opportunities as they arose. Only months beforehand one such opportunity knocked at her door. It was in the

---

14. Bryant, "Library Manager's Report," Aug. 22, 2002, 4.

form of a simple idea from one of the faculty who had noticed some of the Korean students struggling to complete their compulsory reading in time for classes and wondered if the library might be able to obtain key historical and theological texts in Korean in order to help them.[15] The feasibility of this suggestion was quickly picked up by Bryant and explored initially with the support of faculty. With the additional support from Korean candidates and ministers, Korean congregations in Canberra and Sydney, the Korean Presbytery, the Korean Students Association, senior academics from Hannam University in South Korea, and Charles Sturt University, the Korean collection steadily grew from a single copy of St. Augustine's *Confessions* in 2001 to a "cutting-edge Collection" of over six thousand books, seven Korean theological journals, and two full-text Korean databases in 2024.[16]

The Korean Collection has now become "a core part of the Library."[17] It is the largest specialist collection in the library and the forerunner to the much smaller and more recently developed Pacifika, Arabic, Indonesian, and Indigenous collections. What began as an idea for helping Korean students with English as a second language improve their educational experience and, hopefully, their educational outcomes has developed well beyond replicating English texts with identical Korean ones. The collection now includes a broad range of quality books written by Korean-speaking theologians and scholars who bring their own unique perspective and concerns to theology. With scarcely any regular funding source (apart from the five or six years when Charles Sturt University allocated fifteen thousand dollars per annum for the Korean Collection), only so-called "soft money"—modest grants from the Uniting Church's Stamp Committee, donations, and bequests—has enabled its ongoing development. It is an initiative of the Camden Theological Library that has attracted interest from theological libraries within Australia and overseas and, even more importantly, attracted Korean lay people and ministerial candidates, supported Korean-speaking ministers, resourced Hannam University doctoral students studying in Australia, generated a richer learning culture, and admirably modeled the multicultural ethos and aspirations of the college and the wider Uniting Church.[18]

15. Bryant, "Library Manager's Report," May 10, 2001, 3.

16. On the creation of the Korean Collection, see Bryant, "Oak Trees," and "Korean Collection."

17. Bryant, "Library Manager's Report," May 12, 2011, 5.

18. Bryant, "Survey of UME," July 2016, 2.

Developing Culturally Sensitive Library Services

The emergence of the Korean Collection in the Camden Theological Library set a pattern for a multicultural emphasis in the collection. It also alerted Bryant and her staff to the digital divide among the student body and the need to provide more targeted culturally sensitive services and support for students who came from countries outside of Australia. In the first decade of the twenty-first century, over 50 percent of the students at UTC came from an Asian or Pacific background, along with a sprinkling from Africa and the Middle East. For many overseas students English is not their first language, and some have had very little experience of using a library. One student, the Reverend (now Bishop) Zebedee Padokana, from the Solomon Islands, was typical of the latter. He came from a village where there was only one telephone. He had never caught a train before coming to Sydney, and the idea of using a modern computerized library was totally foreign and equally as fearful as his first train journey.

In an attempt to overcome library fear or anxiety, a real and prevalent problem especially for different language and cultural groups, Bryant first engaged two part-time staff who reflected the cultural diversity of the student body. One staff member, Seforosa Carroll, was a PhD candidate of Pacific Island heritage, and the other was Phoebe (Dong Suk) Kim, a Korean who also cataloged the Korean Collection. Both enhanced the library's ability to help a significant number of culturally and linguistically diverse (CALD) borrowers learn how to use the library better. Later, Adele Smith was employed as the library confidence facilitator to assist with this service.

Besides being intentional about offering a high level of service to people from other countries, the physical space of the library was made more welcoming and user friendly for them. The library staff went to considerable efforts to create a multicultural library for a multicultural and diverse community. It regularly hosted displays of art and artifacts from various cultures represented by the library's patrons. These displays are usually held on or around the national day of the particular country represented (for example, Niue, Rotuma, Tonga, South Korea, Indonesia, Fiji, and Kiribati) and also in NAIDOC Week (National Aborigines and Islanders Day Observance Committee), which celebrates the history, culture, and achievements of Aboriginal and Torres Strait Islander Australians. Probably the most far-reaching and expensive initiative has been the creation of a truly bilingual catalog. Now all the Korean language resources in the library can be searched online using a Korean keyboard. The library is now exploring ways of developing online access to resources in other languages such as Indonesian and Arabic. With these initiatives, it comes as no surprise that in

2011 the Camden Theological Library was recognized by the Australia and New Zealand Theological Library Association as "the best expression of a multicultural theological library in Australia and New Zealand."[19]

Managing the Synod Archives

The relocation of the NSW and ACT (New South Wales and Australian Capital Territory) Synod Archives from the Archives and Research Centre at "Eskdale House," one of the Burnside Homes in North Parramatta, to the Centre for Ministry nearby is another example of Bryant's efforts to serve the wider church. For years there were concerns about Eskdale as a long-term location for the archives. The rental for Eskdale (over sixty-five thousand dollars per annum in 2005, plus 2 percent annual indexation) was one concern; substandard air-conditioning was another.[20] The high cost of electricity, an asbestos problem, and difficulties installing compactus shelving presented other challenges. However, the most pressing and recurring concern was the threatened discontinuance of the tenancy of Eskdale.[21] This uncertainty was unsettling for the Uniting Church Records and Historical Society (UCRHS), the body that managed the synod's archives, and the failure to make a decision eventually became a headache for the synod.

The situation came to a head in 2009 when the synod decided to establish a formal Archive Unit under the management of the Board of Education. John Oldmeadow then found himself in the difficult position of having to quickly find a new home for the archives. So he and Bryant visited Eskdale in early May 2009 in order to assess the extent of the task. Soon after that inspection Bryant floated the idea of building a specially designed repository for the synod's archives at the Centre for Ministry, preferably near the Camden Theological Library.[22] Ironically, this solution had been proposed by the church historian, Geoffrey Barnes, in 1977, and it would have saved the synod a great deal of trouble and expense if it had been followed then.

A purpose-built archive was, however, never constructed as Bryant had envisaged because there were too many serious architectural and financial concerns about its feasibility. Eventually, the synod decided to store some high-use records at the Camden Theological Library and to put the low-demand records into off-site commercial storage for retrieval on demand. It involved a significant additional workload for the library staff

19. Byrnes and Balabanski, "Ministerial Education Commission Report," 7.
20. Church Records and Historical Society, "Minutes."
21. Mansfield, "Outline History," 12.
22. Bryant, "Library Manager's Report," May 14, 2009, 4.

and tireless work by Edmund Perrin, Deanna Moore, and other volunteers from the Archives Centre. Gavin Glenn was employed two days a week to work on archive-related tasks especially with IT, and Bryant oversaw the whole operation. Over three thousand boxes of marriage and baptismal registers, journals, congregational records, and photographs of the Uniting Church and its predecessor churches were deposited with FILE Group at Mascot.[23] More than one thousand plans of churches and church buildings were sorted and then collected and scanned by the Department of Lands in Bathurst. Memorabilia was photographed, wrapped in bubble wrap, and carefully stored in itemized boxes. Registers were microfilmed. Photographs were digitized. Card indexes were scanned or photographed. A large number of books in the Swynny Collection from Eskdale were systematically reviewed. Some one thousand of them were cataloged by Bryant outside working hours (there was no funding set aside for cataloging) and incorporated into the Camden Theological Library.

For the first six months of 2010, Bryant had little choice but to give the archives high priority. Then in the second half of the year, she and Gavin Glenn gave their energies to ensuring that there was good electronic access to the additional resources that had come across.[24] It was a massive, time-consuming undertaking, yet as Bryant became more involved with it, she, and even critics of the move, became convinced that it was a good strategy in terms of diversifying the library collection and providing a professional service for researchers. Camden Theological Library "managed" the archives until July 2021; it was a major accomplishment, especially during "uncertain times."[25]

UNCERTAIN TIMES

Uncertain times were about to become even more uncertain. No matter what initiatives Bryant and her staff may have successfully accomplished or at least set in motion, nothing could stem the synod's efforts in 2004 to reduce the available funding for the operation of synod boards and agencies. The synod budget for the 2003 to 2004 financial year rang alarm bells. It showed a deficit of $1,068,780 with no allowance for any growth in existing programs or for initiating new ones.[26] The stricken financial situation facing the synod set loose a merciless juggernaut: a 10 percent budget cut

23. Later, FILE was taken over by Grace Records Management.
24. Bryant, "Library Manager's Report," Aug. 12, 2010, 3.
25. Bryant, "Library Manager's Report," Nov. 12, 2009, 2.
26. Horrocks, "Report to Board."

over three financial years from 2004 to 2007. The library had little choice but to implement the budget restrictions. Notwithstanding well-intentioned efforts to save people's jobs, cuts in staff were inevitable. The 10 percent reduction (4 percent + 3 percent + 3 percent over three financial years) in the library budget translated approximately into fifty thousand dollars. No manner of cost saving could absorb such a figure. By the end of the year, the long-serving, full-time library technician (Lynette Thorn), whose role was primarily servicing the circulation desk, was made redundant. It was a deeply distressing decision, for the full-time library technician herself and other members of the library staff.

Besides attempting to deal with the human cost of implementing the synod's budget reductions in 2004, Bryant had to quickly recalibrate the library's activities. The job descriptions of the remaining staff were revised. Some of their activities, such as the electronic cataloging of material in Stack, were put on hold, and some of the roles of the library technician were absorbed by the remaining staff, including Bryant herself. Most troubling was the regrettable reduction in the library's opening hours. On weekday mornings the library was closed till noon and closed altogether on Saturdays, whereas beforehand Saturday's opening hours were from eleven o'clock in the morning to four o'clock in the evening.

The loss of generous opening hours was a serious blow to Bryant who had worked hard to develop and sustain the Camden Theological Library's reputation for excellence. There was ongoing criticism and concern about the library's opening hours from various quarters. Clive Pearson, the acting principal of the college at the time, expressed "great sadness" that budget cuts had resulted in the closure of the library to the public and for borrowing in the mornings.[27] The student representative at the March 2005 Library Committee voiced the concerns of students, particularly those students who were obliged to work in the library in the mornings because they had no suitable place to study at home. Members of the public and students with families living on campus were also disappointed that the library was closed on Saturdays. Then there was the bittersweet assessment of the 2005 Ministerial Education Commission. It commended the high standard of the collection and the professionalism of the staff, but it also expressed its disappointment and dismay that access to the library and its resources should be so limited. Even Bryant, herself, who one of her librarian colleagues described as a "genius" in her ability to work within the real restraints of funding, felt compelled to voice her disappointment and frustration. In one of those rare moments when Bryant questioned the meaning of the

---

27. Pearson, "Acting Principal's Report."

library itself, she wrote midway through the 2004 to 2007 budget cuts how restricted opening hours were having a deleterious impact on the image of the library:

> Camden Theological Library has been regarded as one of the top three theological libraries in Sydney. Although our collection continues to be one of a high standard, our hours of opening are considerably less well-endowed or supported by their denomination or parent body. Amongst our professional peers, it has been interpreted that the Uniting Church no longer regards CTL as of high a priority as in the past.[28]

In an attempt to minimize the inconvenience of the situation, Bryant consulted with the faculty and student body. An agreement was reached whereby students could prearrange to go into the library for individual study purposes before noon on weekdays, but not on Saturdays when it remained closed. The library was used like a reading room, a quiet place to study and write, but no other library facilities or services were made available. This solution, although not ideal, received a favorable response from students and still operates today even though the library's opening hours were later extended in the mornings.

Some five years after the announcement of the first budget crisis, there was a second lot of budget cuts with potentially far more damaging consequences for the long-term viability of the library. Following a slowing down of the Australian economy and a rise in unemployment after the Global Financial Crisis (GFC) from mid-2007 to early 2009, a nervous meeting of the Synod Fund Management Committee in March 2010 decided to adopt a recommendation that funding for the 2010/11 financial year be cut by 2.53 percent and a further cut of 9.67 percent in 2011/12.[29]

The news of further cuts, the equivalent of forty-five thousand dollars taken from the staffing budget, was devastating for Bryant. Very few economies remained open to her. The library's opening hours had already been cut to the bone. Total staff days worked were reduced from the equivalent of fifteen days to eleven days a week, thus pushing the library to the brink of viability. The budget reductions, she observed, were like lopping off parts of the legs of a table for firewood: it might provide warmth for a short time, but it was no longer effective as a functioning table.[30]

Bryant, however, did manage to navigate around this second round of cuts, partly with a twelve-month grant from the Board of Mission

28. Bryant, "Camden Theological Library."
29. Holden, "Business Manager's Report."
30. Bryant, "Library Manager's Report," Nov. 11, 2010, 6.

multicultural funds to pay the salary of the part-time Korean cataloger, Phoebe Kim, and partly by building up an effective team of part-time library assistants who had the potential and desire to develop professionally when given encouragement, opportunity, and training.

However, with the Board of Mission grant only available for one year, Bryant (now the only full-time staff member) and her loyal team of part-time library assistants were stressed and already stretched to the limit, and with further budget cuts looming on the horizon, the situation for 2012–2013 looked bleak. Feeling most unhappy and disappointed with the uncertainty of the library's funding, Bryant appealed to her advisory committee for their support and understanding. Something had to give. "Previously," she lamented, "I have always been able to report on expanding facilities, and the development of new services in response to newly identified needs of users. Now we are entering a period of needing to review everything which we do, in order to identify services/activities of which we will need to let go."[31]

Clive Pearson, the principal of United Theological College, was equally disconsolate. "I cannot see," he reported to the Ministerial Education Commission, "how the Library can function adequately beyond the end of June 2012 on the basis of the proposed synod fund allocation."[32] The college at that time was also facing significant budget restraints, and for the first time ever in the library's history, there were serious questions being asked as to whether UTC would be able to continue making its indexed annual contribution to the library's so-called "book budget." UTC, however, did contribute $109,000 for collection development in the 2012–2013 financial year and managed a one-off contribution of $107,000 for the following financial year from a special fund built up over many years from bequests and other sources. While this money gave the library some breathing space, that fund was now exhausted, and there was no provision for the 2014–2015 financial year. The very thought of there being no money to buy books and other resources for the library was a difficult pill for the library staff and faculty to swallow. It was made even worse when Andrew Williams, the general secretary of the synod at the time, admitted that the library was not a priority for the church and who also made it clear that the library was expected to raise its own funds for the collection from donations.[33]

---

31. Bryant, "Library Manager's Report," May 10, 2013, 1.

32. Pearson, "Principal's Report."

33. Ross Chambers, quoted in Bryant, "Library Manager's Report," May 9, 2014, 1–2; confirmed by Ross Chambers, email message to author, July 22, 2024.

STILL POINT IN A TURNING WORLD

Fortunately common sense prevailed. The doomsday predictions were averted. From 2014 to the early 2020s, synod funding for library resources has been more or less steady, not indexed to the Consumer Price Index as formerly but, nonetheless, averaging at $125,800 per annum with a median figure of $130,400. Bryant was thus spared the indignity of going cap in hand looking for phantom donations. Perhaps even more importantly, she avoided being channeled into ultimately unhelpful alliances for the sake of short-term revenue streams, and from making hasty decisions that would have proclaimed to the world that the Uniting Church no longer supported serious theological scholarship and quality education for its ministers and lay people.

Even so, during that same period Bryant still had to battle with very real funding constraints and minimal staffing levels hovering just around three full-time equivalent members. And she still had to fend off repeated questioning of the value of the library and whether the synod actually needed a library at all. Bryant's task of advocating for the library at a time when there was not enough funds for all that the synod wanted to achieve was a most unenviable one.

The formation of Uniting Mission and Education (UME) in 2012 brought together the Board of Education with the Board of Mission, which resulted in five or six years of considerable upheaval, an external review, and messy restructuring driven primarily by funding shortfalls. Camden Theological Library, by contrast, provided a place of calm and quiet, attentive support. Playing a generally supporting role quietly on the margins, it avoided most of the turmoil and did what it has done best for more than two decades: valuing excellence, generating an atmosphere of gentle hospitality, and providing the highest quality service it could in situations where the external circumstances were constantly changing, money tight, and the synod's strategic priorities frequently being revised.

Bryant's passion for excellence, with its primary hallmark of service, is what has marked Camden Theological Library as one of the treasures of the Uniting Church. When Ian McCallum and Sherry Quinn from Libraries Alive! conducted an external review of Camden Theological Library in 2021, they observed that it was Bryant's "unrelenting approach to quality service" that made Camden Theological Library "one of the best theological libraries in Australia."[34] In their survey of the library's users, they found no negative comments about the library's service, and in the authors' considered

---

34. McCallum and Quinn, *Camden Theological Library*, 14.

view, the UME received excellent value from the resources it allocated to the library and was "fortunate to have such a committed and effective Library Manager."[35]

Five-Star Service

Since 2017, the staff of Camden Theological Library has been intentional in following Michael Heppell's *Five Star Service: How to Deliver Exceptional Customer Service* (2010). The book is bursting with ideas on how to deliver quality service, as an individual and as an organization, at very low cost. But it is not simply a self-improvement book that motivates the library team. Its caring service is grounded on the Christian ethic of love. "Through the care and nurture of users, by the atmosphere created in the Library, and by the interaction with staff," wrote Bryant for the Good Provider review of UME in 2018, "the 'good feel' that users experience is a living out of a small kingdom community. And so, the Library seeks to be a 'gentle' place, where people and procedures nurture and encourage, where facilities and policies demonstrate compassion."[36] One-time employee of the library Seforosa Carroll, writing from Princeton University in 2018, captures well the distinctive ethos of CTL. While Carroll greatly appreciated the vast resources in the Wright Library at Princeton, considered one of the best theological libraries in the world with its magnificent building and collection of 8.6 million print and electronic books and journals, she missed the warm, friendly service at CTL. Carroll writes,

> CTL is more than just a theological library. For me CTL embodies community through offerings of welcoming spaces to work, the warmth and care of staff and most importantly where each person is known by name where you are never a stranger for too long. . . . CTL may be small in size, but what CTL offers those it is mandated to serve, far outweighs the quality of service of larger libraries, even the "best libraries" in the world! . . . Much is dependent on the quality of service, relationships and the ability to create spaces where people feel a sense of belonging and purpose.[37]

This determination to deliver five-star service was sorely tested when COVID restrictions were introduced in New South Wales in March 2020.

---

35. McCallum and Quinn, *Camden Theological Library*, 3.
36. Bryant, "Report for Good Provider."
37. Carroll, quoted in Bryant's "Camden Theological Library," 18.

No longer able to provide face-to-face services to those groups it normally supported, CTL speedily and creatively used the stimulus of the pandemic to consider ways of functioning differently. To begin, it anticipated correctly a much greater role for digital resources and quickly provided online access to current and new borrowers. Additional e-books and commentaries were purchased. Recommended readings and weekly lectures for subjects offered in the upcoming semester were quickly digitized and made available for UTC students on the online database Quest. Where necessary, the library provided a backup physical delivery service where digitization was not an option. Then, a few weeks before the library reopened on July 6, 2020, one member of the staff was rostered for a period each day to provide a "Click and Collect" service to support students as they sought to complete their final assignments. Finally, using international COVID-safe guidelines, the library was opened for face-to-face services at the start of July 2020 to coincide with UTC's Session 2.

Skillful Use of Technology

CTL's ability to quickly adapt its services during COVID may be attributed to Bryant's long-standing and innovative use of new and existing technologies. According to McCallum and Quinn's review, "The library's computer systems are among the best available and rated highly by their users."[38] Revelation, the CTL's catalog on the library's website, was the first theological library in the world to provide a one-stop twenty-four hour access to a broad spectrum of services and resources, including access to databases of e-books and journals, hard copy books and journals, and the aforementioned database quest. Revelation also provides a gateway to Illuminate, a substantial range of digitized resources relating to the Uniting Church in Australia and its predecessor churches. In July 2024 Illuminate provided access to 20,430 items in the public domain. These include historical material relating to the church's history, parish histories, dissertations, oral histories, Uniting Church publications, minutes, reports, and other key documents coming out of the New South Wales and ACT Synod and the National Assembly. Illuminate was launched in June 2019. Since then it has proven to be a boon for researchers and a key resource for students learning about the Uniting Church. Its creation by Bryant is just one more indication of what a technologically well-equipped library and a librarian with the expertise to manage this technology can do in the creation, preservation, and dissemination of the church's valuable heritage.

38. McCallum and Quinn, *Camden Theological Library*, 3.

Aligning with the Synod's Mission

Not only has CTL demonstrated a remarkable ability to utilize and adapt to modern technology, it has also responded positively and quickly to the strategic directions of the synod and to the mission and education strategies of the library's primary stakeholders. Over the past ten years, for example, the library's collection has focused on small but focused collections for specialist areas of ministry, mission, and outreach. This movement reflects sensitivity to the way the world is changing and expresses itself in greater diversification in the collection. The special collections on "First Peoples" and "Pasifika," already mentioned, have been further developed. The Public and Contextual Theology collection has been considerably strengthened, and newer collections on climate change, globalization, migration, interfaith relations, ecotheology, and LGBTQI+ matters have been created.

In addition to purchasing academic texts and reference materials for CSU courses, more emphasis has been placed on purchasing books and digital resources which are of practical assistance for people in local congregations. Since 2016, this aspect of the library's collection had led to the establishing of Godly Play kits, Messy Church, and other resources for children and young families' ministry, liturgical books for lay leaders of worship, and some sixteen mobile library collections to support UME resourcing programs. For example, the library has prepared resources for UME's Vital Leadership team who, as one aspect of their work, conducts introductory courses for lay pastors on presiding at funerals and weddings. Similarly, the "Saltbush" team takes a traveling collection to rural and isolated communities in New South Wales, and the "Pulse" team draws upon the library's resources for "Growing Young Journey," a program designed for congregations desiring to reorient their ministry alongside young people and families.

Many users of CTL have observed that there is a deep vein of spirituality that runs through everything it does. This vein of spirituality has brought stability to the library over the past twenty-five years and strengthened its deliberate striving for excellence. The library staff, observed McCallum and Quinn in 2021, "live their beliefs in their approach to students: each person is part of the future of the church and is to be supported in accordance with their needs—whether it be producing toys for Godly Play for Sunday's service, or chasing down an elusive reference for a postdoctoral research paper."[39] CTL has admirably demonstrated what a small organization can achieve when there is stable, committed, and professional leadership,

---

39. McCallum and Quinn, *Camden Theological Library*, 7.

adequate resources, and a passion for excellence expressed primarily in service. CTL is a shining example of the way that the Uniting Church might continue to support theological education and research into the future.

BIBLIOGRAPHY

Board of Education. "Camden Theological Library." *Insights* 13.4 (May 2003) 16.

Bryant, Moira. "Camden Theological Library." Working Papers and Reports, Uniting Church in Australia New South Wales Synod, Archives of the New South Wales and ACT Synod, Centre for Ministry, North Parramatta, NSW, 2005.

———. "Korean Collection at Camden Library." *Out & About* 23 (Feb. 2011) 18–19.

———. "Library Manager's Reports." Unpublished reports presented to the Library Committee meetings from 1999–2015, Camden Theological Library, North Parramatta, NSW.

———. "Oak Trees Grow from Acorns." *Out & About* 14 (Mar. 2008) 8.

———. "A Proposal to Upgrade the Library Management System in Operation at the Camden Theological Library." Working paper 10/0400boe, Board of Education, Box 8, 2000.

———. "Report for Good Provider Review 2018." Unpublished report, Miscellaneous Documents (Role of CTL Within Life of NSW and ACT Synod), Archives of the New South Wales and ACT Synod, Centre for Ministry, North Parramatta, NSW, Apr. 2018.

———. "Survey of UME Staff Activities." Unpublished report, Miscellaneous Documents (Role of CTL within Life of NSW and ACT Synod), Archives of the New South Wales and ACT Synod, Centre for Ministry, North Parramatta, NSW, July 2016.

Byrnes, Jennifer, and Vicky Balabanski. "Ministerial Education Commission Report of Visit to the United Theological College, August 2011." Unpublished report, Archives of the New South Wales and ACT Synod, Centre for Ministry, North Parramatta, NSW, Sept. 23, 2011, 1–6.

Church Records and Historical Society. "Minutes of the Church Records and Historical Society, Commenced 16 June 1997." Archives of the New South Wales and ACT Synod, Centre for Ministry, North Parramatta, NSW, 2003.

Holden, David. "Business Manager's Report to Members of the Committee of Finance and Administration, March 10, 2010." Committee of Finance and Administration, Archives of the New South Wales and ACT Synod, Centre for Ministry, North Parramatta, NSW, Feb. 8, 2007–July 15, 2010.

Horrocks, Graham. "Report to Board of Finance and Administration, United Theological College." Unpublished report, Board of Finance and Administration, Agenda, Minutes and Reports, 28 February 2002—24 June 2004, Archives of the New South Wales and ACT Synod, Centre for Ministry, North Parramatta, NSW, Mar. 6, 2003.

Mansfield, Joan. "An Outline History of the Uniting Church Records and Historical Society NSW/ACT to 2009." *Church Heritage* 21.1 (Mar. 2019) 3–20.

McCallum, Ian, and Sherrey Quinn. *Camden Theological Library Review Project Draft Report*. Hackett, ACT: Libraries Alive!, Aug. 2021.

Pearson, Clive. "Acting Principal's Report to Ministerial Education Commission 2006." Reports to MEC 2000–2013, UCA Assembly Archives, State Library of NSW, Sydney.

———. "Principal's Report to Ministerial Education Commission July 11–13, 2011." Reports to MEC 2000–2013, UCA Assembly Archives, State Library of NSW, Sydney.

Pender, John A. *Centering: Bulletin of the Centre for Ministry*. Centre for Ministry bulletin 3, Uniting Church in Australia, 1997.

9

Lifelong Learning
The Contribution of Visiting Scholars and Conferences

Mark Hillis

"Lifelong learning" may read like a well-worn cliché. In this chapter, however, it is my hope that you will discover such learning is a reality, which the stories of participants and presenters at United Theological College (UTC) conferences over the years demonstrate. For some participants, the experience of interacting with visitors and other participants in conferences has been transformative.

The United Theological College and its physical location (since 1987) within the Centre for Ministry at North Parramatta is an institution committed to lifelong learning. Standing in a tradition of ecumenical openness and the pursuit of academic excellence from its earliest days, continuing education has been a goal of UTC.[1] The very architecture and interior design of the Centre for Ministry (CFM) reflected this intention.[2] It is a center that provides hospitality for many different organizations, cultural and religious groups. UTC itself has always envisaged the encouragement

---

1. See Barnes, *Doing Theology*, 80–81.
2. Barnes, *Doing Theology*, 83–99.

of encounter amongst people from all walks of life, diverse ethnicities, and religious traditions in a hospitable meeting space.

When the United Theological College was formed in 1974, it sought to invite scholars of national and international standing to visit, at least annually: a practice not unknown to its preceding Congregational, Methodist, and Presbyterian institutions. Such visiting academics were frequently seen and heard by faculty, students, members of the church, and the general public. In 2007, when Clive Pearson was the principal of UTC, his report to the synod included the following paragraph:

> In keeping with contemporary international thinking the College has also been seeking to address three inter-related audiences: the church, the academy and the public domain. The ways in which each one of these three needs to be served both by theology and the church itself has been deemed faith's "ecology of responsibility."[3]

Pearson's statement clearly enunciates the desired intention of UTC to enable the integration of theological learning and ministry formation with the life of the whole people of God and the wider community. Visiting scholars and conferences have sometimes enabled that vision to be realized, especially when the combination of scholarship and discourse reached beyond the lecture halls and libraries to the "three inter-related audiences" of church, academy, and the public arena. "It is also recognised that formation is a life-long task. We are never fully formed!"[4] Our formation as humans who are disciples of Jesus takes place in a vast diversity of contexts and processes. Nevertheless, there have been occasions when the ongoing offerings provided by UTC through its conferences, seminars, and visiting luminaries have enhanced vital lifelong learning.

The approach in this chapter is to associate particular conferences and encounters with some broad educational terms, such as the nurture and affirmation of faith; wondering and imagining about the implications of experience; disruptive questioning of the status quo; or a transforming impetus to action. These are not to be seen as exclusive or irrefutable categories of learning. They are subjectively based upon the various testimonies of presenters and participants and the inherent qualities of the topics offered. Therefore, rather than following a linear chronology of conferences and visiting luminaries at UTC, the headings provide a schema for organizing this

---

3. Pearson, "United Theological College," 98.

4. Pearson, "Ministry Formation," 8. Readers can find archived copies of *Out&About* sources like this one online through the church's Illuminate database at https://illuminate.recollect.net.au/.

aspect of UTC history. The categories are nurturing and affirming, wondering and imagining, questioning and disrupting, and transforming.

The overall feeling that conferences and encounters with local and global scholars enhanced lifelong learning for individuals and communities has been echoed in numerous conversations about visiting academics and conferences. It has also been an impetus for UTC scholars to publish their own research and to enjoy the interactions that subsequently flow. Chris Budden, an adjunct faculty member and visiting lecturer in theology, has such a view, adding that conferences at UTC were mostly beneficial for the quality of conversation and the subsequent opportunities to add value to the experience of attending:

> So, for me, the best conferences had less to do with major speakers (although there were some good keynotes), and more to do with the topic and the engagement with various papers and people. That was the attraction and value of those gatherings—they built networks and encouraged conversations. I found that helpful both academically and in terms of local engagement.[5]

Budden's decades-long involvement in ministry, as a student, with congregations, serving with various councils of the church (especially with the Uniting Aboriginal and Islander Christian Congress, UAICC), and in academic life, adds weight to the valuing of visitors and conferences.

As the college became increasingly allied with Charles Sturt University in the third millennium, funding for conferences and guest speakers increased markedly, as former faculty member Gerard Moore noted in 2013:

> The University has provided funding for building the academic outreach of the members of faculty through funding for conferences, guest speakers, talks and writing projects that allow the College to influence an ever-widening circle of church members, congregations, and fellow Christians.[6]

The Public and Contextual Theology Strategic Research Centre (PACT at CSU) was a prominent reason for this improvement in resources for conferencing.

> PACT developed from a Research Group in CSU established in 2002. Professor John Painter, the first chair appointed in theology, CSU's first member of the Academy of the Humanities, and an internationally prominent New Testament scholar, was the

---

5. Budden, email message to author, Apr. 10, 2024.
6. Moore, "UTC & CSU," 19.

head of the research group. PACT achieved Strategic Research Centre status in 2007.[7]

PACT became a key generator of research and publication that also fostered numerous seminars and conferences.[8] The visit of William Storrar in 2004 helped to consolidate the role of public theology at UTC. William Emilsen remembers that Dean Drayton, Clive Pearson, and he were nicknamed "The Publicans" at UTC "because of our efforts to get a Master's degree in public theology happening at CSU."[9] The Charles Sturt University School of Theology became part of the Global Network of Public Theology founded in 2007 by William Storrar and Nico Koopman.[10] Storrar's visit was incorporated in the Seminar Week program for 2004, organized jointly by the School of Continuing Education and UTC. It included a public lecture, "Public Spirit: The Citizen's Gift in a Global Era," and was probably one of the last of the endowed Livingstone Lectures.[11]

NURTURING AND AFFIRMING

In the first of the years of the period for this study, 1999, David Jobling came to UTC as an eminent professor of Hebrew Bible from Saint Andrew's Theological College, Saskatoon, Saskatchewan, Canada. He was renowned for his two-volume opus, *The Sense of Biblical Narrative: Structural Analysis in the Hebrew Bible*.[12] He delivered the 1999 Thatcher Lecture, organized by the biblical studies faculty member at the time, Roland Boer. Jobling had recently published a commentary on 1 Samuel, in the Berit Olam series.

Nineteen ninety-nine was also the year of the twelfth May Macleod Lecture.[13] Colin Gibson (1933–2022) was the visiting academic for that

7. Pickard, "ACC&C."
8. Pearson, "Introducing 'PACT,'" 9.
9. Emilsen, email message to author, June 11, 2024.
10. See Global Network for Public Theology, "Mission and History." The GNPT website acknowledges James Haire from the UCA as its second chairperson.
11. Named for David Livingstone (1813–1873), physician, explorer, Congregational (LMS) missionary (in Africa) and abolitionist. "George Durham, a member of Pitt Street [Congregational] Church . . . endowed the Livingstone Lectures of the [Camden] College and provided sums for David Livingstone Bursaries. The total capital of his benefaction now [1964] amounts to £12,000." Garrett and Farr, *Camden College*, 72.
12. Published in 1978 and revised in 1986.
13. The first May Macleod Annual Public Lecture was given in 1987 by John MacIntyre, on the shape of the ministry. May Macleod was the first wife the late Reverend Malcolm Macleod, a former Chair of the UTC Council and of the Synod of NSW (New South Wales) Board of Education.

lecture. At the time he was professor of English at University of Otago, Aotearoa, New Zealand, an internationally renowned composer, and a hymn writer. Gibson's topic was "Laughter in the Presence of God?" The May Macleod Public Lecture Series was established by the Synod of NSW Board of Education, thanks to an endowment by the late Reverend Malcolm Macleod, in honor of his wife, May. The lecture series has, for some years, been acknowledged as an integral part of the UTC calendar.[14] The UTC website claims that it has always hosted the May Macleod Lecture, although it is more accurate to acknowledge that it began as a broader Board of Education initiative.[15]

One of the last of the endowed Thatcher Lectures[16] was held in 2003 at UTC, in conjunction with Seminar Week. James Dunn, renowned New Testament scholar and professor of divinity at Durham University in the United Kingdom, only ever visited seminaries where he had graduate students. He had agreed to supervise Elizabeth Raine's research on the Gospel of Matthew. Since Dunn had many students "from the Far East," as he expressed it, one may rightfully say that his visit to Sydney was thanks to an invitation from Elizabeth Raine. Raine, with John Squires, had come to know Dunn during their 1997 visit to Durham University. Squires remarked,

> This Seminar Week had capacity audiences throughout the week. He was a *name*. Folks from Moore College even came! The story is they usually avoided us, as they called UTC "Heresy House," and labelled Morling (Baptist) College "Heresy on the Hill." Elizabeth and I worked with Rob McFarlane to have a full programme of complementing lectures and workshops on the topic "Jesus Remembered," and it was a great highlight for us— and so many students and ministers who attended.[17]

There was something about James Dunn. He transcended the conservative/critical scholarship divide. Where other visiting lecturers were great but very niche, Dunn was different. Ted Miller, who studied theology at UTC after his retirement from a long and diverse career as an engineer and businessman, was present for the James Dunn visit in Seminar Week 2003.

14. See United Theological College, "Latest Information."

15. See United Theological College, "Latest Information," under the section titled "UTC Annual Lectures."

16. Named after Griffithes Wheeler Thatcher (1863–1950): academic, linguist, theological teacher, Congregational minister, Bible scholar, and Orientalist. Thatcher was a benefactor of the Congregational Camden Theological College. Garrett and Farr, *Camden College*, 73.

17. Squires and Raine, email message to author, Apr. 11, 2024. Rob McFarlane was the director of continuing education.

As I was serving as Minister of the Word in the congregation where Ted belonged, he arranged a meeting with me to discuss what he had learned from Seminar Week. He was energized and excited. In the years that ensued, Ted became a valued lay preacher in that congregation.

The 2007 Seminar Week, organized by Rob McFarlane and William Emilsen, took shape as a conference called Hidden Histories: Untold Stories of the UCA close to the thirtieth anniversary of the Uniting Church in Australia's (UCA) inauguration. It included historians from the Uniting Church and special guest Barbara Brown Zikmund, a prominent American historian of religion and ordained minister of the United Church of Christ in the United States. Zikmund gave four keynote addresses during the conference: on the rise of denominations and the role of ecumenism, how our hidden histories informed the way we shared faith, how the use of the term "ecumenical" had changed, and what language we used to be faithful to God. Among the extensive array of presentations was a Past Presidents Forum, chaired by David Gill, highlighting one achievement of which they were proud and one thing they regretted. The past presidents present were Ian Tanner, D'Arcy Wood, Jill Tabart, James Haire, Dean Drayton, and Gregor Henderson. John Mavor was unable to attend but sent a written paper.[18]

Gordon Lathrop, Evangelical Lutheran pastor from the United States who had held professorships all over the world and written some definitive texts, was invited to UTC in 2009 for The Gospel on Sunday conference by UTC's PACT scholar, Stephen Burns. The conference was greatly appreciated and especially applauded by Ben Myers who summed up the long-term value of the event by saying, "This was brilliant—I kept referring it to it in my classes for years afterwards."[19] Lathrop contributed an article for *Uniting Church Studies*, December 2009, entitled, "The Gospels on Ministry."[20]

How does one encourage children to learn about the Christian faith? Godly Play, described by its founder, Jerome Berryman, as "a way of religious education," was a curriculum derived from a Montessori approach to religious education developed by Sofia Cavalletti.[21] Based in the United Kingdom, Peter Privett, an International Training Consultant for Godly Play, gave the 2011 May Macleod Lecture on the topic, "Supporting Children's

---

18. Gill is a long-serving former general secretary of the UCA Assembly. A few papers from "Hidden Histories" are collected in the *Uniting Church Studies* journal, volume fifteen, from June 2009.

19. Myers, email message to author, May 23, 2024.

20. Lathrop, "Gospels on Ministry."

21. Berryman, *Godly Play*. Berryman went on to produce a whole series of books on curriculum. Cavalletti wrote *Religious Potential of the Child*. Her method is described as "The Catechesis of the Good Shepherd."

Spirituality." The lecture was part of a broader conference, which introduced Godly Play training for many in the Uniting Church and other denominations. Jerome Berryman also attended and was introduced to a number of UTC faculty members. More than a hundred people came from every state to take part. Rachel Kohn, from the ABC radio program *The Spirit of Things* made a program entitled "Play It Again, God."[22]

The Centre for Ministry still holds a very large wooden sculpture representing one of the Godly Play presentations, and for some time after the conference, a lecture room was equipped with Godly Play materials for meditation and loan. The conference included the option of three days Core Training in Godly Play. The event was organized by the Synod Children's Ministry Consultant at the time, Judyth Roberts, and a team of supporters from around the Uniting Church.[23] One of the key concepts in Cavalletti's Catechesis of the Good Shepherd is "education to wonder."[24] Berryman also worked with this approach, developing questions for teachers to ask children that were genuinely open-ended, noncoercive, playful, and yet at the same time, profoundly instructional about Christian faith and practice. Children were encouraged through the process to develop skills in asking theological questions at their own pace and appropriate to their age.

WONDERING AND IMAGINING

Wondering and imagining about the future of Australian society was uppermost in Tim Costello's May Macleod Lecture of 2001 on the topic "What Does a Good Society Look Like?" Other events followed, asking similar questions: a 2006 joint UTC and Synod Board of Mission seminar on forming missional communities, a seminar in 2007 on "Citizenship, Discipleship, and Belonging," and a 2010 PACT-sponsored conference called What Makes for a Good City?

In 2001 UTC was pleased to host John Polkinghorne (1930–2021) as the Livingstone Lecturer. He was professor of mathematical physics at the University of Cambridge, United Kingdom. William Emilsen had invited Polkinghorne, as a leading exponent of the dialogue between science and religion, to be the Livingstone Lecturer for Seminar Week. (The visit occurred before Polkinghorne won the Templeton Prize for Science and Religion.[25])

22. Lewis-Jones, "September," 11; Kohn, "Play It Again."

23. With support from the ELM (once the Education for Lay Ministries, now renamed to Education for Life and Ministry) Centre at the CFM.

24. Cavalletti, *Experiencing Scripture*, 138–50.

25. Polkinghorne won the Templeton Prize in 2002. For further information, see

The topic for the public lecture in 2001 was "The Friendship of Science and Religion." For the remainder of Seminar Week, the theme was "Science and Theology and the Search for Truth."

Two thousand and two saw the visit of Don Saliers, professor of theology and worship at the Candler School of Theology, Emory University, Atlanta, Georgia, for a conference organized by those involved with liturgical and pastoral studies at UTC.[26] Former Lecturer in Pastoral Theology Doug Purnell commented in his diary at the time,

> Don Saliers was wonderful. He affirmed the things I'm battling for—that people "know" through all their senses. If we are to touch people in their deep places, we need to be aware of and address all the senses. I'm left with one important question: What does that mean for pedagogy and theological education?[27]

Saliers gave two sessions on the topic "Word, Bath and Meal in a Culture of Distraction," two sessions on "Liturgy and Seasons of Life: Marriage, Sickness and Health," and two on "Liturgy and Seasons of Life: Finitude and Mortality." Purnell remarked that the latter session "was really grounded, because a close relative of Don's had recently died."[28] Saliers also offered two sessions on "Worship: Humanity at Full Stretch" and two on "Architects and a Theologian in Conversation."[29]

Further impetus for connecting the arts with theological education came from Rod Pattenden who ran an annual Summer School in the Arts for ten years from the opening of the Centre for Ministry, through the Institute for Theology and the Arts. UTC students were able to gain credit for their degree through attendance and extra written work. This was then followed by another series entitled "Wisdom of the Body," which brought together theater skills, expressive arts, and theological reflection and was run by Phil Porter and Cynthia Winton-Henry from the Pacific School of Religion in San Francisco. Porter and Winton-Henry also delivered a performance/lecture for the annual May Macleod Lecture. These innovative programs were the first in Australia to enable a deeper conversation between theological education and the arts.[30]

Templeton Religious Trust, "Areas of Focus." See also https://www.templetonprize.org/.

26. Saliers held the Chair at Candler until 2007. The conference was led by Graham Hughes. Doug Purnell also shared hospitality with Saliers.

27. Purnell, conversation with the author, July 2, 2024.

28. Purnell, conversation with the author, July 2, 2024.

29. Seminar Week record provided by Moira Bryant, librarian, Camden Theological Library.

30. Pattenden, email message to author, July 29, 2024.

A particular highlight of these interactions was the visit by the eminent Filipino artist Emmanuel Garibay, who came for two periods as artist-in-residence and who worked with students and lecturers. His second visit was under the banner of the Pacific Asia Arts Forum, a program funded by the Wallace Foundation, where he worked alongside three significant local artists: Margaret Ackland, Michael Galovic, and Paul Miller. In 2004, this resulted in an exhibition of works, curated by Pattenden, being presented in the Gallery of the Parramatta Heritage Centre. A number of these works remained in the art collection of the Centre for Ministry.[31]

QUESTIONING AND DISRUPTING

A willingness to question everything and to disrupt complacent Christians had been a feature of a number of UTC-sponsored conferences. Among these was Andrew Dutney's May Macleod Lecture in 2003, with the theme "Praying for Peace."[32] Dutney gave an inspiring meditation on the need for Christians to pray for peace, drawing from the fundamental faith assertions in the UCA's *Basis of Union*. He added, "When we pray for peace, we are confessing our faith in God who is at work in our world for peace."[33] In March 2007 Father John Dear, American Jesuit Priest and nonviolent activist for peace, led a PACT-sponsored conference titled Peace and Non-Violence. Australian Catholic peace activist and anarchist Ciaron O'Reilly delivered the 2009 May Macleod Lecture on "Faith and Resistance in a Time of Never-Ending War."[34]

Pete Rollins, Irish activist, philosopher, and theologian, gave the May Macleod Lecture entitled "Fullness of Life on a Journey to Death" in October 2012. Prior to his appearance at UTC, Rollins had been a popular speaker at UCA National Christian Youth Conventions and had built a following in Australia for his radical views. His readiness to question the status quo and to disrupt comfortable Christians was, paradoxically, a point of attraction for many UCA members who heard him.

The visit of Amy-Jill Levine in 2006 created a ripple of excitement and apprehension for a number of people when she led a seminar at UTC on New Testament studies. John Squires comments: "Amy is unique: a Jew

31. Pattenden, email message to author, July 29, 2024.

32. Andrew Dutney was principal of Parkin-Wesley Theological College in Adelaide from 2001 and served as the UCA National Assembly president from 2012 to 2015.

33. Dutney, "Praying for Peace," 16.

34. List of May Macleod Lectures provided by Moira Bryant, librarian, Camden Theological Library.

who holds a tenured position as a Professor of New Testament! She was in Sydney, around 2006 I think, to speak at a conference at ACU, North Sydney."[35] I was present with John Oldmeadow when Levine held a seminar in the NSW Parliament building.[36] A couple of parliamentarians, including Gordon Moyes, MLC (Member of Legislative Council), attended. Levine's confidence and command of New Testament story was enjoyed by all. Elizabeth Raine quoted Levine as saying, "They are not just Christian stories, they're my stories."[37]

Described as "a fine event, with excellent attendance and interaction," the conference in May 2006, Validating Violence—Violating Faith?, asked questions of Judaism, Christianity, and Islam with reference to the description of violence in their respective Scriptures.[38] The guest lecturer was Christopher Stanley, from Saint Bonaventure University, New York. Organized by Emilsen and Squires, the conference featured two lectures from Stanley: "Words of Death: Scriptures and Violence in Judaism, Christianity, and Islam," followed by "Words of Life: Scriptures and Non-Violence in Judaism, Christianity, and Islam."[39] The papers given by many at that conference were published by ATF Press in 2008 as a PACT project.

The March 2008 PACT-sponsored "Religion, Children and Violence" seminar was convened by William Emilsen, with responses to papers from James Haire and Stephen Burns. The intention of the organizers was to follow-on from the Validating Violence—Violating Faith? conference. The guest was Patricia Brennan, a medical doctor and forensic clinical pediatrician who had worked with abused children and who was a practising Christian. Her presentation was confronting for religion and theology, concluding with important questions that needed to be addressed by the churches and all Christians. Brennan's lecture appeared in the *Uniting Church Studies* journal.[40] Elizabeth Raine and John Squires added to the tension of the seminar with a dialogue about whether God should be indicted for child abuse.[41]

On another tack, in exploring religions and their sacred texts, Professors Zeki Saritoprak from John Carroll University, Ohio, and Daniel

---

35. Squires, email message to author, Apr. 11, 2024.

36. Oldmeadow was executive director of the Synod Board of Education at that stage.

37. Raine, email message to author, Apr. 11, 2024.

38. Squires, email message to author, Apr. 11, 2024.

39. Stanley, "Words of Death," 26 and "Words of Life," 46.

40. Brennan, "Religion."

41. Raine and Squires, conversation with the author, July 2, 2004.

Smith-Christopher from Loyola Marymount University, Los Angeles, were guests for the Things That Make for Peace? Sacred Texts and Religious Traditions in a Transforming World conference at UTC in March 2018. It was convened by Anthony Rees.[42] In a gathering which included representatives of other faiths, an expressed hope of the conference was to explore how engaging with the sacred texts and traditions of world religions might demonstrate how religion could contribute to addressing current world affairs, rather than being an aggravation or a problem. Liam Miller, a graduate student in attendance, remarked that he enjoyed the interfaith atmosphere and that it was encouraging personally because he presented his first academic paper at the conference.[43]

There was a demonstrable turn towards the acknowledgment of diversity and difference amongst God's people at UTC through the work of Clive Pearson and collaborators on the concept of "Faith in a Hyphen."[44] That published work, and the subsequent conference in 2006, heralded a number of continuing cross-cultural and intercultural theological explorations that have continued to expand over the years (including, for example, the celebration of Communitas in the UTC community and the Talanoa events initiated by Jione Havea). The 2006 Faith in a Hyphen event was described as "a conference designed to look at what it is like to live in diaspora, to be a migrant, to be second generation and what it means to be part of a dominant majority."[45] For the conference, Pearson had invited Fumitaka Matsuoka from the PANA Institute (Institute for Leadership Development and Study of Pacific and Asian North American Religion) in Berkeley, connected with the Pacific School of Religion, to give the keynote address. Other visitors present included Gary Bouma (Monash University) and Zuleya Keskin (Affinity Intercultural Foundation). Pearson praised the input of Peter Manning from the ABC (Australian Broadcasting Corporation). Manning encouraged the study of cross-cultural theology as imperative to counter a culture of fear that he believed had developed in Australia.[46]

In September 2008, Communitas was inaugurated and aptly described by its incoming director, Katalina Tahaafe-Williams:

> I understand communitas to be about creating the space for the diverse peoples of God to encounter each other, to listen, to

---

42. Anthony Rees teaches Old Testament at UTC and became head of the CSU School of Theology in January 2024.
43. Liam Miller, email message to author, June 25, 2024.
44. See Pearson and Havea, *Faith in a Hyphen*.
45. Pearson, "Forthcoming Events," 15.
46. See Manning, *Us and Them*.

share, to dialogue, to learn, and together act to create new life, a new way of being.⁴⁷

Tahaafe-Williams encouraged an inclusive vision for Communitas as binding all people in the one heart "language of love, compassion, respect and integrity."⁴⁸ The story of the church, and the vision for Communitas in theological education, is to work with integrity on the task of uniting theory and practice, to embody a spirit of community and a readiness to serve one another and the wider community in humility and with mutual respect. Just how that works out in practice has been the concern of leaders amongst the Uniting Church's diaspora communities, and those of other backgrounds who work with them. In a guest editorial for *Uniting Church Studies*, Clive Pearson outlined some concerns for the church which had arisen from what he saw as the "problematic and ambiguous" claim by the Uniting Church Assembly to be "a multicultural church."⁴⁹

Talanoa Oceania conferences have become part of UTC tradition, thanks to the inspiration of biblical scholar and theologian Jione Havea. His intercultural wisdom and insight, and the setting up of the Havea Lecture in honor of his father, has stimulated theological study and community amongst Pacific Islander (PI) people connected with UTC. PI people are not a homogenous people. Their needs and cultural encounters are as varied as their languages and islands. However, they are able to support one another in mutual understanding based upon their oceanic origins and the stories they share about living in different cultural contexts.⁵⁰ A write-up of Talanoa 2008 in *Out & About* indicated that Talanoa Oceania 2008 "generated healthy energy, and one of the participants estimated that we averaged around 80 people each day."⁵¹ Participants included people from various roots/routes: Papua New Guinea, Aotearoa, Rarotonga, Samoa, Niue, Rotuma, Fiji, Tuvalu, India, Tonga, England, New Zealand, Indonesia, Korea, China, and Australia.⁵²

UTC hosted Nāsili Vaka'uta for the Havea Lecture in 2022, on the topic of "Pasifika Theology and Biblical Studies: New Directions for Oceanic Hermeneutics." Vaka'uta is the principal of Trinity Methodist Theological College, Auckland. In a brief evaluative statement about the Havea Lecture, Liam Miller wrote,

47. Tahaafe-Williams, "Vision for Communitas," 4–5.
48. Tahaafe-Williams, "Vision for Communitas," 5–6.
49. Pearson, "Case for a Pasifika Theology," 7.
50. Havea, "Talanoa Oceania (Sept 29–Oct 1)."
51. Havea, "Talanoa Oceania."
52. Havea, "Talanoa Oceania."

This was a special and exciting evening and something new was launched that nonetheless felt like it was connected with a long theological journey and also signalled a beginning of a broader shift in the theological culture, identity, and priorities of the college.[53]

The 2024 Havea Lecture was incorporated into the Talanoa Oceania Conference, convened by Seforosa Carroll at UTC. Its theme was Indigeneity: Belongings and Subversion.[54]

In September 2009 a PACT-sponsored symposium was held at UTC, hosted by the Association of Asian-Australian Theology and Ministry with the Korean Society of Sydney. It was organized by Myong Duk Yang.[55] Listed as an Asian Diaspora in Australia symposium, the topic was Making Space for Christ: Second Thoughts on Crossing Borders. In Jin Yoon, head of the Sociology Department, Korea University, was the keynote speaker, along with Clive Pearson as principal of UTC.

The UTC Korean Fellowship hosted an event in December 2009 to celebrate one hundred and twenty years of Australian mission in Korea. The speakers for the event were John P. Brown,[56] Clive Pearson, and Myong Duk Yang.[57] Volume twenty-one of the *Uniting Church Studies* was devoted to the theme, "The Australian Missionary Movement in Korea." Emilsen's editorial for that edition explores the Australian-Korean connection.[58]

Apart from the many Australian diaspora communities that have Christian connections, UTC has also encouraged relationship building with other faiths. A recent development in this field has been the 2023 appointment of Sathianathan Clarke to UTC as lecturer in theology and mission.[59] Clarke was first introduced to UTC as a May Macleod lecturer in 2017.[60] His topic was "Interfaith Collaboration and Protective Hospitality."[61] Derya

---

53. Miller, email message to author, June 25, 2024. Miller added to his comments about the Havea Lecture that "it was also the best meal I've had at a UTC event."

54. A full report on that event is found on the UTC website, with the revealing title, "Talanoa Is More Than Mere Storytelling" (Carroll, "*Talanoa* Is More").

55. Myong Duk Yang was serving with the UCA Board of Mission in NSW as cross-cultural consultant and synod director of the Asian-Australian Theology and Ministry Association.

56. A former missionary in Korea and Uniting Church minister who has served in many roles for the Church.

57. United Theological College, "120 Years."

58. Emilsen, "Australian–Korean Connection."

59. See United Theological College, "Rev Prof Sathi Clarke."

60. Clarke was on sabbatical from Wesley Theological Seminary, Washington, DC.

61. Clarke pointed out that "protective hospitality is offered unconditionally when

Iner (from the Centre for Islamic Studies at CSU) was the respondent to the lecture. Iner had experience of hostile Islamophobia in Australia and had written for news publications and given support to numerous community organizations.[62]

David Clough visited in 2019. An advocate for treating domestic and farm animals differently on theological grounds, Clough was disarmingly aware and respectful of other views than his own, and perhaps more persuasive for that. Although based in the United Kingdom, Clough's insightful exploration of Australian history and experience with sheep and cattle grazing opened a fascinating discussion with UTC faculty members. Clough was also very aware of the impact of European farming and animal husbandry for Indigenous Australians. His May Macleod Lecture, "Eating More Peaceably: The Christian Ethics of Eating Animals," shared his theological vision with a broader audience.[63]

Human-induced climate change has been a theme UTC has tackled throughout the past twenty-five years.[64] One example occurred in May 2008. It was a conference co-sponsored by PACT, Waterlines, Earth Ministries, and Project Green Church. Michael Northcott, the Edinburgh-based Christian ethicist, Scottish Episcopal priest, and author of *A Moral Climate: The Ethics of Global Warming*, gave two keynote presentations. The conference was organized by Clive Pearson and included seminar streams on ecopraxis, climate justice, interfaith perspectives, and ecotheology. Reviewing the event, David Reichardt, at that stage a PhD candidate in ecotheology, commented, "Northcott used this experience and his facility with data projection to marry science with theology, testimony with a strong biblical emphasis."[65]

A more recent UTC conference dedicated to the climate change issue featured Ernst M. Conradie.[66] His September 2023 May Macleod Lecture title was "In God We Trust? Revisiting God's Providence Amidst the Shift from the Holocene to the Anthropocene." Peter Walker, UTC principal, wrote a review of it, commenting that "listeners were shaken by the reality

---

your neighbour is in trouble," and is contrasted with promotional hospitality. Foye, "May Macleod Lecture."

62. See Charles Sturt University, "Teaching and Research Staff."

63. Clough is professor of theological ethics in the Department of Theology and Religious Studies at the University of Chester, and he is a lay preacher in the Methodist Church in the United Kingdom. See Creature Kind, "Regular Contributors."

64. Including frequent courses in ecotheology.

65. Reichardt, "Moral Climate?," 6.

66. From the Department of Religion and Theology at the University of the Western Cape in South Africa.

of climate change yet given hope by Conradie's probing into the question of how God is with us and moving us."[67] UTC also sponsored a two-day conference with Conradie, which attracted a wide variety of attendees from different denominations and locations.[68]

The Calvin Quincentenary conference (2009) is rightly placed under this "Questioning and Disrupting" heading because it offered a forum for scholars, who had been revisiting the importance of John Calvin for the church, to share their different perspectives. The conference allowed new generations of scholars to challenge old assumptions about Calvin and what it meant to be "Calvinist." Papers at the conference asked questions of Calvin's relevance for theological exploration today: in public theology and secularity, science, religion and the Bible, human rights, women in the church, attitudes to Islam, and for biblical interpretation in the Korean church and society.[69] For Michael Earl, the hard work of helping organize a conference was also an opportunity for personal encounter and growth. Earl was impressed with the input of visiting academic Randall Zachman.[70] The opportunity to engage with scholarship relevant to one of the founders of Protestantism, John Calvin, was highly significant.

> It is a pity that not more people, especially younger people, are appreciative of the radical reforms that Calvin introduced into the church. It is often forgotten that the Reformation was to a large degree led by young people, often in their twenties and thirties. As a young person myself, the Calvin 500 conference was a stimulating experience and one which reaffirmed for me the great Protestant principle of the Reformation: *ecclesia reformata semper reformanda* (the church, under the word of God, is always in the process of reforming itself).[71]

One may well assert that several of the visitors to UTC were encouraging the church to engage in reform, specifically with reference to questions about its cultural biases and settler-colonial assumptions. In 2011, Anthony Reddie, then research fellow with the Queen's Foundation for Ecumenical Theological Education in the United Kingdom, gave a keynote address at a conference sponsored by UTC, PACT, and the National Council of Churches. His

---

67. Walker, "Ernst Conradie."
68. Walker, "Ernst Conradie."
69. A selection of the papers are available in a Calvin Quincentenary edition of the *Uniting Church Studies* journal (vol. 17.1, June 2011).
70. See Zachman, "Astronomy." Zachman was professor of reformation studies at the University of Notre Dame in Indiana.
71. Earl, "Reflections." Michael Earl was a UTC student at the time.

topic, "The Myths of Whiteness: Truth, Knowledge and Power," included insights from his publication *Is God Colour-Blind?*[72] Reddie's question brings to mind the insights of a 2024 visiting scholar, Grace Ji-Sun Kim, on whiteness, as seen in her work *When God Became White: Dismantling Whiteness for a More Just Christianity*. Ji-Sun Kim examines the roots of the perceived theological distortion, drawing from her Korean and Canadian experience, demonstrating its harmful impact on the church and the world.[73]

In sympathy with these thoughts is the work of Anastasia Boniface-Malle, who visited UTC in 2006 for Seminar Week and who also contributed a chapter to the *Validating Violence—Violating Faith?* publication that followed the eponymous 2006 UTC/PACT conference. Boniface-Malle's message from her own context resonates not only with Reddie and Ji-Sun Kim, but also with the concern expressed in first-world countries about the societal threat of domestic violence:

> Both African culture and the biblical culture demean a woman's image. A woman must be submissive to her husband or father. Christianity and most major religions of the world concede and justify male supremacy and the submission of the woman.[74]

A timely and significant conference on neoliberalism, its economic philosophy, its effects, influence, and collisions within the church and theology was held at UTC in June 2018. The follow-up in *Uniting Church Studies* highlighted that economic theory and practice was a concern for theology. The conference engaged with serious concerns about economic theory and practice at work in social service and welfare sectors, the environmental field, and Indigenous affairs.[75]

TRANSFORMING

In 2000 Sir Ronald Wilson gave the May Macleod Lecture, "The Healing of a Nation."[76] The lecture was delivered just a few days before the people's Walk for Reconciliation across the Sydney Harbour Bridge and elsewhere in

---

72. Reddie, *Is God Colour Blind?*
73. Kim, *When God Became White*.
74. Boniface-Malle, "From Violence," 77.
75. See the insightful essay by Ji Zhang on the significance of the revised Preamble in the UCA Constitution for Christology, in "Christology of the Preamble."
76. The lecture appeared in *Uniting Church Studies* volume twenty-two, first issue. Wilson, former judge of the High Court of Australia, was the first layperson to be elected president of the Uniting Church Assembly, serving 1988–1991.

Australia. Wilson declared that "despite the disappointments, I am unshakeable in my belief that the Council's vision of a united Australia, which respects this land of ours, which values its Aboriginal and Torres Strait Islander heritage, and provides justice and equity for all will come to pass."[77] There was so much hope expressed in that lecture, which did not shy from laying out the necessary steps to achieve reconciliation. For Christians, Wilson argued, it was the love of Christ that urged us on to reconciliation, not guilt or self-satisfaction.[78]

When Lowitja O'Donoghue delivered the May Macleod Lecture in 2002, it was very much in continuity with that of Ronald Wilson. There was a strong desire to see the findings of the *Bringing Them Home Report* acted upon as part of an Australia-wide movement towards national reconciliation. O'Donoghue stated, movingly, that passages from Isaiah (61:1) and Matthew's Gospel (25:35–36) framed a "social agenda that has relatively recently made Christianity a possibility for me.

> I had to be able to reconcile my commitment to social justice with my growing belief in Christian spirituality. I could not belong to a Church that did not practice what it preached.[79]

In keeping with Wilson's belief and O'Donohue's statement, it is important to record that the seventeenth Assembly meeting of the UCA, in 2024, included a resolution to revive and redefine the Covenant between Indigenous and non-Indigenous Uniting Church members.[80] Also significant was the July 2024 UTC conference entitled the Preamble 15 Years On. It marked the advent of the revised Preamble of the UCA Constitution in 2009, which honors the Indigenous heritage of Australia and the UCA. The conference transpired well as a simultaneous multi-sited and hybrid gathering.[81]

Even though Christine Gapes knew that her post at UTC as lecturer in youth ministry and field education was soon to conclude, she passionately sought to ensure that there would be a Seminar Week in 2005 with a focus on youth ministry. Gapes wanted Kenda Creasy-Dean from Princeton

---

77. Wilson, "Healing of a Nation," 19. The "Council" to which Wilson refers is the Council for Aboriginal Reconciliation.

78. Wilson, "Healing of a Nation."

79. O'Donoghue, "Our Father's Business."

80. See "Revival and Redesign."

81. Confirmed by Chris Budden in a conversation with the author, July 24, 2024. The Sydney site had thirty attending; Adelaide twenty-five; and on Zoom from all over Australia, an additional fifteen attended. An edition of *Uniting Church Studies* will publish the presentations of the conference, and complement the existing *Uniting Church Studies* volume sixteen, issue one, from June 2010.

Theological Seminary to be the keynote speaker. Working with the continuing education director and applying for funding through the UTC Board of Finance and Administration (BFA), as well as writing to the College Council about her concern, Gapes ensured that the event would transpire.[82]

Phil Newton, an ordained deacon of the Uniting Church in ministry, offers a powerful testimony to the value of well-resourced conferences and inspirational visitors:

> I was at UTC from 2005 to 2007. My strong memories are the "Hidden Histories" seminar week. I still recall Peter Walker (then a visiting academic) talking about the theological antecedents of the UCA in Barth, Bonhoeffer, and Newbigin. I have that paper, having chased it up with Peter years later. At that same conference, Andrew Dutney presented on the value of a more Methodist theological formation, which was compelling. At the Youth Ministry Seminar Week, Kenda Creasy-Dean was a stand out. She spoke about finding God in the wilderness and it changed my life.[83]

For Newton, events like conferences and encounters with visiting lecturers added a dimension that differed from the routine of classes and the ministerial formation program. The occasions he outlined did more than complement the college curriculum. They also nurtured and grew his faith.

Kyounghee Cho is another UTC student who discovered that by organizing and participating in conferences, horizons were broadened and theological imaginations were stimulated. Cho was initially reluctant and apprehensive about participating in the Coming Out conference at UTC in December 2007.[84] Her lecturer in biblical studies, Jione Havea, had been impressed with a final paper Cho had written and encouraged her to present it at the conference he was organizing. While attending the conference, Cho felt "surprised and shocked" at such diverse readings of the Bible, yet she was also inspired.[85] In time, Cho came to the view that the presentations which inspired her were shared with a conviction and integrity she could respect. Subsequently, Cho accepted an invitation from a publisher to translate Jack Rogers's book *Jesus, the Bible and Homosexuality: Explode the Myths, Heal the Church* into Korean. Cho explains that Rogers's book is

---

82. Gapes, "Proposed Budget"; Gapes, "Letter to Larry Beal."
83. Newton, email message to author, May 28, 2024.
84. Cho, email message to author, June 17, 2024.
85. Cho, conversation with the author, June 28, 2024.

regarded as very radical in Korea, adding, "I learned so many things from that book!"[86] Reflecting upon these events in conversation, Cho remarks,

> Although my own presentation at the Coming Out conference was not about homosexuality, being part of the conference challenged me to learn from others.[87]

UTC faculty spent months preparing for a conference on faith and atheism, held in October 2011, with the theme of Questioning God: Faith and Atheism in Australia. The conference was very well attended and received beyond the confines of college life. William Emilsen tells the story of how the faculty of UTC conceived the idea of engaging respectfully and theologically with the phenomenon that came to be known as the "New Atheism."[88] The conference and other projects emerged from discussion at a faculty retreat in 2009. One of the highlights of this multipronged initiative was the Questioning God: Faith and Atheism in Australia conference at UTC.

Professor David Fergusson, from the University of Edinburgh, was the keynote speaker for the conference. The participation of faculty and others was also strong. Before the event, Emilsen wrote that Fergusson's approach to atheism was close to the conversational tone for which organizers were hoping and that the conference would not be seen as a "gladiatorial contest."[89] It was a conference where atheists, agnostics, and representatives of different religious communities could feel welcome and included. It allowed Christians and others to grapple with the challenges they were facing without mutual misrepresentation.[90] The then premier of NSW, Kristina Keneally, gave the address at the opening dinner. Robert Banks's book *And Man Created God* was launched on the first of the four conference days. Scott Stephens, respected ABC *Religion and Ethics* presenter, chaired the closing panel session.[91] In reflecting upon that conference and its aftermath, Clive Pearson has said, "This is a much-neglected item in the Uniting Church, which really needs more attention."[92]

If there were any need of evidence that the Questioning God conference struck the right note in terms of dialogical tone and hospitality, one

86. For an Evangelical Presbyterian minister's biographical account of a transformational experience, see Rogers, *Jesus*.
87. Cho, conversation with the author, June 28, 2024.
88. Emilsen, *I Believe in God*, ix–xiii.
89. Emilsen, "Faith and Atheism," v.
90. Emilsen, "Why Bother," 7.
91. Emilsen, "Faith and Atheism," v.
92. Pearson, note to the author, May 31, 2024.

anecdote provides it. In a break during the conference, Carolyn Craig-Emilsen found herself in the company of an atheist representative. He remarked that the Centre for Ministry was a "lovely venue" and wondered about its availability for a conference; without hesitation, Craig-Emilsen suggested the inquirer approach the helpful staff at the Centre for Ministry office.[93] Emilsen had also encouraged the UTC faculty to extend the engagement with atheism by preparing and preaching sermons in three strategic church locations, addressing the topic "I Believe in God."[94] The *Uniting Church Studies* volume eighteen was devoted to the topic of faith and atheism. It included thoughtful articles from presenters at the conference.

Czech theologian Tomáš Halík made an appearance at UTC in June 2011, prior to the Questioning God conference, invited by Ben Myers.[95] Halík's broad and deep reflections on the encounter between Jesus and Zacchaeus provide an antidote to both triumphalist and defensive Christian apologetics.[96] In weaving his exploration of relationships between human beings of religious and no faith, Halík's central narrative was Jesus' response to Zacchaeus. He also explored the work of Nietzsche, Thérèse of Lisieux, Simone Weil, and other significant Christian texts.

The XIV International Bonhoeffer conference, Crisis and Hope: Reading Bonhoeffer for Today, was to be held at the UTC campus in January 2024, but capacity became an issue, and it was transferred to the Wesley Centre in Sydney. Di Rayson, the author of *Bonhoeffer and Climate Change: Theology and Ethics for the Anthropocene*, attended along with several other Bonhoeffer scholars, including Clifford Green, Paul Chung, Lisa Dahill, Willie Jennings, Kung Lap-yan, Anne Pattel-Gray, and Peter Walker.

Kim Langford, who attended the conference, commented that having attended previous Bonhoeffer conferences, she was keen to "sharpen my theological thinking ahead of commencing graduate theological studies at UTC this year."[97] Langford admired the ethical responsibility taken by all presenters in their representation and interpretation of Bonhoeffer. She added, "The presenters responded to a vast range of comments and questions, and throughout the congress I experienced a real sense of learning together."[98] A professional pastoral supervisor and university chaplain,

---

93. Craig-Emilsen, conversation with the author, Feb. 16, 2024.
94. Emilsen, *I Believe in God*.
95. Myers, "Tomas Halik."
96. Halík, *Patience with God*. For the story of Zacchaeus, see Luke 19: 1–10.
97. Langford, email message to author, July 10, 2024.
98. Langford, email message to author, July 10, 2024.

Langford reflected upon the potential value of the conference for her ministry practice:

> The congress experience was theologically stimulating and provided me with rich resources for collegial and pastoral conversations across university, community, and congregational settings. I have experienced afresh the relevance of Bonhoeffer's writings for developing approaches to courageous decision-making. This has shaped my commitment to supporting others refine their questions and explore their choices amid times of significant life choices and ethical conundrums.[99]

Looking back across the last twenty-five years, one may easily identify the COVID-19 epidemic as a threat to the quality of engagement and learning at UTC during the years 2020–2022. Staff and students attested to the difficulties created by the sudden shift to online modes of teaching and learning. Lecturers at the time expressed their concerns for the present and future of the college as they experienced the consequences of the pandemic.[100] Recent evaluative comments from UTC principal, Peter Walker, have clarified matters about the impact of the epidemic upon UTC's capacity to host conferences:

> Because of COVID, we moved quite quickly to hosting conferences in hybrid mode: some folks in person and others joining online. We have not held a conference since 2020 that was not hybrid. This has become the "new normal."[101]

GIFTS FROM THE PAST AND AN EYE ON THE FUTURE

In the history of UTC, endowed lectureships were an assured way of encouraging the continuation and broadening of contact with ideas and theological developments. In the early years of focus for this chapter, some of the legacy funding for visiting scholars remained, under the Livingstone and Thatcher Lectures. More recently there have been endowments in memory of May Macleod and Sione Havea.[102] As mentioned earlier, the PACT arrangement with Charles Sturt University became an important source of support for visiting academics, conferences, and publications. UTC could

---

99. Langford, email message to author, July 10, 2024.
100. Hillis, "Hardened Hearts," 340.
101. Walker, email message to author, July 6, 2024.
102. Father of former UTC lecturer, and global academic, Jione Havea.

only ever provide conferences and invite visitors, based on the inspiration and goals of staff and students employed or enrolled at any given time. This chapter has endeavoured to tell some of the story of how the United Theological College used its resources to gather leading scholars, the theological college community, and the wider church and society in dialogue and learning together.

BIBLIOGRAPHY

Banks, Robert. *And Man Created God: Is God a Human Invention?* Oxford: Lion Hudson, 2011.

Barnes, Geoffrey. *Doing Theology in Sydney: A History of United Theological College, 1974–1999*. Adelaide, SA: Openbook, 2000.

Berryman, Jerome W. *Godly Play: A Way of Religious Education.* San Francisco: HarperSanFrancisco, 1991.

Boniface-Malle, Anastasia. "From Violence and War to Shalom in the Hebrew Bible." In *Validating Violence—Violating Faith? Religion, Scripture and Violence*, edited by William W. Emilsen and John T. Squires, 77–94. Adelaide, SA: ATF, 2008.

Brennan, Patricia. "Religion, Children and Violence: Fallen Angels or Risen Apes?" *Uniting Church Studies* 14.2 (2008) 1–14.

Budden, Chris. "Introduction: Exploring the Implications of the New Preamble." *Uniting Church Studies* 16.1 (2010) 1–5.

Carroll, Seforosa. "*Talanoa* Is More Than Mere Storytelling." United Theological College, Apr. 29, 2024. https://www.utc.edu.au/blog/talanoa-is-more-than-mere-storytelling/.

Cavalletti, Sofia. *The Religious Potential of the Child: Experiencing Scripture and Liturgy with Young Children.* Translated by Patricia M. Coulter and Julie M. Coulter. Chicago: Liturgy Training, 1992.

———. *The Religious Potential of the Child 6 to 12 Years Old: A Description of An Experience.* Translated by Rebekah Rojcewicz and Alan R. Perry. Chicago: Liturgy Training, 2002.

Creature Kind. "Regular Contributors." https://www.becreaturekind.org/our-team.

Dutney, Andrew. "Praying for Peace." Illuminate. Released 2003. https://illuminate.recollect.net.au/nodes/view/24088.

Earl, Michael. "Reflections on Calvin 500." *Out & About* 20 (Nov. 2009) 17.

Emilsen, William W. "Australian-Korean Connection." *Uniting Church Studies* 21.2 (Dec. 2017) 5–8.

———. "Faith and Atheism." *Uniting Church Studies* 18.2 (Dec. 2012) v–vi.

———, ed. *I Believe in God.* North Parramatta, NSW: United Theological College, 2011.

———. "Why Bother with a Conference on the New Atheism." *Out & About* 25 (Sept. 2011) 6–7.

Emilsen, William W., and Elizabeth A. Watson, eds. *Growing Up Uniting.* Richmond, SA: MediaCom Education, 2021.

Emilsen, William W., and John T. Squires, eds. *Validating Violence—Violating Faith? Religion, Scripture and Violence.* Adelaide, SA: ATF, 2008.

Emilsen, William W., and Patricia Curthoys, eds. *Growing Up Uniting: The Proceedings of the Third Uniting Church National History Society Conference 11–13 June 2021.* Hoppers Crossing, VIC: Uniting Church National History Society, 2021.

Foye, Jonathan. "Hearing Scripture's Diverse Voices." *Insights*, July 2022. https://www.insights.uca.org.au/hearing-scriptures-diverse-voices/.

———. "May Macleod Lecture Calls for Interfaith Collaboration." *Insights*, Nov. 2017. https://www.insights.uca.org.au/may-macleod-lecture-calls-for-interfaith-collaboration/.

Gapes, Christine. "Letter to Barry Leal." UTC Council Correspondence 2003–2005, Sept. 8, 2004.

———. "Proposed Budget for Seminar Week 2005." Letter to the Board of Finance and Administration, UTC Council Correspondence 2003–2005, June 23, 2004.

Garrett, John, and L. W. Farr. *Camden College: A Centenary History.* Glebe, Sydney: Camden College, 1964.

Global Network for Public Theology. "Mission and History." https://www.gnpublictheology.net/about.

Halík, Tomáš. *Patience with God: The Story of Zacchaeus Continuing in Us.* New York: Doubleday, 2009.

Havea, Jione. "Talanoa Oceania." *Out & About* 17 (Dec. 2008) 14.

———. "Talanoa Oceania (Sept 29–Oct 1)." *Out & About* 16 (Sept. 2008) 14.

Hillis, Mark K. "Hardened Hearts and Cries for Freedom: Interpreting Biblical Narratives in a Pandemic." *British Journal of Religious Education* 46.3 (2024) 337–47.

Human Rights and Equal Opportunity Commission. *Bringing Them Home.* Australian Human Rights Commission, 1997. https://humanrights.gov.au/sites/default/files/content/pdf/social_justice/bringing_them_home_report.pdf.

Kim, Grace Ji-Sun. *When God Became White: Dismantling Whiteness for a More Just Christianity.* Downer's Grove, IL: InterVarsity, 2024.

Kohn, Rachel, presenter. "Play It Again, God." In *The Spirit of Things.* ABC Radio National. Sydney: RN, July 24, 2011.

Lathrop, Gordon. "The Gospels on Ministry: On Recovering the Paradoxical Authority of the Ordained Minister." *Uniting Church Studies* 15.2 (2009) 1–10.

Lewis-Jones, Marjorie. "September: Godly Play." *Insights*, Sept. 2011. https://www.uca.org.au/september-godly-play/.

Manning, Peter. *Us and Them.* Milsons Point, NSW: Random House, 2006.

Moore, Gerard. "UTC & CSU." *Out & About* 26 (Apr. 2013) 18–19.

Myers, Ben. "Tomas Halik in Sydney." Faith and Theology, May 20, 2011. https://www.faith-theology.com/2011/05/tomas-halik-in-sydney.html.

O'Donoghue, Lowitja. "Our Father's Business: An Agenda for the Church in Contemporary Australia." May Macleod Lecture transcript, UCA Synod Board of Education Papers, May 2002.

Pearson, Clive. "The Case for a Pasifika Theology." *Uniting Church Studies* 23.1 (2021) 5–8.

———. "Forthcoming Events." *Out & About* 3 (Dec. 2005–Jan. 2006) 14–15.

———. "Introducing 'PACT'." *Out & About* 10 (Feb. 2007) 7–9.

———. "Ministry Formation." *Out & About* 2 (Aug.–Sept. 2005) 8–11.

———. "United Theological College." In *2007 Working Papers and Reports*, compiled by the Uniting Church in Australia NSW/ACT Synod, 98–102. https://illuminate.recollect.net.au/nodes/view/11957.

Pearson, Clive, and Jione Havea, eds. *Faith in a Hyphen: Cross Cultural Theologies Down Under*. Adelaide, SA: Openbook, 2004.

Pickard, Stephen, "ACC&C; PACT and School of Theology: Origins, Relationships, Trajectories." Unpublished paper for Synod Executive Committee, United Theological College Archives, North Parramatta, NSW, Apr. 2016.

Rayson, Dianne. *Bonhoeffer and Climate Change: Theology and Ethics for the Anthropocene*. New York: Rowman & Littlefield, 2021.

Reddie, Anthony. *Is God Colour Blind? Insights from Black Theology for Christian Faith and Ministry*. Rev. ed. London: SPCK, 2020.

Reichardt, David. "A Moral Climate?" *Out & About* 16 (May 2008) 5–6.

Rogers, Jack. *Jesus, the Bible, and Homosexuality: Explode the Myths, Heal the Church*. Louisville: Westminster John Knox, 2006.

Stanley, Christopher. "Words of Death: Scriptures and Violence in Judaism, Christianity and Islam." In *Validating Violence—Violating Faith? Religion, Scripture and Violence*, edited by William W. Emilsen and John T. Squires, 17–38. Adelaide, SA: ATF, 2008.

———. "Words of Life: Scriptures and Non-Violence in Judaism, Christianity and Islam." In *Validating Violence—Violating Faith? Religion, Scripture and Violence*, edited by William W. Emilsen and John T. Squires, 39–56. Adelaide, SA: ATF, 2008.

Tahaafe-Williams, Katalina. "A Vision for Communitas." *Out & About* 16 (Sept. 2008) 4–7.

Templeton Religious Trust. "Areas of Focus." https://templetonreligiontrust.org/areas-of-focus/.

United Theological College. "Latest Information." https://www.utc.edu.au/news-events/.

———. "120 Years Australian Mission in Korea." *Out & About* 20 (Nov. 2009) 15.

———. "Rev Prof Sathi Clarke." https://www.utc.edu.au/people/rev-prof-sathi-clarke/.

Uniting Church in Australia. "A Revival and Redesign of the Covenant." July 13, 2024. https://uniting.church/congress-proposals/.

Charles Sturt University. "Teaching and Research Staff." Centre for Islamic Studies and Civilization. https://arts-ed.csu.edu.au/centres/cisac/staff/profiles/teaching-and-research-staff/derya-iner.

Walker, Peter. "Ernst Conradie Delivers May Macleod Lecture." *Insights*, Oct. 2023. https://www.insights.uca.org.au/ernst-conradie-delivers-may-macleod-lecture/.

Wilson, Ronald. "The Healing of a Nation." *Uniting Church Studies* 6.2 (2000) 1–19.

Zachman, Randall C. "'Astronomy is the Alphabet of Theology': Calvin and the Natural Sciences." *Uniting Church Studies* 17.1 (2011) 23–32.

Zhang, Ji. "Christology of the Preamble: An Antidote to Neoliberalism." *Uniting Church Studies* 22.1 (2019) 61–73.

10

With Heart and Mind
Research and Publications at UTC

JOHN T. SQUIRES

AN ANCIENT SCRIBE, WRITING an account of events in his society in a time long before his life, reports the instruction that King David spoke to his chosen successor, his son, Solomon: "Set your mind and heart to seek the Lord your God" (1 Chr 22:19 NRSV[1]). He reinforces that in a later address, telling Solomon to "know God . . . and serve [the Lord] with single mind and willing heart" (1 Chr 28:9). The book of Proverbs (attributed by tradition to Solomon) then advocates both attending to the mind (Prov 22:17; 23:12, 19) and "inclining your heart" towards God (Prov 2:2; 3:1–6; 4:4, 20–23; 6:21; 7:3) as integral parts of the life of faith.

The injunction of David is echoed in the way that Jesus extends the traditional commandment to "love the Lord your God with all your heart and with all your soul and with all your might" (Deut 6:5), adding "and with all your mind" (Mark 12:30). Setting mind and heart, together, to love God and serve the people of God has been integral to United Theological College (UTC) throughout its fifty years. This chapter explores that conjunction through the research undertaken and publications produced within UTC since 1999.

---

1. Scripture quotations in this chapter are all from the NRSV.

A clear commitment to academic rigor had been integral to United Theological College from its very beginning. The inaugural teaching faculty (Barnes, Dicker, Loy, Maddox, Peterson) was comprised of ordained ministers with pastoral experience who each had earned a PhD in their field, from highly reputable American universities. The blend of pastoral experience and academic qualifications was a mix that continued to be important for subsequent appointments. This signaled an intention to ensure that academic insights were relevant to pastoral ministry in the church.

In the following years, additions to the faculty almost all had similar experience and qualifications, with universities from the United Kingdom soon represented (Ferguson, Carley, Hughes). It would be some years before members of faculty were appointed holding doctoral qualifications from Australian universities (the first being the joint appointment of Susan and William Emilsen). Nevertheless, the commitment to developing a theology and practice of ministry that was strongly contextualized for Australian society remained strong—the early work of Loy and Dicker was subsequently developed and expanded by the Emilsens, Pearson, Havea, Mawson, and now Carroll.

From the beginning, the UTC Council put in place elements which would allow for the gradual development of the academic resources of the college, alongside the important ministry formation processes. UTC faculty were eligible to take a regular sabbatical leave, to step out of their routine teaching, formation, and administrative responsibilities for a period of research and writing. Support could include assistance with travel costs, allowing research to take place in overseas locations—an important consideration in earlier days, when international travel was more expensive and less commonplace and before the internet allowed for far more regular international connections.

Such periods of leave have resulted in a steady, and growing, stream of publications from faculty members, which has built the research culture of the college over time.[2] Publications by faculty members have ranged across the traditional academic forms—journal articles, chapters in books, and monographs—as well as in writing oriented more specifically to the life of the church—in church magazines, newspapers, and blogs.

Initially, faculty publications were displayed in a modest display board outside the Faculty Common Room. Later, a much larger showcase was placed in the atrium of the Centre for Ministry. It was a strong public statement about the importance of "the life of the mind" in theological education.

---

2. In 2000, Geoffrey Barnes wrote, "UTC Faculty has tried to maintain the relevance of scholarship to the church's mission." Barnes, *Doing Theology*, 58.

The prolific research output of UTC faculty members will be explored in detail later in this chapter.

Alongside these periods of leave, regular faculty colloquia were held during term time, for members of faculty to share their current research by presenting a short paper and then receiving feedback from colleagues about the ideas presented. These gatherings were intended to build cohesion amongst faculty and expose specialists in one field to current thinking in another field; and they held faculty members to account for their intellectual life. Adjunct faculty and ministry colleagues from nearby pastoral placements would also be invited to these gatherings on occasion; some colloquia featured scholars visiting from afar, presenting their work for discussion. At the start of each academic year, in conjunction with the opening service of the college, an inaugural lecture was presented by a member of faculty on a rotational basis.

UTC set up its own organizational infrastructure to support and encourage a strong educational and research culture. A Board for Studies (later Committee for Studies) oversaw all the internal academic arrangements relating to all students at the college. This ran in parallel to the original Board for Ministerial Formation (also later a committee) which had oversight of candidates for ministry who were in formation under the faculty.

In the Sydney College of Divinity (SCD), UTC always had a representative on the Academic Standards Committee, which scrutinized the proposals for teaching subject units in all the member institutes of the SCD. The academic credibility and educational experience of UTC members was always valued in that context, especially as newly introduced member institutes often had a rather uncritical "bible college" feel about their proposals.

A key transition in the life of UTC took place from the last years of the 1990s into the next decade, culminating in the admission of UTC as a full member of the School of Theology in the Faculty of Arts of Charles Sturt University in 2007. In preparation for this transition, members of faculty prepared short papers on "academic excellence" and shared them in discussion with colleagues. What emerged was a clear resolution to move from the Sydney College of Divinity, the initial tertiary authorizing body for UTC diplomas and degrees, into a fully accredited university.

The first step in this transition was recognition of UTC faculty as accredited supervisors of MTh(Hons) and PhD students. Beginning in the late 1990s, this aspect of the college grew exponentially over the ensuing decade, with benefits in a number of key areas. First, the church benefitted as students researched issues which could enhance biblical literacy, theological understanding, and pastoral ministry within the church. Regular Research Seminars for such students mirrored the faculty colloquia already noted;

research students were expected to attend and engage with the presentations of fellow students from across the theological disciplines.

Second, the college benefitted financially, as doctoral supervision attracted government funding—and as published research was assessed in terms of "research points," which also garnered financial support from the Commonwealth Government. The financial viability of the college would come to depend more and more on this stream of income—as has been the case in all the theological colleges across Australia which are embedded in the tertiary system.

Third, the university connection allowed for work to be undertaken with ISRA (Islamic Science and Research Academy), a Muslim organization offering educational courses in Islam. UTC faculty members took the lead in the early years as the educational arm of the organization was fostered through Charles Sturt University (CSU). This led to the development of a bachelor of Islamic studies under the energetic leadership of Associate Professor Mehmet Ozalp, who has been a regular participant in seminars at UTC and within the CSU School of Theology. A regular program of "scriptural reasoning" seminars with Muslim students has been a significant development.

Finally, CSU was able to broker a connection between UTC and Hannam University in Korea, enabling Korean-speaking students in Australia to pursue graduate studies in Korean while a resident in Australia. The burgeoning collection of Korean-language theological works in Camden Theological Library attest to the vigor of this initiative.

In terms of administration, on becoming a member of the CSU School of Theology, UTC faculty contributed as full members both to the school board and to the Academic Board of the Faculty of Arts, and then to the various reinventions of those bodies in the changes that ensued in subsequent years. A highly significant element in the CSU connection was the Public and Contextual Theology (PACT) Research Group, one of the flagship research groups within the university. This was both an intellectual and a financial stimulus to research strategies and publication possibilities.

UTC faculty participated in PACT seminars, contributed to PACT publications, and played essential roles in the administrative management of the research group. A number of international scholars took part, along with CSU faculty members, in such seminars; members of the UTC faculty and specific postgraduate students were both able to engage in person with such visitors and also were able to have their research critiqued by scholars of international standing. Already in 2008, Professor Tom Frame, head of the School of Theology, had claimed that "the university has become a premier venue for theological learning and research in Australia."[3] What emerged in the following fifteen years has indicated that although this claim may have been somewhat premature, nevertheless UTC faculty have played key roles in the development of theological research within CSU.

Susan and William Emilsen had worked hard to establish both a creditable journal, *Uniting Church Studies*, and an in-house publications venture, *UTC Publications*. The fully-refereed, multidisciplinary journal launched in 1995 provided an avenue for members of faculty and others across the Uniting Church to publish their research. The journal is continuing with strength as an avenue for research relating especially to uniting and united churches. The first volume produced by *UTC Publications* was the Bible studies presented by Vicky Balabanski at the 1997 Assembly;[4] however, after some years, this publishing venture has found it difficult to maintain the sales required to sustain it.

The intellectual life of the church as a whole has also been fostered through scholarship funding provided by a scholarship fund set up by *With Love to the World* (WLW), a joint enterprise of the Strathfield-Homebush Parish and UTC. Since its founding, the income received from subscribers of this unique daily Bible study resource has been carefully stewarded, such that the committee began awarding scholarships from 1982. Scholarship recipients who later were appointed as faculty members have included Howard Wallace, John Squires, Susan Emilsen, William Emilsen, Jione Havea, Ian Robinson, Peter Walker, Seforosa Carroll, and Rebecca Lindsay.

Another group of WLW scholarship recipients served at the college as "visiting lecturers"; the impressive list includes Robert McFarlane, John Hoskin, Elizabeth Raine, Malcolm Coombs, David Reichardt, Katherine Grocott, Myong Duk Yang, Ki Soo Jang, and Helen Richmond. Some of these individuals have taught multiple subjects over an extended period of years, making substantial contributions to the teaching offered at UTC. Alongside these people are scholarship holders whose ministry has been exercised in other places.[5] Four scholarship recipients later served as principals of UCA (Uniting Church of Australia) theological colleges—Victoria Balabanski in South Australia, Geoff Thompson in Queensland, John Squires in Western Australia, and Peter Walker in New South Wales (NSW) and the ACT (Australian Capital Territory)—while a fifth scholarship recipient, Xavier Lakshmanan, is serving as principal of the Australian College of Christian

---

3. See Charles Sturt University, "Theology Students."

4. Balabanski, *Lose the Way*.

5. In other UCA synods: Peter Trudinger, Anna Grant-Henderson, Julia Pitman, Sarah Agnew; in other denominations: Peter Ralphs, Andrew Curtis, Craig de Vos, Lindsay Carey; in overseas university positions: Andrew Irvine and Wesley Wildman.

Studies in Burwood, NSW. The contribution to the intellectual life of the church has been wide and deep.

Integral to the role of theological colleges in the twenty-first century has been the development of a strong "research culture," encouraging quality thinking about life, faith, and discipleship in the Australian context. Supervising doctoral students in their research has become a key component within the overall program of the college; UTC has seen a strong development in this area over the decades.[6]

Adjunct to the college program, the option of a doctor of ministry (DMin) professional degree, including research relating to an aspect of practical ministry, had been introduced to UTC through a partnership with the San Francisco Theological Seminary. This degree gave ministers in placement a pathway to engage in wider reading and deeper thinking about an area of ministry that held particular interest to them, and to write a dissertation that, it was hoped, would better inform and equip others in their own practice of ministry.

A DMin was also available within the CSU School of Theology, and although there was a move to strengthen this degree with a more rigorously academic research component, this degree is now no longer offered by CSU. Nevertheless, over a number of decades, Uniting Church ministers have found this to be a pathway to enrich their ministry practice in practical ways.

In endeavoring to serve "with heart and mind," UTC faculty have sought to serve the church at every point, with a culture that values research and encourages publications. Indeed, the academic rigor of UTC has been first and foremost intended for the life of the church, knitting heart and mind together in that enterprise. Theological education is a discipline that requires immersion in a number of subject areas, with a view to generating an appreciation for the Christian tradition, sharpening skills in a range of methods of understanding and interpretation, and developing abilities in listening and encouraging, as well as speaking and inspiring. In short, it is a multipronged enterprise across a range of subject areas, thus requiring those who teach to have expertise in their specialized areas.

With that in mind, the research activities of those bearing the responsibility to teach in theological education are significant; they provide the stimulus and capacity to convey knowledge about their specialization, as well as the empathy to offer appropriate encouragement along the way. The research undertaken by members of the UTC faculty is thus the

---

6. All the CSU PhD dissertations referred to in this chapter can be accessed online through the Illuminate program of the Camden Theological Library; see https://illuminate.recollect.net.au.

fundamental platform upon which their teaching rests; the academic rigor of their research activities blends both heart and mind so that those they teach might serve church and community effectively and faithfully.

THEOLOGICAL STUDIES

A "thorough grounding in theological and biblical disciplines" (as the UTC website puts it)[7] has been conveyed by teachers who themselves have continued to explore those fundamental disciplines in their research. Just after concluding his term on faculty (2009–2017) Ben Myers published his study of *The Apostles' Creed*.[8] The material had been developed through his UTC teaching and was presented in a nine-part sermon series at Leichhardt Uniting Church, Sydney, during 2013. The videos of this sermon series are available on YouTube, a relatively recent platform for the "publication" (or, making public) of one's academic work.[9] These videos are as much a resource for the church as the published book.

Understanding this creed is a matter of central importance in theology and, indeed, in worship. My own experience of inviting Myers to a rural presbytery to lead sessions about the creed in a regular in-service training was that his insights were wonderfully inspiring and energizing for the lay leaders who were part of that week. He brought a fine combination of scholarship and spirituality to his teaching. The skills of the lay people in theology, preaching, spirituality, and pastoral care were all nurtured through this experience.

During his time on the UTC faculty, Myers continued his practice of regular blogging—another relatively recent development in making public the fruits of academic research. While his blog *Faith and Theology* is now dormant,[10] in its heyday it was reaching thousands of readers on a regular basis. He reflected theologically on this activity in "Theology 2.0: Blogging as the Theological Discourse."[11] Alongside this, Myers published *Christ the Stranger* in 2012 and *Salvation in My Pocket* in 2013, as well as a number of journal articles on the *Basis of Union*, Calvin's political theology, marriage,

7. United Theological College, "Place for You."
8. Myers, *Apostles' Creed*.
9. Myers, "Apostles' Creed."
10. For reference, see https://www.faith-theology.com. A post on August 29, 2018 announced, "Fourteen years and 2600 posts later, this blog is now closed." Myers, "Faith and Theology." There was a brief revival of the blog by Matt Wilcoxen in 2019, posting some of his doctoral research, but nothing since September 23, 2019.
11. Myers, "Theology 2.0."

atonement, Bonhoeffer and community, Karl Barth, Rowan Williams, T. F. Torrance, Milton (the topic of his own 2005 PhD dissertation), and Augustine.[12]

Myers attracted a good number of doctoral students who produced dissertations on various theological matters. He remembers this period of time as "something special—we attracted some really impressive doctoral students from all kinds of ecclesial, theological, and cultural backgrounds, in a way that wouldn't normally be possible in a denominational seminary."[13] Myers ran a theology discussion group for PhD students, remembering that "there was a youthful buzz somehow around systematic theology, especially in relation to classic Christian texts."[14] The list of PhD students whose dissertations he supervised cover a range of theological topics: transcendence, ontology, the episcopacy, feminist theology, themself, ecumenism, and the doctrine of faith.[15] Myers notes that the work of Damian Palmer, now a visiting lecturer at UTC, on "Negotiating the Historic Episcopate," was a highlight, "a groundbreaking contribution to its field."[16]

Dean Drayton (1999–2010) offered his explorations in theology in a way that was accessible and clear in *Which Gospel?*;[17] his later work, *Apocalyptic Good News*, has drawn on his earlier professional work as a geophysicist and his first book, *Pilgrim in the Cosmos*, to explore matters of faith and spirituality in the contemporary context.[18] What appears in these works well reflects the teaching that Drayton provided during his decade as a faculty member. Articles published during Drayton's time on the faculty addressed "the greening of evangelism,"[19] public theology, and the Protestant mission in Korea. Drayton supervised two PhD dissertations on theology[20] and

12. Myers, *Christ the Stranger*; Myers, *Salvation in My Pocket*.
13. Myers, email message to author, Aug. 10, 2024.
14. Myers, email message to author, Aug. 10, 2024.
15. Myers supervised PhD dissertations by Thomas Philip, "Exegeting the World"; Stephen Wright, "Creator Sings"; Janice Rees, "Difference, Doctrine and Discourse"; Ryan Green, "Kenosis and Ascent"; Jae In Yu, "Doctrine of Faith"; Matthew Wilcoxen, "Morally Perfect Being Theology"; Brian McKinlay, "Rowan Williams' Theory"; Grahame Rosolen, "Theological Geometry and Its Application to Classic Christology"; and Xavier Lakshmanan, "Narrative and Ontology," subsequently published as *Textual Linguistic Theology*. He was co-supervisor with William Emilsen of Damian Palmer, "Negotiating the Historic Episcopate."
16. Myers, email message to author, Aug. 10, 2024.
17. Drayton, *Which Gospel?*
18. Drayton, *Apocalyptic Good News*; Drayton, *Pilgrim in the Cosmos*.
19. Drayton, "Greening of Evangelism."
20. Eun Soo Kim, "From the Denominational Church"; Katharine Grocott, "Theological Critique."

co-supervised (with Pearson) the dissertation of David Reichardt, subsequently published as *Release the River!*,[21] as well as three PhD dissertations on ecotheology[22] and a DMin dissertation.[23]

During his time at UTC, Drayton served a three-year term as the national president of the Uniting Church, during which he continued half-time as a member of faculty. Two significant addresses that he gave in relation to this position—in 2003, on his installation, and then in 2006 at the conclusion of his term—are published, along with articles by other faculty members and colleagues from the wider church, in *Witness the Glory of God*.[24] Drayton's presidency was marked by the ongoing controversy and conflict relating to a decision by the Assembly at which he presided, relating to sexuality and leadership.[25]

Peter Walker, appointed as principal in 2019, also teaches theology. He completed his own PhD dissertation on Nicholas of Cusa in 2020 and, in the ensuing years, has published a small number of articles on topics such as sin and the Anthropocene, Gandhi, spirituality in theological education, and "Public Theology and the Modern Democratic State."[26] He has coedited with Jonathan Cole *Theology on a Defiant Earth* and is currently preparing a book on religious diversity, *Enfolded and Unfolding*.[27]

Recent appointments in theology also include Ockert Meyer (2020 onwards), who has taught preaching as well as theology and whose seven published articles during that time all relate to preaching, and Sathianathan Clarke (2024 onwards), whose publications prior to his appointment have addressed contextual theology, constructive global theology, and the theology of religions.

BIBLICAL STUDIES

The publications of Anthony Rees (from 2015 onwards), according to his UTC website, are marked by "diversity in relation to both content and

21. Reichardt, "Release the River!," published as *Release the River!*
22. Matagi Vilitama, "Singing the Niuean '*Fetuiaga Kerisiano*'"; Christopher Dalton, "Mining Coal Seam Gas"; and Thomas Emeleus, "Divine and Human Creativity."
23. Hawea Jackson, "Niuean Cultural Values."
24. Walker, *Witness the Glory*.
25. His own reflections on his term as president are in Drayton, "Assembly's Tenth Triennium."
26. Walker, "Vision of God" (under the supervision of Stephen Pickard and Scott Cowdell); Walker, "Public Theology."
27. Walker and Cole, *Theology*; Walker, *Enfolded and Unfolding*.

methodology, in each case aiming to be historically informed, theoretically infused and contextually relevant."[28] This varied approach is evident in his three monographs, utilizing "a mosaic reading," an ecological reading, and more recently "the theory of hegemonic masculinity and homosociality."[29] The UTC website for Rees notes that "these concerns also inform his teaching across the range of degrees offered at UTC."[30] He has published a good collection of articles on various Hebrew Bible matters and supervised two completed PhD dissertations.[31]

In New Testament, John Squires (1990–2010) continued his earlier doctoral work on Luke-Acts, producing a full commentary on the Acts of the Apostles, published in the *Eerdmans Commentary on the Bible*, and an introduction to the Gospel of Luke in the *Cambridge Companion to the Gospels*.[32] He offered detailed exegesis of texts with a strong awareness of their historical, cultural, and literary contexts, a characteristic which marked his teaching and is conveyed in some of his articles.[33] Squires had supervised a number of postgraduate students when UTC belonged to the SCD; in CSU, he worked with three PhD graduates.[34]

Squires collaborated with his wife, Elizabeth Raine, who taught as a visiting lecturer at UTC for over a decade, to develop a series of "Biblical Culture Days," which were presented at the college, at synod meetings, and at a number of churches around Sydney and in rural areas over the course of a number of years from 1998 onwards. These days were designed as offering a "cultural immersion" into the period of time when ancient Israelite festivals were being celebrated, or in churches which had received a letter from Paul. After teaching at the college for over two decades, Squires accepted a call to ministry in church placements, where he has continued an educational ministry in conjunction with Raine, teaching lay leaders training

28. United Theological College, "Assoc. Prof."
29. Rees, *[Re]Reading Again*; Rees, *Voices of the Wilderness*; Rees, *Moses*.
30. United Theological College, "Assoc. Prof."
31. Yung Hun Choi, "Movement Pattern," published as *Patterns of Movement*; and John Brunton, "Theology in Planning" (co-supervised with Myers), a dissertation which explores how "interdisciplinary research in the field of public theology brings a different perspective to the theory and practice of urban and regional planning." Brunton, "Theology in Planning," abstract. (For more on public theology, see the corresponding section further on.)
32. Squires, *Plan of God*; Squires, "Acts"; Squires, "Luke."
33. Squires, "Singing"; Squires, "Interpreting Galatians."
34. Malcolm Coombes, "Literary Relationship," subsequently published as *1 John*; Matthew Wilson "Place of the 'Religious Outsider'"; Karl Hand, "Proto-Luke." All three have taught as visiting lecturers at UTC.

courses. He continues to offer biblical scholarship in an accessible form for lay people in his blog, *An Informed Faith*.[35]

Squires's successor, Jeffrey Aernie (2011–2022) produced two substantial treatments of biblical material: *Is Paul Also Among the Prophets?* and *Narrative Discipleship*.[36] His published articles covered 2 Corinthians and a number relating to Mark;[37] Aernie was also co-supervisor of a PhD dissertation.[38] In more recent years, Ali Robinson (from 2020 onwards) has written on ancient trust networks and associations[39] while Bec Lindsay (2024 onwards) is working, at the time of writing, on a series of articles relating to Ruth and termination of pregnancies.

PASTORAL THEOLOGY

The discipline of pastoral theology provides an important foundation for pastoral ministry; the emphasis has generally been more practical than academic, so this area is represented only sparsely in this chapter. While teaching in this area at UTC, Douglas Purnell (1996–2004) published *Conversation as Ministry* and subsequently *Being in Ministry*, reflecting the methods and ideals that he communicated in his teaching.[40] Amongst the articles published by Purnell was "Why We Do What We Do When We Teach Pastoral Theology at United Theological College (UTC) Sydney."[41]

Also responsible for teaching pastoral theology was Kenneth Brown (2007–2008) and Rhonda White (2000–2006, 2015 onwards) while Christine Gapes (1996–2004) taught youth ministry subjects. Both White and Gapes had responsibility also for field education; White had an article published on the "Integration Journal" that she developed for use in the formation program, while Gapes published a number of articles on youth ministry while at UTC. After the shootings at Port Arthur in 1996, Gapes found herself in a unique position to do grief research in two high schools in Tasmania, to which she then applied a theological lens.[42]

35. Squires, *Informed Faith*.
36. Aernie, *Is Paul*; Aernie, *Narrative Discipleship*.
37. Aernie, "Borderless Discipleship"; Aernie, "Cruciform Discipleship."
38. Matthew Anslow, "Prophetic Vocation" (co-supervisor with David Neville and Greg Jenks), later published, Anslow, *Fulfilling the Law*.
39. Robinson and Llewelyn, "Life in Roman Galilee," and Llewelyn and Robinson, "Life in Roman Egypt."
40. Purnell, *Conversation as Ministry*; Purnell, *Being in Ministry*.
41. Purnell, "Why We Do."
42. Gapes, "Severed Connections."

More recently, in a partnership with the Alan Walker College of Evangelism, Ian Robinson (2017–2022) was responsible for teaching mission, leadership, and evangelism, bringing his extensive work across the church and his practical publications on prayer, leadership, evangelism, and spirituality into his teaching.

LITURGICAL STUDIES

Leading worship is a fundamental of ministry in pastoral contexts, so a strong program of preparation in this area is vital. Graham Hughes (1977–2002) had initially been appointed to teach New Testament, but his focus shifted as he began to develop subjects in liturgical theology after a sabbatical devoted to that in the mid-1980s. Hughes ultimately produced a major contribution to liturgical studies in *Worship as Meaning*, utilizing semiotic theory to analyze the construction, transmission, and apprehension of meaning within an actual worship service.[43] The practical outworking of this approach had been evident in earlier decades in the subjects taught by Hughes, in his writings on "liturgical excellence," and in a locally circulated newsletter, "The Gifts of God," advocating for liturgical renewal within the Uniting Church.[44] On his retirement in 2002, Hughes was honored by a series of essays in *Prayer and Thanksgiving*, a volume coedited by his colleagues (and former students) Emilsen and Squires.[45]

Sarah Mitchell (1997–2006), although bearing the large administrative load of principal, found time to attend to matters of worship, a staple area of learning for ministry candidates. Mitchell published the provocatively named article "Together in Song: An Ecumenical Si(g)n?,"[46] noting that here she "brought together my theological thinking, my background in sociolinguistics and my love of music."[47] This offered a model for other researchers in terms of integrating different areas of interest and expertise. Mitchell published other articles on worship as well as theological education and ministry training.

Stephen Burns (2007–2012) and Anita Monro (2003–2009) both came to their appointments with strong liturgical credentials. They collaborated on a number of projects—one, relating to worship, provided a series of

---

43. Hughes, *Worship as Meaning*.

44. A significant article by Hughes, "Limping Priests," received later attention in an article by Stephen Burns, "'Limping Priests' Ten Years Later."

45. Emilsen and Squires, *Prayer and Thanksgiving*.

46. Mitchell, "Together in Song."

47. Mitchell, email message to author, Aug. 8, 2024.

essays exploring the distinctive flavours of worship, in *Christian Worship in Australia*.[48] Burns commented to me that "I was new to the country and noticing all kinds of things in worship that were different for me (mainly to do with massive differences in seasons and climate). I would never have been able to write about most things in this book, but loved that the chapters could be invited/commissioned."[49]

While at UTC, Burns published two works offering liturgical analysis;[50] he has since continued this line of research in his subsequent position at the University of Divinity with a prolific number of articles on worship, feminist theologies, baptism, daily prayer, liturgical gestures, "mission-shaped worship," worship in the public square, and most recently Anglican theology.[51] From his time at UTC, Burns nominates as his favorite an article on "Presiding Like a Woman," which became the basis for a collection of essays he edited with Nicola Slee.[52] While at UTC, Burns was co-supervisor for three PhD dissertations.[53]

While teaching at UTC, Anita Monro published *Resurrecting Erotic Transgression*, a feminist theological methodology based on the work of Julia Kristeva.[54] Feminist theology was not always to the liking of UTC students, nor indeed did it always sit well with the emerging focus on "public theology," which Monro and Burns subsequently critiqued in their *Public Theology and the Challenge of Feminism*; the articles in this book (including contributions by Carroll and Havea) argue that "public theology risks re-inscribing traditional constructs of public and private, civic and domestic, and uncritical notions of gender and the work and worth of people."[55] The book seeks to demonstrate "how constructive feminism can be for the future of public theology." (For more on public theology, see below.)

During and just after her time at UTC, Monro published articles on feminist theology and on liturgy, reflecting her research while at UTC.[56]

48. Monro and Burns, *Christian Worship*.
49. Burns, email message to author, Aug. 7, 2024.
50. Burns, *SCM Studyguide*; Burns, *Living the Thanksgiving*.
51. Burns, "Mission-Shaped Worship."
52. Burns, "'Presiding Like a Woman'"; Slee and Burns, *Presiding Like a Woman*.
53. Burns co-supervised with Pearson the PhD work of Sioeli F. Vaipulu, "Towards an '*Otua*logy'" with Pearson, Drayton, and Monro; Matagi Vilitama, "Singing the Niuean '*Fetuiaga Kerisiano*'"; and (with Robert Gribben and Stephen Reid) Christine Senini, "Munus Triplex Nauticus." (*Munus Triplex* is the threefold office of Christ as prophet, priest, and king.)
54. Monro, *Resurrecting Erotic Transgression*.
55. See publisher's blurb for Monro and Burns, *Public Theology*.
56. Monro, "Juxtaposing Dingo and Baby"; Monro, "'And Ain't I a Woman'"; and in

Monro was a member of the Worship Working Group of the Uniting Church and contributed significant work on "The Second Service of the Lord's Day," published in *Uniting in Worship 2*.[57] In addition, Monro co-supervised a candidate for the doctor of professional studies through Middlesex University.[58] With Havea, Monro co-presented the Inaugural Lecture in 2008 on "Mother and Son at the Foot of the Cross." With funds from UTC they commissioned the glass artwork in the chapel based on the John 19:25–27 text.[59]

Gerard Moore (2008–2019), teaching in liturgy and theology, published *Earth Unites with Heaven*,[60] an insightful work which shaped the guidance that was offered to students in his classes. A year later saw the appearance of another publication with immediate practical relevance, *The Disciples at the Lord's Table*.[61] Moore published a number of journal articles, which treat a range of topics relating to worship; he supervised the PhD dissertation of Cristina Lledo Gomez[62] and co-supervised a PhD dissertation[63] as well as a DMin dissertation.[64] Also under Moore's supervision was Dr. Ruth Sheridan, a PACT scholar who published on John's Gospel.[65] During his time at UTC, Moore served as the Chair of the Project Team for the national ecumenical Transforming Theology project.[66]

---

a cross-disciplinary collaboration, Monro, "Pursuing Feminist Research."

57. National Working Group on Worship, *Uniting in Worship 2*.

58. Drene Somasundram, "Gender Inclusive Model," which used aspects of Monro's PhD dissertation to build a Tri-Space Model based on "third-space" methodology. From the United Kingdom, Drene was working at Avondale College (NSW) at the time.

59. The artist is Peng Mo, an Asian-Australian glasswork artist who had previously exhibited in the Ranamok Glass Prize in 2007.

60. Moore, *Earth Unites with Heaven*.

61. Moore, *Disciples*.

62. Lledo Gomez, "Mother Church," later published, Lledo Gomez, *Church as Woman*.

63. Moore co-supervised with Stephen Burns the work of Eojin Lee, "Theology of the Open Table," a dissertation which explores "how, liturgically and practically, a theology of the open table might be embodied and enacted in actual worship [of the PCK] through examining the Uniting Church in Australia (UCA) practising an open table." Lee, "Theology of the Open Table," abstract.

64. Ki Soo Jang, "Korean Migrant Churches."

65. Sheridan, *Retelling Scripture*. Sheridan also published a number of related articles.

66. Published as *Transforming Theology: Student Experience and Transformative Learning in Undergraduate Theological Education*, edited by Les Ball.

CHURCH HISTORY

Susan and William Emilsen shared a joint appointment in church history from 1993 until Susan's death in 2003; William continued in this position until he retired in 2014. William Emilsen had begun with an intention to be "a historian for and of the Uniting Church," and ensure that material from the early time of the Uniting Church was documented and made widely available.[67] Susan and William gathered much significant Uniting Church material in their initial 1997 collection, *Marking Twenty Years*, followed in 2003 by *Mapping the Landscape*, which surveyed the broad scope of Australian and New Zealand Christianity.[68] *The Uniting Church in Australia: The First 25 Years* appeared in 2003, the year of Susan's death. William followed this up with *An Informed Faith* and, after retirement, with *Growing Up Uniting*.[69] Together, these five works offer a remarkable collection of articles by significant people within the Uniting Church and beyond; they are essential reading for anyone serious about understanding this unique church.

Susan and William Emilsen modeled exactly what they asked of their students in the core course required of all ministry candidates, Uniting Church Studies, in their documenting of the story of the O'Connor Congregation in Canberra, one of the most controversial—and important—congregations of the early years of the church, as well as Pitt Street in Sydney, a most historic congregation.[70] Anyone serious about understanding the context in which the church was born, and the ethos of the church that developed over the years, would do well to note this excellent model. (For more on William Emilsen's research and extensive publications, see below.)

PUBLIC THEOLOGY

One of the immediate benefits from the CSU connection was the establishment of the Public and Contextual Theology Research Group. PACT research seminars supported faculty research, while interest in the area among students led to a number of research students working towards an MTh (honors) or a PhD. In parallel to this development, two new master of arts degrees were introduced in the early 2000s, one focused on public

---

67. Emilsen, email message to author, Aug. 9, 2024.

68. Emilsen and Emilsen, *Marking Twenty Years*; Emilsen and Emilsen, *Mapping the Landscape*.

69. Emilsen, *First 25 Years*; Emilsen, *Informed Faith*; Emilsen and Watson, *Growing Up Uniting*.

70. Emilsen and Emilsen, *O'Connor*; Emilsen et al., *Pride of Place*.

theology, the other on contextual theology. Clive Pearson (1997–2011), along with Drayton and Emilsen, formed the driving force for the development of public theology offerings. Key planning sessions took place in the courtyard beside the faculty offices in North Parramatta. By the end of the first decade of the twenty-first century, a full range of subject units in this area were in place.[71]

A regular stream of articles with "public theology" in their title was published by members of PACT. Pearson sat on the editorial board of the *International Journal of Public Theology*, where many PACT articles appeared; he was editor-in-chief for seven years. Along with other faculty members, Pearson participated in the Global Network of Public Theology, which had been formed in 2007.[72] Public theology was a "natural" for Pearson; his Cambridge PhD dissertation had been on Henry Major, an "Anglican Modernist" in New Zealand.[73] Major (1871–1961) was a member of the Modern Churchmen's Union, which was active in advocating on various matters in society; a precursor, perhaps, to a "public theology"? In the following years, Pearson's publications reflect a clear emphasis on public theology.

Pearson had offered an initial article in this area in 2001 bringing together public theology and ecotheology;[74] Drayton contributed two initial articles[75] as well as subsequent articles,[76] while Emilsen contributed two early articles on indigenous matters in the public realm.[77] Pearson continued with a string of articles from 2007 onwards; more recently he has consolidated his work in this area with *Enacting a Public Theology*.[78] During the early years of development of this area, Pearson supervised two PhD students who produced dissertations exploring ecotheology, a significant area in public theology.[79] Pearson has since supervised or co-supervised another twenty doctoral students; a number of these dissertations, noted

---

71. Some years later, the two MA degrees were collapsed into a single MA in public and contextual theology.

72. https://www.gnpublictheology.net.

73. With Allan Davidson and Peter Lineman, Pearson coedited *Scholarship and Fierce Sincerity* to which he contributed four chapters.

74. Pearson, "On Being Public."

75. Drayton, "Public Theology"; Drayton, "Religion."

76. These articles by Drayton canvased Wesley at Aldersgate, evangelist Arthur Jackson, the Protestant Mission in Korea, and the theology of grace.

77. Emilsen, "On Being Very Visible"; Emilsen, "March for Justice."

78. Pearson, *Enacting a Public Theology*.

79. Barry Leal's 2005 SCD dissertation on the wilderness was the foundation for two subsequent books, *Wilderness in the Bible* and *Through Ecological Eyes*. David Reichardt's dissertation "Release the River!" was published under the same title.

below in the discussion of Contextual Theology and more extensively in the chapter on Pasifika in this volume, have also addressed ecological and other strands in public theology.

Pearson identifies some of the significant contributions that he has made in this area in more recent years as the introductory chapter in the 2017 anthology he edited, *Imagining a Way*[80] and an article on providence,[81] as well as articles on providence and climate change, cities and climate change, low-lying islands and climate change, and theology and the Anthropocene.[82] He has been a prolific contributor over the years.

CONTEXTUAL THEOLOGY (1)

Understanding the context is vital in preparing for, and offering, effective pastoral ministry; so, too, when "doing theology," due attention is to be given to the context in which it takes place. In fostering this element of the college's teaching, much faculty research undertaken across the years has attended to the fascinating dynamic of understanding and communicating the Christian tradition in the complex situation of the Australian context.

A commitment to contextual theology, as already noted, had been integral to the teaching of theology at UTC from the start; Loy and Dicker had co-taught subjects exploring "the Australian context" from the 1970s.[83] (I personally learned much from this opportunity to engage theologically with Australia's history and culture.) A more developed approach to contextualization was evident two decades later in the work of two key members of faculty who were appointed in the late 1990s.

In teaching theology, Clive Pearson pressed on his students the importance of engaging in a fully informed contextual learning, as Myers demonstrates in his chapter in this book. All of Pearson's students know what it means to identify "allies" and "aliens" in relation to their own theological understanding. Alongside Pearson, in his teaching of Hebrew Scripture, Jione Havea (2000–2015) brought his unique insider/outsider understanding of Pasifika culture to bear on exegesis and interpretation. The research of these two scholars informed and enriched the teaching that they undertook. Pearson, in his chapter in this book, has well documented the articulation of Pasifika theologies through the various doctoral students he supervised, as well as in the undergraduate classes he taught. The interactive dynamic

80. Pearson, *Imagining a Way*.
81. Pearson, "God's Continued Providence."
82. Personal communication.
83. Barnes, *Doing Theology*, 74.

of teacher and student together exploring, learning, and articulating could not be clearer.

In like fashion, Havea notes that the main inspiration for his research and publications comes from "Talanoa (conversations) with students around biblical texts and theological issues, during and after class sessions. We often disagree and debate, and in the process find more matters to reflect on and debate around."[84] He also derives inspiration from "talanoa with folx in public places, including with people in prison and in community functions, mostly around their struggles and disempowering societal realities"; and third, from academic literature and conferences.[85] The groundedness of his research in the realities of everyday life is evident in many ways.

The early research output of Pearson and Havea attests to the centrality of "contextual theology" at UTC. A 2004 collection, *Faith in a Hyphen*, set the theme.[86] Pearson edited the collection, Havea wrote a "sub-version" in place of a preface, and they each contributed a number of chapters. The book includes a chapter by Mitchell on "*Communitas* of Christ: Risking the Cross-Cultural Way," a theme which was prominent during her time as principal. The hyphen motif signals the intersection of two different cultures as a person in diaspora develops "the construction of hybrid identities in a new land."[87] Pearson further utilized this motif in two 2004 articles while the hyphen motif (working in the intersection of two cultures) plays a significant role in a number of the PhD dissertations which Pearson has supervised.[88]

For some years from 2007, Katalina Tahaafe-Williams served on faculty as the director of Communitas, the Contextual and Mission Programme. After a conference held in 2009, she coedited with visiting scholar Steven Bevans a volume which contained papers given at that conference, *Contextual Theology for the Twenty-First Century*.[89] Havea and Tahaafe-Williams contributed to the volume, as did visiting lecturer Chris Budden, writing on "The Necessity of a Second Peoples' Theology in Australia."

The preface explains that "Communitas enables the people of God to join God's missiological adventure of kingdom building in the world, by learning with gusto how to live and act together across the many different cultural backgrounds that are God's gift in creation"; the words are from

---

84. Havea, email message to author, Aug. 12, 2024.
85. Havea, email message to author, Aug. 7, 2024.
86. Pearson and Havea, *Faith in a Hyphen*.
87. Mitchell, "*Communitas* of Christ," publisher's blurb.
88. Pearson, "Telling Tales"; Pearson, "Encountering Christ."
89. Bevans and Tahaafe-Williams, *Contextual Theology*.

Mitchell's article, "*Communitas* of Christ," in *Faith in a Hyphen*.⁹⁰ The Communitas program did not last beyond the time that Tahaafe-Williams was in the role. However, Pearson and Havea continued the cross-cultural theme as they coedited *Out of Place*, while Burns and Pearson coedited another collection of cross-cultural essays in *Home and Away*.⁹¹

Pearson had come to Australia from Aotearoa–New Zealand, via studies in the United Kingdom. Another Pākehā Kiwi who likewise arrived in Sydney via studies in the United Kingdom, Michael Mawson (2019–2022), has reflected on the significance of entering the enriched intercultural environment that had been fostered at UTC for some years, noting how his earlier work on Bonhoeffer had been enriched and expanded (see the chapter by Myers).⁹² This signaled a rich engagement that has been fruitful for Mawson, as is evident in his book of essays on Bonhoeffer, *Standing Under the Cross*; his parallel interest in ethics is reflected in *The Ethics of Grace*.⁹³ Mawson began as supervisor for five PhD students, whose work is continuing (three under new supervisors).

CONTEXTUAL THEOLOGY (2)

Jione Havea's work is characterized by puns and playfulness in words used or reframed, as was evident early when his PhD was published as *Elusions of Control: Biblical Law on the Words of Women*. The blurb for the book also sets out the method Havea would refine and develop in future works; "inspired by the transoceanic experiences of South Pacific islanders, Havea explores the circularity of vow-making and vow-breaking," from Numbers 30 into other biblical narratives.⁹⁴

---

90. Bevans and Tahaafe-Williams, *Contextual Theology*, 9; Mitchell, "*Communitas* of Christ," 175–84.

91. Havea and Pearson, *Out of Place*; Burns and Pearson, *Home and Away*.

92. "In this new context, I began discovering and learning from some of the rich, concrete scholarship that was emerging in the region. . . . I soon read work by indigenous scholars Anne Pattel-Gray, Garry Deverell, Hirini Kaa and Naomi Wolfe, who highlighted the devastating effects of missionary Christianity on First Peoples, as well as ongoing problems being caused by imported forms of Western theology and education. Friends like Jione Havea and Brian Kolia introduced me to the dynamic, creative work being done by Pasifika scholars in the areas of hermeneutics and biblical studies. And students at the college pressed me to give greater attention to disruptive and marginal voices and positions (e.g., indigenous, Pasifika, Minjung, Dalit, womanist and queer theologies)." Mawson, *Standing Under the Cross*, 5–6.

93. Mawson, *Standing Under the Cross*; Mawson, *Ethics of Grace*.

94. Havea, *Elusions of Control*.

Havea produced some initial articles: "Boring Readers, Forgotten Readers," "Would the Real Native Please Sit Down!" and "Reading the Bible Across Cultures: The Bible in Multiple Cultures," this last in an important work edited by two PhD candidates and visiting lecturers at UTC, Helen Richmond and Myong Duk Yang, *Shaping Faith, Ministry and Identity in Multicultural Australia*.[95] There followed a string of contextually-oriented articles, some of which presaged the growing tide of anxiety and anger across Oceania regarding the rising tides of water threatening Islander life—a matter taken up with vigorous commitment by Uniting Church leaders in recent years. Havea has continued his relentless program of collaborative publications with Oceania/Pasifika as a focus into the present.

In 2010, Havea collaborated with Monica J. Melanchthon and Richard E. A. Rodgers to produce *Women in the Bible and in Theological Education*.[96] Within the space of just a few years, there followed collections which he edited, each with a clear cross-cultural orientation.[97] A particularly important volume that he edited was *Indigenous Australia and the Unfinished Business of Theology*. This collection included his own article "Forgive Us Our Trespasses," as well as an article by Chris Budden, "Migration and Rudd's Apology."[98] Budden, who has taught Christian Ethics at UTC for many years, as well as the CSU theology unit on indigenous issues, has been persistent over the years in asking the fundamental indigenous question for Second Peoples: How do we do theology on land that has been stolen from the First Peoples?

Budden's teaching at UTC and beyond has been nourished by his two books, *Following Jesus in Invaded Space* and *Why Indigenous Sovereignty Should Matter to Christians*, as well as a number of journal articles on sovereignty, public theology, and acknowledgement of country.[99] In this regard, also, the biography of Charles Harris by Emilsen should be noted, as well as some of his work published in articles relating to indigenous history.[100] Havea has continued his focus on indigenous matters with "Postcolonize

---

95. Richmond and Yang, *Shaping Faith*.

96. Melanchthon and Havea, *Women in the Bible*.

97. Havea, *Talanoa Ripples*; *Out of Place* (with Pearson; see above); *Colonial Contexts* (with Mark G. Brett); *Indigenous Australia* (2014); *Bible, Borders, Belonging(s)* (with David Neville and Elaine Wainwright); *Reading Ruth* (with Peter H. W. Lau); and *Islands, Islanders* (with Steed Vernyl Davidson and Margaret Aymer).

98. Havea, "Forgive Us"; Budden, "Migration."

99. Budden, *Following Jesus*; Budden, *Why Indigenous Sovereignty*.

100. Emilsen, *Charles Harris*. See also Emilsen, *Goldfields Journal*.

Now," the opening article in a 2017 volume he edited, *Postcolonial Voices from Downunder*.[101]

In terms of PhD supervision, Havea has covered an astonishingly wide range of topics. He commented to me that "the range of topics that came my way included: Feminist Pentecostal hermeneutics, mosaic reading, religious outsiders and postcolonial criticism, pastoral-liturgical identity, feminist diasporic and pasifika theologies, public theologies, remigrant theology, Australian-Samoan reading, Tongan 'otuaology, ecological justice, suffering God, jeoung reading, occupied Korea, solesolevaki reading, Pasifika feminist criticism, and Moana criticism."[102]

WORLD RELIGIONS

The multicultural and multifaith nature of Australian society has been another influence on the development of contextual theology at UTC. For many years William Emilsen taught a subject on world religions, drawing initially from his own doctoral study of Mahatma Gandhi and his impact on missions and missionaries in India. "Gandhi was my entry point into understanding other religions," Emilsen told me; "his understanding of truth and non-violence being at the core of religion is important to me."[103]

Emilsen's study of Gandhi's life and thought is evident in a number of his publications.[104] His doctoral supervision included a number of interfaith dissertations. Helen Richmond's dissertation exploring Christian-Muslim marriages was revised and published under the title *Blessed and Called to Be a Blessing*.[105] A connection with ISRA led to Emilsen supervising a

---

101. Havea, "Postcolonize Now."

102. Havea, email message to author, Aug. 12, 2024. Havea co-supervised with Squires the 1996 CSU dissertation by Jacqueline Grey on Pentecostal hermeneutics, later published as *Three's a Crowd*, and was co-supervisor with Squires for Matthew Wilson's 2012 dissertation (see above) and with Pearson, Burns, and/or Monro for multiple PhD dissertations. Havea supervised the dissertation of Anthony Rees, "*[Re] Reading Again*"; Rees, of course, succeeded Havea as the Hebrew Bible lecturer at UTC in 2015.

103. Emilsen, conversation with the author, Aug. 9, 2024.

104. Emilsen, "Gandhi"; his book *Violence and Atonement*; a chapter on Gandhi and violence in *Validating Violence—Violating Faith?*; *Gandhi's Bible*, a book on Gandhi's interpretation of the Bible; a chapter on Gandhi as leader in *Great Spiritual Leaders*; and most recently, a reflection on terrorism in the book *Gandhi's Truths in an Age of Fundamentalism and Nationalism*.

105. Richmond, "Living Together" (co-supervised with Drayton and Robert McFarlane).

number of Muslim women.¹⁰⁶ He had also earlier supervised Manas Ghosh in a DMin dissertation on Rabindranath Tagore and Interfaith Dialogue (2011). Ghosh subsequently received an award of "Community Fellow" from Western Sydney University, recognizing his "contribution to social justice, peace and communal harmony in Western Sydney" at the time of a fatal terrorist incident in 2015.¹⁰⁷ Emilsen also drew together speakers from across religious traditions for seminars on the topics of violence in religion and violence against women and children. The papers for the former seminar, sponsored by PACT, were published in a volume coedited with Squires, *Validating Violence—Violating Faith?*¹⁰⁸

Responding to another dimension of the multifaith nature of Australian society through his involvement in the UCA national dialogue with the Jewish community over many years, Squires published a study of the public stances of churches towards Judaism and the Jewish people since the Vatican II statement, *Nostra aetate* (1965).¹⁰⁹ In his teaching from the early 1990s onwards, Squires had arranged regular lectures from Rabbi Jeffrey Kamins on "Jesus the Jew." In subsequent decades, the regular presence of faith leaders from other religious traditions became a staple part of the course for ministry candidates.

Seforosa Carroll (2023 onwards) continues responsibility for this element in today's college teaching. In her doctoral dissertation, Carroll had advocated that "the practice of interfaith encounters in this country requires more intentional theological work to be done within the Christian faith itself";¹¹⁰ this work is being carried through in her classes at UTC. Her emphasis is that there is a strong case for "welcoming those of a different faith to practice their faith in this country on the basis of the oikonomia, economy of God."¹¹¹ Most recently, Carroll has coedited volumes on climate change, the Pacific region, and "the Capitalocene," as well as articles on "Coconut Theology," experiences of racializing, and "Jesus Through Pacific Eyes."¹¹²

---

106. Rawaa Gebara's dissertation, "Ijtihad" was published as *Ijtihad*. Emilsen supervised Nada Roude, who had a role in advising State and Federal Governments and police on how best to relate to the Muslim community; Roude wrote on "Muslim Leaders' Perspectives."

107. Emilsen, email message to author, Aug. 9, 2024.

108. Emilsen and Squires, *Validating Violence*.

109. Squires, "Christians Relating to Jews."

110. Carroll, "Making Room," abstract.

111. Carroll, email message to author, Aug. 23, 2024.

112. Shibata et al., *Climate Change*; Martinez Andrade and Carroll, *Facing Climate Collapse*.

Emilsen and Carroll had previously collaborated to draw together essays for a book on "great spiritual leaders"; the book includes essays by Squires, Aernie, Myers, Emilsen, and Carroll.[113] Earlier, Emilsen edited a collection of essays by faculty members under the simple title, *I Believe in God*.[114] The book includes chapters by Pearson, Myers, Havea, Moore, and Hughes. And so we come full circle, back to theological studies!

CONCLUSION

This outline of research undertaken and publications produced by UTC faculty over the past twenty-five years sits within a book that is entitled *Things That Matter*. There would be no doubt that some would argue that these matters are not to be numbered amongst the "things that matter" for the church as a whole. What matters in a church institution dedicated to theology, they might say, is surely teaching subjects that sharpen the minds of students at the college to equip them for deeper thinking about matters of faith. What matters in an institution focused on forming candidates for ministry within the Uniting Church, they could suggest, is surely providing reflective experiences that are transformative for those candidates, strengthening their hearts in order that they might meet the challenges of ministry in the years ahead.

Also noted are the number of the research dissertations that have been completed under the supervision of UTC faculty. Many of those who wrote PhD and DMin dissertations went on to contribute to the church in significant educational and resourcing roles. CSU doctoral graduates from UTC have taught at Uniting Church theological colleges in Sydney and Brisbane, in a number of theological colleges of UCA partner churches in Oceania and in positions in the United Kingdom, and in ministry leadership roles in the Uniting Church and other denominations. The research culture developed at UTC has been a gift to the wider church.

The proposition that undergirds this chapter is that sharpening the life of the mind and strengthening the capacity of the heart are each integral to what has been canvased in terms of research and publications. Both of these are "things that matter." Agility in teaching theology requires persistence in reading and questioning, formulating hypotheses and developing arguments, to sharpen the mind of the teacher themselves. So the question for the reader is, has the research identified in this chapter met this brief? Sensitivity in forming candidates and encouraging more effective reflective

---

113. Carroll and Emilsen, *Great Spiritual Leaders*.
114. Emilsen, *I Believe in God*.

practitioners likewise requires exploration of ideas and deepening of practices to strengthen the heart of the teacher themselves. Have the publications that have been documented in this chapter demonstrated that this has indeed been taking place?

Depth in research and breadth in publications across the faculty is one measure of a faithful and effective institution—one measure amongst a number. Nurturing the heart and the mind alike are each things that matter. Through the research and publications of UTC faculty, there is surely some part achieved of the things that matter for this institution.

BIBLIOGRAPHY

Aernie, Jeffrey. "Borderless Discipleship: The Syrophoenician Woman as a Christ-Follower in Mark 7:24–30." In *Bible, Borders, Belonging(s): Engaging Readings from Oceania*, edited by Jione Havea et al., 191–207. Atlanta: SBL, 2014.

———. "Cruciform Discipleship: The Narrative Function of the Women in Mark 15–16." *Journal of Biblical Literature* 135.4 (2016) 779–97.

———. *Is Paul Also Among the Prophets? An Examination of the Relationship Between Paul and the Old Testament Prophetic Tradition in 2 Corinthians*. New York: T&T Clark, 2012.

———. *Narrative Discipleship: Portraits of Women in the Gospel of Mark*. Eugene, OR: Pickwick, 2018.

Amosa, Faala Faamatuainu. "Courting a Public Theology of *Fa'a-vae* for the Church and Contemporary Samoa." PhD diss., Charles Sturt University, 2020.

Anslow, Matthew. *Fulfilling the Law and the Prophets: The Prophetic Vocation of Jesus in the Gospel of Matthew*. Eugene, OR: Pickwick, 2022.

———. "The Prophetic Vocation of Jesus in the Gospel of Matthew: A Narrative and Socio-Historical Study." PhD diss., Charles Sturt University, 2017.

Balabanski, Vicky. *"That We May Not Lose the Way": Bible Studies of the 8th Assembly of the Uniting Church in Australia, Perth, July 1997*. North Parramatta, NSW: United Theological College, 1997.

Ball, Les, ed. *Transforming Theology: Student Experience and Transformative Learning in Undergraduate Theological Experience*. Preston, VIC: Mosaic, 2012.

Barnes, Geoffrey. *Doing Theology in Sydney: A History of United Theological College, 1974–1999*. Adelaide, SA: Openbook, 2000.

Bevans, Stephen B., and Katalina Tahaafe-Williams, eds. *Contextual Theology for the Twenty-First Century*. Eugene, OR: Pickwick, 2011.

Brett, Mark G., and Jione Havea, eds. *Colonial Contexts and Postcolonial Theologies: Storyweaving in the Asia-Pacific*. New York: Palgrave Macmillan, 2014.

Brunton, John. "Theology in Planning: An Integrated Theological Framework for the Planning Process." PhD diss. abstract. Charles Sturt University (website), 2014. https://researchoutput.csu.edu.au/en/publications/theology-in-planning-an-integrated-theological-framework-for-the-.

———. "Theology in Planning: An Integrated Theological Framework for the Planning Process." PhD diss., Charles Sturt University, 2022.

Budden, Chris. *Following Jesus in Invaded Space: Doing Theology on Aboriginal Land.* Eugene, OR: Pickwick, 2009.

———. "Migration and Rudd's Apology: Whose Voices Are Heard and What Do They Mean for the Christian Community?" In *Indigenous Australia and the Unfinished Business of Theology: Cross-Cultural Engagement,* edited by Jione Havea, 97–111. New York: Palgrave Macmillan, 2014.

———. *Why Indigenous Sovereignty Should Matter to Christians.* Unley, SA: MediaCom Education: 2018.

Burns, Stephen. "'Limping Priests' Ten Years Later: Formation for Ordained Ministry." *Uniting Church Studies* 17.2 (2011) 1–16.

———. *Living the Thanksgiving: Exploring the Eucharist.* London: Canterbury, 2006.

———. "Mission-Shaped Worship." *Anvil* 22.3 (2005) 185–98.

———. "'Presiding Like a Woman': Feminist Gestures for Christian Assembly." *Feminist Theology* 18.1 (2009) 29–49.

———. *SCM Studyguide to Liturgy.* London: SCM, 2006.

Burns, Stephen, and Clive Pearson, eds. *Home and Away: Contextual Theology and Local Practice.* Eugene, OR: Pickwick, 2013.

Carroll, Seforosa. "Making Room for the Religious Other: Reading Interfaith Dialogue and Encounters in the Australian Context from a Feminist Diasporic Perspective." PhD diss. abstract. Charles Sturt University (website), 2015. https://researchoutput.csu.edu.au/en/publications/making-room-for-the-religious-other-reading-interfaith-dialogue-a-3.

———. "Making Room for the Religious Other: Reading Interfaith Dialogue and Encounters in the Australian Context from a Feminist Diasporic Perspective." PhD diss., Charles Sturt University, 2015.

———. "Strangers and Frangipani *Lei*: Exploring a Christology of Hospita*leity*." In *Faith in a Hyphen: Cross-Cultural Theologies Down Under,* edited by Clive Pearson and Jione Havea, 145–57. Adelaide, SA: Openbook, 2004.

Carroll, Seforosa, and William W. Emilsen, eds. *Great Spiritual Leaders: Studies in Leadership in a Pluralist Society.* Canberra ACT: Barton, 2014.

Charles Sturt University. "Theology Students Graduate in Sydney." June 10, 2008. https://news.csu.edu.au/local-news/dubbo/theology-students-graduate-in-sydney.

Choi, Yung Hun. "The Movement Pattern of the Hebrew Psalter: A Holistic Thematic Approach with an Exemplar, Psalms 69–87." PhD diss., Charles Sturt University, 2019.

———. *Patterns of Movement in the Hebrew Psalter: A Holistic Thematic Approach with an Exemplar, Psalms 69–87.* New York: Lang, 2021.

Coombes, Malcolm. *1 John: The Epistle as a Reflecture of the Gospel of John.* Preston, VIC: Mosaic, 2013.

———. "The Literary Relationship Between the Gospel of John and 1 John and Its Implications for Interpreting 1 John." PhD diss., Charles Sturt University, 2006.

Dalton, Christopher. "Mining Coal Seam Gas: An Exhibition in the Divine Art Gallery: How an Australian Theology of Land Can Inform the Public Debate Surrounding the Coal Seam Gas Industry." PhD diss., Charles Sturt University, 2015.

Drayton, Dean. *Apocalyptic Good News: Christ in the Cosmos.* Eugene, OR: Resource, 2019.

———. "The Assembly's Tenth Triennium (2003–2006): Reflections of a President." *Uniting Church Studies* 12.2 (2006) 1–18.

———. "The Greening of Evangelism." *Uniting Church Studies* 13.1 (2007) 18–38.

———. *Pilgrim in the Cosmos (A Spirit Journey)*. Adelaide, SA: Openbook, 1996.

———. "Public Theology in the Market State." *International Journal of Public Theology* 2.2 (2008) 203–22.

———. "Religion in the Public Press: August–September 2007." *Uniting Church Studies* 14.2 (2008) 25–37.

———. *Which Gospel? Three New Testament Perspectives*. Adelaide, SA: MediaCom Education, 2005.

Emeleus, Thomas George. "Divine and Human Creativity and the Blessing and Curse of Fossil Carbon." PhD diss., Charles Sturt University, 2016.

Emilsen, Susan, and William W. Emilsen, eds. *Mapping the Landscape: Essays in Australian and New Zealand Christianity*. New York: Lang, 2000.

———. *O'Connor: Exploring the History of a Uniting Church Congregation*. North Parramatta, NSW: United Theological College, 1997.

Emilsen, Susan, et al. *Pride of Place: A History of the Pitt Street Congregational Church*. Beaconsfield, VIC: Circa, 2008.

Emilsen, William W. *Charles Harris: A Struggle for Justice*. Unley, SA: MediaCom Education, 2019.

———. "Gandhi and 'Lead, Kindly Light.'" In *This Immense Panorama*, edited by Carole Cusack and Peter Oldmeadow. Sydney: School of Studies in Religion, University of Sydney, 1999.

———, ed. *Gandhi's Bible*. Delhi: ISPCK, 2001.

———, ed. *The Goldfields Journal of William Diaper (Alias "Cannibal Jack") 1851–1853*. Carlisle, WA: Hesperian, 1999.

———, ed. *I Believe in God*. North Parramatta, NSW: United Theological College, 2011.

———, ed. *An Informed Faith: The Uniting Church at the Beginning of the 21st Century*. Preston, VIC: Mosaic, 2014.

———. "The March for Justice, Freedom and Hope, 26 January 1988." *Uniting Church Studies* 16.2 (2010) 45–71.

———. "On Being Very Visible: 'Rollie' Busch as a Public Theologian." *Uniting Church Studies* 14.1 (2008) 43–53.

Emilsen, William W., and Elizabeth A. Watson, eds. *Growing Up Uniting*. Richmond, SA: MediaCom Education, 2021.

Emilsen, William W., and John T. Squires, eds. *Prayer and Thanksgiving: Essays in Honour of Rev. Dr Graham Hughes*. North Parramatta, NSW: United Theological College, 2003.

———. *Validating Violence—Violating Faith? Religion, Scripture and Violence*. Adelaide, SA: ATF, 2008.

Emilsen, William W., and Susan Emilsen, eds. *Marking Twenty Years: The Uniting Church in Australia, 1977-1997*. North Parramatta, NSW: United Theological College, 1997.

———. *The Uniting Church in Australia: The First 25 Years*. Armadale, VIC: Circa, 2003.

Gapes, Christine. "Severed Connections: Using Theological Imagination to Explore Youth's Response to Violence at Port Arthur." *Journal of Youth and Theology* 2.2 (2003) 47–63.

Gebara, Rawaa El Ayoubi. "Ijtihad and Its Relevance to Muslims in Australia." PhD diss., Charles Sturt University, 2015.

———. *Ijtihad: Independent Legal Reasoning and Muslims in Australia*. Saarbrücken: Lambert Academic, 2017.

Green, Ryan. "Kenosis and Ascent: The Trajectory of the Self in the Writings of John Milbank and Rowan Williams." PhD diss., Charles Sturt University, 2017.

Grocott, Katharine. "A Theological Critique of Joseph Campbell's Monomyth as a Source for Meaning Making in American Film." PhD diss., Charles Sturt University, 2012.

Hand, Karl. "Proto-Luke and Its Sources." PhD diss., Charles Sturt University, 2014.

Havea, Jione. *Elusions of Control: Biblical Law on the Words of Women*. Atlanta: SBL, 2004.

———. "Forgive Us Our Trespasses: Black Australia, Peopled Wilderness, Eroding Islands." In *Indigenous Australia and the Unfinished Business of Theology: Cross-cultural Engagement*, edited by Jione Havea, 207–19. New York: Palgrave Macmillan, 2014.

———, ed. *Indigenous Australia and the Unfinished Business of Theology*. New York: Palgrave Macmillan, 2014.

———. "Postcolonize Now." In *Postcolonial Voices from Downunder: Indigenous Matters, Confronting Readings*, edited by Jione Havea, 1–14. Eugene, OR: Pickwick, 2017.

———, ed. *Talanoa Ripples: Across Borders, Cultures, Disciplines*. Albany, NZ: Masilamea, 2010.

Havea, Jione, and Clive Pearson, eds. *Out of Place: Doing Theology on the Crosscultural Brink*. Sheffield, UK: Equinox, 2011.

Havea, Jione, and Peter H. W. Lau, eds. *Reading Ruth in Asia*. Atlanta: SBL, 2015.

Havea, Jione, et al., eds. *Bible, Borders, Belonging(s): Engaging Readings from Oceania*. Atlanta: SBL, 2014.

Havea, Jione, et al., eds. *Islands, Islanders, and the Bible: RumInations*. Atlanta: SBL, 2015.

Hawea, Jackson. "Niuean Cultural Values and Their Relationship to the Gospel of Jesus Christ." DMin diss., Charles Sturt University, 2016.

Hughes, Graham. "Limping Priests: Ministry and Ordination." *Uniting Church Studies* 13.1 (2002) 1–13.

———. *Worship as Meaning: A Liturgical Theology for Late Modernity*. Cambridge: Cambridge University Press, 2003.

Jang, Ki Soo. "The Role of Korean Migrant Churches in Australia in Welfare Service Provision and Social Action." DMin diss., Charles Sturt University, 2018.

Kim, Eun Soo. "From the Denominational Church to the Missional Church." PhD diss., Charles Sturt University, 2012.

Kioa, Isileli Jason. "The Role of the Tongan National Conference in the Uniting Church in Australia." DMin diss., Charles Sturt University, 2020.

Lakshmanan, Xavier. "Narrative and Ontology: Paul Ricoeur's Hermeneutic Philosophy as a Guide to Theological Method." PhD diss., Charles Sturt University, 2013.

———. *Textual Linguistic Theology in Paul Ricoeur*. New York: Lang, 2016.

Leal, Robert Barry. *Through Ecological Eyes: Reflections on Christianity's Environmental Credentials*. Strathfield, NSW: St. Pauls, 2006.

———. *Wilderness in the Bible: Toward a Theology of Wilderness*. New York: Lang, 2004.

Lee, Eojin. "A Study of the Theology of the Open Table: Researching the Eucharist of the Presbyterian Church of Korea." PhD diss. abstract. Charles Sturt University (website), 2004. https://researchoutput.csu.edu.au/en/publications/a-study-of-the-theology-of-the-open-table-researching-the-euchari-3.

———. "A Study of the Theology of the Open Table: Researching the Eucharist of the Presbyterian Church of Korea." PhD diss., Charles Sturt University, 2014.

Lledo Gomez, Cristina. *The Church as Woman and Mother: Historical and Theological Foundations*. New York: Paulist, 2018.

———. "Mother Church as Metaphor in Key Early Patristic Writers and Vatican II." PhD diss., Charles Sturt University, 2015.

Llewelyn, Stephen, and Alexandra Robinson. "Trust Networks and Village Life in Roman Egypt: A Case Study of Tebtunis." In *The Village in Antiquity and the Rise of Early Christianity*, edited by Alan Cadwallader et al., 127–53. London: T&T Clark, 2024.

Martinez Andrade, Luis, and Seforosa Carroll, eds. *Facing Climate Collapse: Ecology, Theology and Capitalocene*. London: SCM, forthcoming.

Mawson, Michael. *Standing Under the Cross: Essays on Bonhoeffer's Theology*. London: Bloomsbury, 2023.

Mawson, Michael, and Paul Martens, eds. *The Ethics of Grace: Engaging Gerald McKenny*. London: T&T Clark, 2023.

McKinlay, Brian. "Rowan Williams' Theology of Conflict, Unity, and Solidarity." PhD diss., Charles Sturt University, 2020.

Melanchthon, Monica Jyotsna, and Jione Havea. *Women in the Bible and in Theological Education*. Edited by Richard E. A. Rodgers. Delhi: ISPCK, 2010.

Mitchell, Sarah. "*Communitas* of Christ: Risking the Cross-Cultural Way." In *Faith in a Hyphen: Cross-Cultural Theologies Down Under*, edited by Clive Pearson and Jione Havea, 175–84. Adelaide, SA: Openbook, 2004.

———. "Together in Song: An Ecumenical Si(g)n?" *Ecumenical Review* 54 (2002) 353–68.

Monro, Anita. "'And Ain't I a Woman': The Phronetic Dramaturgy of Feeding the Family." In *Presiding Like a Woman: Feminist Gesture for Christian Assembly*, edited by Nicola Slee and Stephen Burns, 123–32. London: SPCK, 2010.

———. "Pursuing Feminist Research: Perspectives and Methodologies." In *Researching Practice: A Discourse on Qualitative Methodologies*, edited by Joy Higgs et al., 289–98. Rotterdam: Sense, 2010.

———. *Resurrecting Erotic Transgression: Subjecting Ambiguity in Theology*. Sheffield, UK: Equinox, 2006.

———. "A View from the Antipodes: Juxtaposing Dingo and Baby; A Consideration of the Cycle of Light in the Australian Summer." *Studia Liturgica* 40.1-2 (2010) 94–101.

Monro, Anita, and Stephen Burns, eds. *Christian Worship in Australia: Inculturating the Liturgical Tradition*. Strathfield, NSW: St Pauls, 2009.

———. *Public Theology and the Challenge of Feminism*. London: Routledge, 2015.

Moore, Gerard. *The Disciples at the Lord's Table: Prayers over Bread and Cup Across 150 Years of Christian Church (Disciples of Christ) Worship*. Eugene, OR: Pickwick, 2015.

———. *Earth Unites with Heaven: An Introduction to the Liturgical Year*. Northcote, VIC: Morning Star, 2014.

Myers, Benjamin. "The Apostles' Creed." Recorded by Leichhardt Uniting Church. May–July 2013. Video. https://www.youtube.com/playlist?list=PLg4FvsplYA9fEqZOxgjP4Yyj6DS-gXois.

———. *The Apostles' Creed: A Guide to the Ancient Catechism*. Bellingham, WA: Lexham, 2019.

———. *Christ the Stranger: The Theology of Rowan Williams*. Edinburgh: T&T Clark, 2012.

———. "Faith and Theology Is Closed." *Faith and Theology*, Aug. 29, 2018. https://www.faith-theology.com/2018/.

———. *Salvation in My Pocket: Fragments of Faith and Theology*. Eugene, OR: Cascade, 2013.

———. "Theology 2.0: Blogging as the Theological Discourse." *Cultural Encounters* 6 (2010) 47–60.

National Working Group on Worship. *Uniting in Worship 2*. Sydney: Uniting Church in Australia, 2005.

Palmer, Damian. "Negotiating the Historic Episcopate: Christian Unity Discussions Between the Anglican and Non-Episcopal Communions, 1888–1938." PhD diss., Charles Sturt University, 2014.

Pearson, Clive, ed. *Enacting a Public Theology*. Stellenbosch, SA: Sun Media, 2019.

———. "Encountering Christ in a Hyphen." *CTC Bulletin* 20.1 (2004) 1–13.

———. "On Being Public About Ecotheology." *Ecotheology* 6.2 (July 2001) 42–59.

———. "God's Continued Providence." In *T&T Clark Handbook of Christian Theology and Climate Change*, edited by Ernst M. Conradie and Hilda P. Koster, 395–405. New York: T&T Clark, 2020.

———. *Imagining a Way: Exploring Reformed Practical Theology and Ethics*. Louisville: Westminster John Knox, 2017.

———. "Telling Tales: Following the Hyphenated Jesus-Christ." *Studies in World Christianity* 10.1 (2004) 31–46.

Pearson, Clive, and Jione Havea, eds. *Faith in a Hyphen: Cross-Cultural Theologies Down Under*. Adelaide, SA: Openbook, 2004.

Pearson, Clive, et al., eds. *Scholarship and Fierce Sincerity*. Auckland, NZ: Polygraphia, 2006.

Philip, Thomas. "Exegeting the World: M. M. Thomas's Secular Commentaries on Scripture." PhD diss., Charles Sturt University, 2022.

Purnell, Douglas J. *Being in Ministry: Honestly, Openly, and Deeply*. Eugene, OR: Wipf & Stock, 2010.

———. *Conversation as Ministry: Stories and Strategies for Confident Caregiving*. Cleveland, OH: Pilgrim, 2003.

———. "Why We Do What We Do When We Teach Pastoral Theology at United Theological College (UTC) Sydney." *Pastoral Psychology* 53.1 (2004) 87–94.

Rees, Anthony. *Moses: Man Amongst Men?* Lanham, MD: Lexington, 2023.

———. *[Re]Reading Again: A Mosaic Reading of Numbers 25*. London: Bloomsbury, 2015.

———. *Voices of the Wilderness: An Ecological Reading of the Book of Numbers*. Sheffield: Sheffield Phoenix, 2015.

Rees, Janice. "Difference, Doctrine and Discourse: A Contribution to Feminist Systematic Theology." PhD diss., Charles Sturt University, 2014.

Reichardt, David. *Release the River! An Ecotheological Reading of How the Murray-Darling Basin's Human Inhabitants Have Affected Its Waterways*. Delhi: ISPCK, 2015.

———. "Release the River! An Ecotheological Reading of How the Murray-Darling Basin's Human Inhabitants Have Affected Its Waterways." PhD diss., Charles Sturt University, 2009.

Richmond, Helen. "Living Together as Friends and Partners: Implications of Muslim-Christian Marriage in Indonesia and Australia for Our Understanding of Christian Mission and Da'wah." PhD diss., Charles Sturt University, 2010.

Richmond, Helen, and Myong Duk Yang. *Shaping Faith, Ministry and Identity in Multicultural Australia*. Sydney: Uniting Church in Australia Assembly and NSW Board of Mission, 2006.

Robinson, Alexandra, and Stephen Llewelyn. "Trust Networks and Village Life in Roman Galilee: A Case Study of the Gospel Narratives and Acts." In *The Village in Antiquity and the Rise of Early Christianity*, edited by Alan Cadwallader et al., 173–98. London: T&T Clark, 2024.

Roude, Nada. "Australian Muslim Leaders' Perspectives on Countering Violent Extremism: Towards Developing a Best Practice Model for Engaging the Muslim Community." PhD diss., Charles Sturt University, 2017.

Senini, Christine. "Munus Triplex Nauticus Kaleidoscope: Priest, Pastor, and Porthole as the Pastoral-Liturgical Identity of a Royal Australian Navy Chaplain." PhD diss., Charles Sturt University, 2014.

Sheridan, Ruth. *Retelling Scripture: "The Jews" and the Scriptural Citations in John 1:19—12:15*. Leiden: Brill, 2012.

Shibata, Ria, et al., eds. *Climate Change and Conflict in the Pacific: Challenges and Responses*. London: Routledge, 2023.

Slee, Nicola, and Stephen Burns, eds. *Presiding Like a Woman: Feminist Gesture for Christian Assembly*. London: SPCK, 2010.

Somasundram, Drene. "A Gender Inclusive Model in Theological Education for the Seventh-Day Adventist Church." PhD diss., Middlesex University, 2007.

Squires, John T. "Acts." In *Eerdmans Commentary on the Bible*, edited by James D. G. Dunn and John Rogerson, 1213–67. Grand Rapids: Eerdmans, 2003.

———. "Christians Relating to Jews: Key Issues in Public Statements." *Journal of Ecumenical Studies* 44.2 (2009) 180–202.

———. "The Gospel According to Luke." In *The Cambridge Companion to the Gospels*, edited by Stephen C. Barton, 158–81. Cambridge: Cambridge University Press, 2006.

———. *An Informed Faith*. https://johntsquires.com/.

———. "Interpreting Galatians 3:27–28 in the Uniting Church: A Relational and Contextual Perspective." *Uniting Church Studies* 15.2 (2009) 11–24.

———. *The Plan of God in Luke-Acts*. Society for New Testament Studies Monograph Series 76. Cambridge: Cambridge University Press, 1993.

———. "Singing, Streaking, Shocking: Reading the New Testament with a Youth Hermeneutic." *Uniting Church Studies* 10.1 (2004) 36–52.

Talia, Maina Vakafua. "Am I Not Your *Tū/akoi*? A Tuvaluan Plea for Survival in a Time of Climate Emergency." PhD diss., Charles Sturt University, 2015.

Tuiai, Aukilani. "The Congregational Christian Church of Samoa, 1962–2002: A Study of the Issues and Policies that Have Shaped the Independent Church." PhD diss., Charles Sturt University, 2012.

Tupu, Charles Uesile. "*Fa'aola Fanua*: A Samoan Public Theology of Taking Care of Customary Land (*fanua faa-le-aganu'u*)." PhD diss., Charles Sturt University, 2021.

United Theological College. "Assoc. Prof. Anthony Rees." https://www.utc.edu.au/people/assoc-prof-anthony-rees/.

———. "A Place for You." https://www.utc.edu.au/about-us/.

Vaipulu, Sioeli Felekoni. "Towards an '*Otua*logy: Revisiting and Rethinking the Doctrine of God in Tonga." PhD diss., Charles Sturt University, 2013.

Vilitama, Matagi. "On Becoming a Liquid Church: Singing the Niuean '*Fetuiaga Kerisiano*' on a Distant Shore." PhD diss., Charles Sturt University, 2015.

Walker, Christopher C., ed. *Witness the Glory of God in the Face of Jesus Christ: Papers in Honour of Dean Drayton*. Unley, SA: MediaCom Education, 2014.

Walker, Peter. *Enfolded and Unfolding: Christian Theology and Religious Diversity*. Lanham, MD: Lexington, forthcoming.

———. "On the Vision of God: An Historical and Theological Inquiry into the Significance of Nicholas of Cusa's De Visione Dei for Christian Theology of Religions and Interreligious Dialogue." PhD diss., Charles Sturt University, 2020.

———. "Public Theology and the Modern Democratic State." In *Enacting a Public Theology*, edited by Clive Pearson, 29–40. Stellenbosch, SA: Sun Media, 2019.

Walker, Peter, and Jonathan Cole, eds. *Theology on a Defiant Earth: Seeking Hope in the Anthropocene*. Lanham, MD: Lexington, 2022.

Wilcoxen, Matthew. *Divine Humility: God's Morally Perfect Being*. Waco, TX: Baylor University Press, 2019.

———. "Morally Perfect Being Theology: A Doctrine of Divine Humility." PhD diss., Charles Sturt University, 2017.

Wilson, Matthew Barrington. "The Place of the 'Religious Outsider' in the Kingdom of God: A Biblical Response to Relations with Other Faiths." PhD diss., Charles Sturt University, 2012.

Wright, Stephen. "The Creator Sings: A Wesleyan Rethinking of Transcendence with Robert Jenson." PhD diss., Charles Sturt University, 2012.

Yu, Jae In. "The Doctrine of Faith in John Calvin, Karl Barth, and Korean Reformed Theology." PhD diss., Charles Sturt University, 2019.

Index

Aboriginal Australians. *See* indigenous Australians
accountability, 6–7, 61, 64–65
Ackland, Margaret, 153
Aernie, Jeffrey, 179, 191
Agnew, Sarah, 173n5
Alan Walker College of Evangelism, 14, 180
All Saints Missionary College Library, 126–27
American Theological Library Association (ATLA), 129
Amosa, Faala Faamatuainu (Sam), 106
Amyraut, Moses, 32
animal welfare, 158
Ansari, Mahsheed, 35
Anselm of Canterbury, 30
Anslow, Matthew, 179n38
Aotearoa-New Zealand, 26, 35, 78, 97–98, 149, 184, 187
applied theology, 17
Arabic-language resources, 132, 133
archives, 134–35, 141, 146n4, 153n34, 174n6
the arts, 152–53
Asian Diaspora in Australia symposium, 157
Assembly of the Uniting Church. *See* National Assembly of the Uniting Church
Association of Asian-Australian Theology and Ministry, 157
Association of College and Research Libraries in America, 128

Athanasius of Alexandria, 30, 31, 32
atheism, 163–64
Atrium, 73–74, 170
Augustine of Hippo, 31, 32, 34, 119, 132, 176
Aulén, Gustaf, 30
Australian and New Zealand Theological Library Association (ANZTLA), 129, 134
Australian National University (ANU), 3
Australian Research Council (ARC), 19
autoethnography, 55–56

bachelor's programs, 1, 3–4, 10, 11, 12–14, 44
Balabanski, Vicky, 35, 173
Banks, Robert, 163
baptism, 103
Barnes, Geoffrey, 69, 72, 134, 170, 170n2
Barth, Karl, 29, 30, 31, 32, 116–17, 162, 176
Basis of Union (Uniting Church in Australia)
  Centre for Ministry's architecture and, 72
  ecclesiology in, 32, 99
  ministry of scholarship in, 4, 13
  ordained ministry responsibilities and, 41, 43
  in peace activism, 153
  publications on, 175
Being the Church course, 31, 37

Berryman, Jerome, 150, 151
Bert Hely and Associates, 72
Bertelsmeier, Diane, 126n1, 129n9
Bevans, Steven, 186–87
Biblical Culture Days, 178
biblical studies
 colonialism and decolonization in, 91–92, 118, 185–86, 187n92
 in CSU School of Theology's curriculum, 13
 research and publications on, 148, 154, 162–63, 173, 177–79, 185–86, 187–88, 187n92
 visiting scholars and conferences on, 148, 149, 153–54, 162–63, 178
Bielefeld University, 19
Black Americans, 31, 33, 34, 37, 98
blogging, 175, 179
Blue Mountains Library, 80
Board for Ministerial Formation (United Theological College), 171
Board for Studies (United Theological College), 171
Board of Education (Synod of NSW and ACT), 139, 148n13, 149
 See also Uniting Mission and Education (UME)
Board of Finance and Administration (United Theological College), 162
Board of Mission (Synod of NSW and ACT), 137–38, 139, 151, 157n55
 See also Uniting Mission and Education (UME)
Boase, Liz, 35
Boer, Roland, 148
Bonhoeffer, Dietrich
 Ben Myers' instruction and publications on, 30, 31, 32, 176
 on community, 47, 84
 in contextual theology, 28, 33, 34, 35, 36, 99, 187
 visiting scholars and conferences on, 47, 162, 164–65
Boniface-Malle, Anastasia, 160
Bouma, Gary, 155

Brennan, Patricia, 154
Brett, Mark, 34
Brewers of Hope, 83
Brown, John P., 157
Brown, Kenneth, 179
Brunton, John, 178n31
Bryant, Moira, as library manager. *See* Camden Theological Library
Budden, Chris, 147, 161n81, 186, 188
Bultmann, Rudolf, 30
Burns, Stephen
 in conferences, 150, 154
 in contextual theology, 36–37, 187, 189n102
 in liturgical studies, 78–79, 180–81, 182n63

Calvin, John, 30, 31, 32, 159, 175
Calvin Quincentenary conference, 159
Camden Theological Library
 archival management by, 134–35, 141, 146n4, 153n34, 174n6
 budgetary constraints faced by, 130–31, 132, 135–39
 as church resource, 119, 130–31, 142
 CSU School of Theology and, 8, 129, 132
 diversity in patrons of, 80, 119, 133
 overview of upgrades to, 126–28
 service in, 128, 139–41, 142–43
 special collections in, 8, 58, 104, 118–19, 131–34, 142, 172
 in Student Support Team, 83
 vision of excellence for, 128–30
Carey, Lindsay, 173n5
Carley, Keith, 170
Carroll, Seforosa
 at Camden Theological Library, 133, 140
 as high-profile Pasifika graduate, 90
 on Pasifika issues, 93, 96, 97, 103, 157, 190–91
 research and publications by, 181, 190–91
 as scholarship recipient, 173
 in student support programs, 71, 82–83, 133

in UTC's theology instruction, 27, 38, 51, 170
casual staffing, 9
Catechesis of the Good Shepherd, 150n21, 151
Cavalletti, Sofia, 150, 151
Centre for Ministry (CFM)
  architectural design of, 72–73, 74, 145
  Camden Theological Library and, 131, 134
  as conference venue, 164
  displays in, 151, 153, 170
  "green-chair" theology in, 58, 60, 65–66
Centre for Religion, Ethics, and Society (CRES), 18–19
Chang, HeeWon, 111, 113–14, 118, 121
chapel, 60, 62, 72, 74, 81, 124, 182
chaplains, 3, 15, 85, 123
Charles Sturt University (CSU) School of Theology
  Camden Theological Library and, 8, 129, 132
  curriculum and instruction in, 9, 10–14, 148, 174
  establishment of, 2–4, 6–9
  Korean universities' links with, 15, 20, 111, 123, 124, 132, 172
  leadership positions held by graduates of, 191
  research and publications in, 17–20, 92, 147–48, 178
  students and demand in, 14–17
  in UTC's First Year Mentoring Program, 82
  UTC's intersection of church and university in, 20–22, 171–72
children's and youth ministries, 142, 150–51, 154, 161–62, 179
Cho, Kyounghee, 35, 162–63
Choi, Jason Chong Bok, 111, 120, 124–25
Choi, Yung Hun, 178n31
Christ and Creation course, 27–28
Christchurch earthquake, 62
Christology. *See* Jesus
Chung, Paul, 164
church history, 13, 38, 104, 117, 150, 162, 183
churches
  in Australian public life, 2–3
  Camden Theological Library as resource for, 119, 130–31, 142
  children's and youth ministries in, 142, 150–51, 154, 161–62, 179
  in Korea, 112, 117
  for Korean immigrants, 112, 115–16, 119, 123, 124
  multicultural leadership in, 90–91, 110
  ordained ministry in (*see* formation for ordained ministry; ordained ministers)
  social change and, 69
  See also Uniting Church in Australia (UCA); worship services
Clarke, Sathianathan, 35, 38, 157, 177
climate change. *See* ecotheology and climate action
Clough, David, 158
Coakley, Sarah, 31, 32
Cole, Jonathan, 177
Coleman, Milton, 52
Colgan, Emily, 35
Collection Development Policy, 127, 128
College Council, 4, 16, 21, 162
colloquia, 35, 171
colonialism and decolonization
  in biblical studies, 91–92, 118, 185–86, 187n92
  in community of the heart, 64–65, 66
  research and publications on, 36, 50–51, 160, 185–86, 187n92, 188–89
  in systematic theology, 34, 35, 36, 38
  visiting scholars and conferences on, 159–61
Coming Out conference, 162–63
Committee for Ministerial Formation (United Theological College), 171

Committee for Studies (United Theological College), 171
Commonwealth Supported Places (CSPs), 5
Communitas program, 58, 91, 155–56, 186–87
community of the heart
  background on, 54–56
  commitment to, 59–61
  "green-chair" theology in, 58, 60, 65–66
  importance of in formation, 56–59
  marginalized groups in, 63–65
  tears and joys in, 61–63
computers, 126, 127, 141
Cone, James, 31, 33, 37
conferences. *See* visiting scholars and conferences
Conradie, Ernst M., 158–59
contextual theology
  Clive Pearson's instruction and research supervision in, 25–29, 32, 36–37, 78, 115, 116–17, 185–86
  at CSU School of Theology, 13–14, 17, 18, 92
  Michael Mawson's instruction on, 33, 34–35
  migrants in, 26, 94–96, 97, 101, 103, 116–17, 121, 155, 186
  overview of UTC's research and publications on, 185–89
  PACT in (*see* PACT (Public and Contextual Theology Strategic Research Centre))
  Pasifika peoples in (*see* Pasifika peoples)
  under Sarah Mitchell's principalship, 78
continuing professional development, 8, 10, 11, 16, 17, 21, 85–86, 174
  See also School of Continuing Education
Coolamon College, 131
Coombes, Malcolm, 173, 178n34
Core Phase Formation. *See* formation for ordained ministry
Costello, Tim, 151

Council for Aboriginal Reconciliation, 161n77
Covenant with the Uniting Aboriginal and Islander Christian Congress, 43, 161
COVID-19 pandemic, 10–11, 34, 35, 63, 140–41, 165
Craig-Emilsen, Carolyn, 71, 83, 164
Creasy-Dean, Kenda, 161–62
creation doctrine, 27
Crisis and Hope: Reading Bonhoeffer for Today conference, 164
Critical Theology course, 26–27, 28
Critical Thinking course, 71
culture. *See* multiculturalism
Cupitt, Don, 26
Curtis, Andrew, 173n5

Dahill, Lisa, 164
David (biblical figure), 169
Davidson, Allan, 184n73
Davies, Henry, 110
de Vos, Craig, 173n5
deacons, 41, 44–45
Deane-Drummond, Celia, 94
Dear, John, 153
decolonization. *See* colonialism and decolonization
Deed of Agreement, 6–9, 10, 20
Department of Foreign Affairs (Australia), 18
Department of Lands (Australia), 135
designated research areas, 18
Deverell, Gary, 33, 35, 187n92
DeYmaz, Mark, 101
diaspora. *See* migrants
Dicker, Gordon, 26, 103, 170, 185
Directorate of Vital Ministry (Synod of NSW and ACT), 16, 17, 21
dissertations. *See* research and publications
distance education, 10–11, 14, 17, 49, 65–66, 161n81, 165
diversity. *See* multiculturalism
doctoral programs. *See* postgraduate programs
doctrine, 26, 27–28, 38
Doing Theology on Indigenous Land course, 73

Dong San Korean Uniting Church, 112
Drayton, Dean, 62, 148, 150, 176–77, 181n53, 184
Dunn, James, 149
Durham, George, 148n11
Dutney, Andrew, 153, 162

Earl, Michael, 159
Earth Ministries, 158
economic theory, 160
ecotheology and climate action
   in Camden Theological Library's special collections, 142
   community of the heart in, 62
   indigenous peoples and, 26, 35, 91, 93–94, 185, 188
   Koreans in, 123
   research and publications on, 26, 93–94, 177, 184–85, 188
   in systematic theology instruction, 27, 28, 34, 35
   visiting scholars and conferences on, 35, 158–59
Education for Lay Ministries (ELM), 72, 131, 151n23
ego-histoire, 55–56
Elia, Samata, 97
Emilsen, Susan, 70n7, 71, 170, 173, 183
Emilsen, William
   in conferences, 148, 150, 151, 154, 157, 163, 164
   as instructor and research supervisor, 38, 70n7, 176n15, 183, 189–90
   Korean students and, 112, 119
   as pioneering Australian faculty member, 170
   research and publications by, 180, 183, 184, 188, 190, 191
   Uniting Church Studies journal established by, 173
employment, for ministry candidates, 46
endowed lectureships, 165
   See also Havea Lectures; Livingstone Lectures; May Macleod Lectures; Thatcher Lectures

English language. *See* non-native English speakers
episcopacy, 176
Eskdale House, 134
Ete, Risatisone, 97, 98
ethics, 12, 13, 18–19, 33, 34
evangelism and mission work, 38, 110, 112, 157, 184n76, 187n92, 189
Evans, James, Jr., 31, 98

faculty
   as accredited postgraduate supervisors, 171–72
   in church councils, 16
   in community of the heart, 56, 60–61, 63
   in developing Camden Theological Library's collections, 119, 128, 132
   in formation for ordained ministry, 45, 56
   at intersection of church and university, 21
   qualifications and performance review for, 2, 6–7, 8–9, 170
   research and publications by (*see* research and publications)
   in supporting international students, 29, 75–77, 79–80, 82–83, 115, 116–17, 120, 122–23, 132
   in systematic theology instruction (*see* systematic theology)
   as visiting scholars (*see* visiting scholars and conferences)
Faculty Common Room, 170
Faith in a Hyphen conference, 155
faka'apa'apa (respect), 96
farming, 158
fatele (dance music), 94
Faupula, Salesi, 90
feminism, 64–65, 92, 96
Ferguson, Graeme, 170
Fergusson, David, 163
fetuiaga Kerisiano (liquid church), 98, 105
field-based learning, 44–45, 46, 49
Fiji, 20, 91, 92, 94
FILE Group, 135

Finau, Salesi, 97
First Peoples. *See* indigenous Australians; Pasifika peoples
First Year Mentoring Program (FYM), 82–83
first-generation migrants, 96, 103
Fleming, Nicole, 60n19
Floyd, George, 34
Floyd, Tony, 102
Foiakau, Inise, 92
Ford, David, 56–57, 58, 61, 62, 63, 64
Formation Day, 45
formation for ordained ministry
    community of the heart in (*see* community of the heart)
    CSU School of Theology and, 2, 5, 8, 11, 12, 13, 14
    flexibility in, 48–52
    formative tension in, 46–48
    multiculturalism in, 12, 43, 46–48, 49–52, 64–65, 68–69, 88
    oversight for, 8, 171
    UCA's standards for, 41–44, 49, 68–69, 88
    UTC's program for, 44–46
fourth-year honors programs, 11
Frame, Tom, 172–73
frangipani *lei*, 97
"free and friendly space", 74–75
Friday Groups, 45
Frisch, Michael, 70

Galovic, Michael, 153
Gandhi, Mahatma, 177, 189
Gapes, Christine, 52, 73, 78, 161–62, 179
Garibay, Emmanuel, 153
Gebara, Rawaa, 190n106
gender
    in domestic violence, 160
    feminist perspectives on, 64–65, 92, 96
    in ordination, 48, 112, 118, 124
    research and publications on, 92, 181, 187, 188
    in UTC's student body, 14, 48
Ghosh, Manas, 190
Gibson, Colin, 148–49
Gill, David, 150
Gillespie Presbyterian Collection, 130
Glenn, Gavin, 135
Global Financial Crisis (GFC), 15–16, 137
Global Network for Public Theology (GNPT), 19–20, 148, 184
Godly Play, 142, 150–51
Goh, Paul, 50
Gosbell, Louise, 35
The Gospel on Sunday conference, 150
graduate programs. *See* postgraduate programs
Grant-Henderson, Anna, 173n5
Green, Clifford, 164
Green, Ryan, 176n15
"green-chair" theology, 58, 60, 65–66
Gregory of Nazianzus, 31
Grey, Jacqueline, 189n102
Gribben, Robert, 181n53
Griffith, Colleen, 75
Grocott, Katherine, 173
Growing Young Journey program, 142

Haire, James, 150, 154
Halapua, Winston, 33, 93
Halík, Tomáš, 164
Hall, Douglas John, 27, 28, 36, 103
Hand, Karl, 178n34
Hannam University, 111, 123, 124, 132, 172
Harris, Charles, 188
haua (wanderer), 97
Havea, Jione
    in biblical studies, 78, 91–92, 118, 162, 185–86, 187–88, 187n92
    in conferences, 156, 162
    in formation programs, 51
    glass artwork commissioned by, 182
    research and publications by, 181, 185–86, 187–89, 191
    as scholarship recipient, 173
    in systematic theology instruction, 27, 34, 35, 170
    talanoa methodology of, 91–94, 118, 186
Havea, Sione 'Amanaki, 34, 92, 165
Havea Lectures, 92, 156–57, 165

Henderson, Gregor, 150
Heppell, Michael, 140
Herbert, Meg, 52
Hidden Histories conference, 150, 162
Higher Education Board (HEB), 5
Higher Education Contribution Scheme (HECS), 5
Higher Education Participation and Partnerships Program (HEPPP), 82
Hiliau, Faaimata Havea, 90
Holden, David, 80
holy insecurity, 98–99
Hong Kong, 15, 33
Horizon (library management system), 127
Hornsby College (TAFE NSW), 118
Hoskin, John, 173
hospitality, 60, 74–75, 114, 157n61
Hughes, Graham, 115, 152n26, 170, 180, 191
Humphries, Jon, 100, 102–3
hybrid learning, 65–66, 161n81, 165
hyphenated/hybrid identities, 26, 95–96, 103, 121, 155, 186

Ieli, Hani, 74, 75–76, 84, 85, 86
Illuminate database, 141, 146n4, 174n6
immigrants. *See* migrants
Indigeneity: Belongings and Subversion conference, 157
Indigenous Australian Cultures and Spiritualities course, 73
indigenous Australians
  in Camden Theological Library's special collections, 132, 133, 142
  in CSU School of Theology curriculum, 12, 73
  theological colleges' efforts to increase enrollment by, 15
  in UTC curriculum, 33, 73, 116
  in UTC student body, 73, 74, 117
  visiting scholars and conferences on, 65, 158, 160–61
  See also Pasifika peoples
Indonesians, 18, 81, 132, 133
Iner, Derya, 158
Inge, John, 71, 72, 83, 85

Institute for Mission, 72, 131
Institute for Theology and the Arts, 127, 152
integration, 45, 60
intensives, 10–11
interfaith dialogue
  Camden Theological Library collection on, 142
  in conferences, 35, 154, 155, 157–58, 163–64, 190
  in CSU School of Theology, 18
  in formation for ordained ministry, 78, 190
  research and publications on, 154, 189–91
  See also atheism; Islamic studies and Muslim-Christian dialogue; Jews
International Bonhoeffer Congress, 47, 164–65
International Journal of Public Theology, 19–20, 184
Introduction to Theology course, 33–34
Irenaeus, 31
Irvine, Andrew, 173n5
Islamic Science and Research Academy (ISRA), 172
Islamic studies and Muslim-Christian dialogue
  in conferences, 35, 154, 158
  in CSU School of Theology, 3, 12, 18, 158, 172
  research and publications on, 154, 189–90

J., Professor, 120
Jackson, Arthur, 184n76
Jackson, Hawea, 105
Jang, Ki Soo, 173
Jennings, Willie James, 34, 50–51, 64, 65, 164
Jenson, Robert, 32
Jesus
  in community of the heart, 57, 61
  in formation for ordained ministry standards, 42
  on heart and mind, 169

Jesus (*continued*)
   multiculturalism and, 94, 97, 99, 100–101, 105, 106, 190
   in systematic theology instruction, 27–28, 32
   Zacchaeus and, 164
Jews, 153–54, 190
Jobling, David, 148
Johnson, Elizabeth, 31, 32
Johnson, Lydia, 101
Joso, Raymond, 76, 77, 79, 80, 81, 83–84
journals, 19–20, 126, 132, 179, 184
   See also Uniting Church Studies (journal)
joy, 63
Jubilee, 125
Julian of Norwich, 31

Kaa, Hirini, 35, 187n92
Kailahi, Haloti, 90
Kamins, Jeffrey, 190
Kardashian, Levon, 101, 102
Kärkkäinen, Veli-Matti, 35
Kelly, Renee, 83
Keneally, Kristina, 163
Keskin, Zuleya, 155
Kim, Ace, 111, 117, 124
Kim, Do Young, 111, 114, 118, 120–21
Kim, Grace Ji-Sun, 160
Kim, Phoebe Dong Suk, 111, 118–19, 133, 138
Kioa, Isileli Jason, 105–6
Kiribati, 91, 94
Kohn, Rachel, 151
Kolia, Brian Fiu, 36, 187n92
Koopman, Nico, 148
Korea and Koreans
   Australian missionaries in, 110, 157, 184n76
   Camden Theological Library's collection for, 8, 58, 118–19, 131–32, 172
   comfort and discomfort at UTC for, 113–16, 122–25
   in contextual theology, 97, 101, 116–17
   in demography of UTC, 73
   in multicultural context, 50, 111–13, 116–23
   as ordained ministers, 110–11, 115–16, 117, 118, 120, 123–24
   translation work by, 162–63
   UTC's links with universities in, 15, 20, 111, 123, 124, 132, 157, 172
Korean Presbytery, 123, 132
Korean Society of Sydney, 157
Kristeva, Julia, 181
Kung Lap-yan, 164
Kwok Pui-Lan, 33

ladders of learning, 16–17
Lakshmanan, Xavier, 74, 75, 79–80, 86, 173–74, 176n15
Langford, Kim, 164–65
language education requirements, 13
   See also non-native English speakers
Lathrop, Gordon, 150
lay education, 16, 17, 142, 175, 178–79
Leal, Barry, 184n79
lecturers. See faculty
Lee, Aeryun R.
   contextual theology of, 96–97, 98, 99, 101
   formation experiences of, 111, 112, 114–15, 116–17, 120
Lee, Eojin J., 111, 115–16, 122–23, 182n63
Lee, Jung Young, 27
Lee, Sang Taek, 111, 124
Lee, Steve, 73–74, 76, 80–81, 85
Lee, Sunny Kyung Hee, 111, 112, 118, 124
Leichhardt Uniting Church, 175
Levine, Amy-Jill, 153–54
LGBTQI+ people, 48, 112, 142, 162–63, 177
liberation and resistance theologies, 33, 34, 36
libraries, 7–8
   See also Camden Theological Library
Libraries Alive!, 139–40, 141, 142
Library Committee (Camden Theological Library), 136

library management systems, 127
lifelong learning, 83–87
  See also visiting scholars and conferences
Lima, Peletisala, 94
Lindsay, Rebecca, 173, 179
Lineman, Peter, 184n73
liquid church (*fetuiaga Kerisiano*), 98, 105
little acorns, 123–24
liturgical studies, 13, 60–61, 79, 152, 180–82
Livingstone, David, 148n11
Livingstone Lectures, 148, 151–52, 165
Lledo Gomez, Cristina, 182
Lopez, Mark, 100
Loy, Allan, 170, 185
Luther, Martin, 34, 35

MacIntyre, John, 148n13
Macleod, Malcolm, 148n13, 149
Macleod, May, 148n13, 149, 165
Maddox, Robert, 170
Major, Henry, 26, 184
majors of study, 12–13
Manning, Peter, 155
Mansfield, Bruce, 4
Mar, Jo, 99
master's programs, 11–12, 15, 148, 183–84
Matsuoka, Fumitaka, 98–99, 155
Mavor, John, 150
Mawson, Michael, 33–35, 36, 38, 170, 187
May Macleod Lectures
  the arts in, 152
  on children's ministries, 150–51
  on ecotheology, 158–59
  history of, 148–49, 165
  on indigenous reconciliation, 160–61
  interfaith dialogue in, 157
  peace activism in, 153
McCallum, Ian, 139–40, 141, 142
McFarlane, Rob, 149, 150, 173
McGrath, Alister E., 33
McKee, Elsie, 31
McKinlay, Brian, 176n15

Melanchthon, Monica J., 188
Meyer, Ockert, 35, 38, 86, 177
Migliore, Daniel, 33, 98
migrants
  Camden Theological Library's collection on, 142
  churches for, 112, 115–16, 119, 123, 124
  in contextual theology, 26, 95–96, 97, 101, 103, 116–17, 121, 155, 186
  in formation for ordained ministry, 49–50
  hyphenated/hybrid identities of, 26, 95–96, 103, 121, 155, 186
  Pasifika peoples as, 94–96
  in UCA's declaration on multiculturalism, 99–100
  visiting scholars and conferences on, 155, 157
  See also Korea and Koreans; multiculturalism; non-native English speakers; Pasifika peoples
Miller, Liam, 35, 155, 156–57
Miller, Paul, 153
Miller, Ted, 149–50
Milton, John, 30, 176
Ministerial Education Board (Synod of NSW and ACT), 8, 21
Ministerial Education Commission (Uniting Church in Australia), 68–69, 127, 136, 138
ministers. *See* formation for ordained ministry; ordained ministers
ministry of scholarship, 4, 13, 16
Minjung theology, 34, 36
mission work and evangelism, 38, 110, 112, 157, 184n76, 187n92, 189
Mitchell, Sarah, 45, 78, 91, 180, 186, 187
Mo, Peng, 182n59
Modern Churchmen's Union, 184
Moltmann, Jürgen, 28, 31
Monro, Anita, 180–82, 181n53, 189n102
Moore, Deanna, 135
Moore, Gerard, 147, 182, 191

Moore Theological College, 149
Morling College, 149
Morris, Jocelyn, 126n1
Mostert, Christiaan, 25, 98
Moyes, Gordon, 154
Mud Flower Collective, 64–65
multiculturalism
   at Camden Theological Library, 8, 58, 118–19, 131–34, 138, 142, 172
   in church leadership, 90–91, 110
   in conferences, 154, 155–58, 159–61, 162–63, 178
   in contextual theology (*see* contextual theology)
   in formation for ordained ministry, 12, 43, 46–48, 49–52, 64–65, 68–69, 88
   in growth and lifelong learning, 83–87
   importance of in theological education, 68–72
   intersections of learning, culture, and faith in, 75–83
   Jesus and, 94, 97, 99, 100–101, 105, 106, 190
   Koreans in, 50, 111–13, 116–23
   National Assembly of the Uniting Church and, 47, 68–69, 90, 102, 156, 161
   Pasifika peoples in, 96–104
   in pastoral care, 101–2
   in rise of theological studies at public universities, 3
   in Synod of NSW and ACT, 79, 87, 90, 110, 120
   UCA's declaration on, 43, 87, 99–100, 103–4, 105
   in UTC's student body, 72–75
   See also indigenous Australians; interfaith dialogue; Korea and Koreans; migrants; non-native English speakers; Pasifika peoples
muna o te fale (wisdom of the household), 93
music, 93, 94

Muslims. *See* Islamic studies and Muslim-Christian dialogue
Myers, Ben
   in conferences, 150, 164
   as instructor and research supervisor, 29–33, 37–38, 79–80, 150, 176, 178n31
   research and publications by, 47, 58, 175–76, 191

NAIDOC (National Aborigines and Islanders Day Observance Committee) Week, 133
Nam, Sang Hyun, 111, 115, 116, 122
National Assembly of the Uniting Church
   archives of, 141
   Bible studies presented at, 173
   multiculturalism and, 47, 68–69, 90, 102, 156, 161
   on ordained ministry and formation, 41, 42–43, 48, 49, 68–69, 177
National Council of Churches, 159
neoliberalism, 160
New South Wales Synod. *See* Synod of NSW (New South Wales) and ACT (Australian Capital Territory)
New Zealand, 26, 35, 78, 97–98, 149, 184, 187
Newbigin, Lesslie, 162
Newton, Phil, 162
Nicholas of Cusa, 177
Niebuhr, H. Richard, 37
Nietzsche, Friedrich, 164
9/11, 103
Niue, 93, 98, 105
non-native English speakers
   in addressing language gaps in Korean churches, 115–16
   challenges faced by, 30, 77, 81, 95, 101, 122–23
   supports for, 14, 71, 79–80, 82, 115, 132
   in UCA resolution, 69
Northcott, Michael, 158
Northern Synod, 90
Nouwen, Henri, 74–75

O'Connor Congregation, 183
O'Donoghue, Lowitja, 161
off-campus (distance) study, 10–11, 14, 17, 49, 65–66, 161n81, 165
Oh, Myeong Cheol, 111, 113, 119, 122, 124
oikeiosis (homemaking), 96
Oldmeadow, John, 130, 134, 154
Olivetti, Filimone, 98
One Heart Faith Community, 117, 124
open table theology, 182n63
Openbook Annual Theological Essay Award, 96–97, 114
oral history, 69–71
ordained ministers
  continuing professional development for, 10, 11, 16, 85–86, 174
  cultural models of supervision for, 101
  formation for (*see* formation for ordained ministry)
  gender and sexual orientation of, 48, 112, 118, 124, 177
  Korean UTC graduates as, 110–11, 115–16, 117, 118, 120, 123–24
  in Samoan society, 106
  as UTC faculty members, 9
O'Reilly, Ciaron, 153
Origen, 31, 32
Ormerod, Neil, 29n5
Ospino, Hosffman, 75
'otualogy (Tongan "God talk"), 95
Overseas Students Committee (United Theological College), 82
overwhelmings, 56–57, 58
Ozalp, Mehmet, 172

Pacific and Asian North American (PANA) Institute, 98, 155
Pacific Asia Arts Forum, 153
Pacific School of Religion, 98, 152, 155
Pacific Theological College, 20, 91
PACT (Public and Contextual Theology Strategic Research Centre)
  background on, 18, 147–48
  Camden Theological Library's collection from, 142

  in conferences, 147–48, 150, 151, 153, 154, 157, 158, 159
  international collaboration by, 18, 19–20
  in rise of public theology research at UTC, 183, 184
  in UTC's connection to CSU School of Theology, 92, 172
Padokana, Zebedee, 91, 133
Painter, John, 147–48
Palmer, Damian, 176, 176n15
Palmer, Parker, 84
Palu, Ma'afu, 92
Pannenberg, Wolfhart, 25, 30
Park, Myung Hwa, 110, 111
Parliament of New South Wales, 154
Parramatta Heritage Centre, 153
"Pasifika" label, 92, 94
Pasifika peoples
  in biblical studies, 91–92, 118, 185–86, 187–88, 187n92
  Camden Theological Library's support for, 132, 133, 142
  Clive Pearson's mentorship for, 29, 181n53
  in colonialism and decolonization, 34, 35, 91–94, 118, 187n92, 188–89
  in demography of UTC, 73
  in ecotheology and climate action, 26, 35, 91, 93–94, 185, 188
  in high-profile leadership positions, 90–91
  as migrants, 94–96
  in multicultural context, 96–104
  in Pasifika countries, 104–6
  visiting scholars and conferences on, 35, 91–92, 156–57
  See also indigenous Australians
Past Presidents Forum, 150
Pastoral Groups, 45
pastoral studies, 13, 101–2, 150, 152, 179–80
  See also formation for ordained ministry; ordained ministers
Pattel-Gray, Anne, 33, 65, 66, 164, 187n92
Pattenden, Rod, 152, 153

peace activism, 153, 154–55, 160, 189, 190
Pearson, Clive
   in conferences, 155, 156, 157, 158, 163
   in public theology, 148, 184–85
   research and publications by, 184–85, 186, 187, 191
   as research supervisor, 29, 32, 33, 177, 181n53, 189n102
   in systematic theology instruction, 25–29, 30, 36–37, 78, 115, 116–17, 170, 184–85
   as UTC principal, 51, 136, 138, 146
Period of Discernment, 55
Perrin, Edmund, 135
Peterson, Geoffrey, 52, 170
Phan, Peter, 27
PhD programs. *See* postgraduate programs
Philip, Thomas, 176n15
Pickard, Stephen, 25–26
pikipikihama (outrigger) understanding of supervision, 92–93
Pitman, Julia, 173n5
Pitt Street Congregational Church, 148n11, 183
place, 71–72, 73–74, 83, 85
Polkinghorne, John, 151–52
Port Arthur shootings, 179
Porter, Phil, 152
postcode theology, 26, 37
postcolonialism. *See* colonialism and decolonization
postgraduate programs
   in continuing education for ministers, 11, 85–86, 174
   at CSU School of Theology, 11–12, 15, 16, 17, 148
   CSU School of Theology's bachelor's program as preparation for, 13
   decline of systematic theology applicants to, 38
   Korean students in, 110, 111, 119, 120, 122–23
   leadership positions held by graduates of, 191
   in rise of theological studies in public universities, 2
   UTC faculty as accredited supervisors in, 171–72
power differentials, 50, 63
practical theology, 13, 17, 86–87
Preamble 15 Years On conference, 161
presbyteries, 42, 49, 123, 132, 175
Princeton University, 19, 29, 90, 140, 161–62
principals, 16, 21
   See also Dicker, Gordon; Mitchell, Sarah; Pearson, Clive; Walker, Peter
private students, 57–58, 60
Privett, Peter, 150–51
Project Green Church, 158
prophetic criticism, 36, 37
Protestant Reformation, 159
   See also Calvin, John; Luther, Martin
public theology
   conferences on, 148
   ecotheology in, 123, 177, 184–85
   in indigenous issues, 106, 184–85, 188–89
   PACT in (*see* PACT (Public and Contextual Theology Strategic Research Centre))
   research and publications on, 177, 178n31, 181, 183–85, 188–89, 190n106
publications. *See* research and publications
pule fakalaga (indigenous survival values), 94
Pulse team, 142
Purnell, Douglas, 52, 152, 179

Quest database, 141
Questioning God: Faith and Atheism in Australia conference, 163–64
Quinn, Sherry, 139–40, 141, 142

Raine, Elizabeth, 149, 154, 173, 178–79
Ralphs, Peter, 173n5
Rayson, Dianne, 35, 164

Reasoning, Values, and Writing
  course, 71
Reconciliation course, 73
Reddie, Anthony, 118, 159–60
Rees, Anthony, 155, 177–78, 189n102
Rees, Janice, 176n15
Reformation, Protestant, 159
  See also Calvin, John; Luther,
  Martin
Reformed doctrine, 26, 159
regional formation, 11
Reichardt, David, 158, 173, 177,
  184n79
Reid, Stephen, 181n53
religious freedom legislation, 18
Relph, Edward, 71–72
remigrants, 94
research and publications
  biblical studies in, 148, 154,
    162–63, 173, 177–79, 185–86,
    187–88, 187n92
  in Camden Theological Library (*see*
    Camden Theological Library)
  church history in, 150n18, 183
  at CSU School of Theology, 17–20,
    92, 147–48, 178
  in fourth-year honors programs, 11
  liturgical studies in, 180–82
  for Openbook Annual Theological
    Essay Award, 96–97, 114
  overview of contextual theology
    in, 185–89 (*see also* contextual
    theology)
  pastoral studies in, 101, 150,
    179–80
  public theology in, 177, 178n31,
    181, 183–85, 188–89, 190n106
  theological colleges' increased
    participation in, 2, 174
  theological studies in, 26, 29, 30,
    32–33, 36–37, 47, 58, 174–77
  translation work in, 162–63
  in *Uniting Church Studies* (*see Unit-
    ing Church Studies* (journal))
  UTC's history of, 169–75
  world religions in, 154, 189–91
research centers, 18

research higher degree (RHD)
  programs. *See* postgraduate
  programs
research seminars, 17, 171–72
Revelation (Camden Theological
  Library's catalog), 141
Richmond, Helen, 69, 79, 173, 188,
  189
Ricoeur, Paul, 32
Roberts, Judyth, 151
Robinson, Ali, 179
Robinson, Ian, 173, 180
Rodgers, Richard E. A., 188
Rogers, Jack, 162–63
Rogoimuri, Sitiveni, 99
Rollins, Pete, 153
Rosolen, Grahame, 176n15
Roude, Nada, 190n106
Rountree, Te Aroha, 35
Ruddock inquiry, 18

Saliers, Don, 152
Saltbush team, 142
Samoans, 91, 94, 97, 106
San Francisco Theological Seminary,
  174
Saritoprak, Zeki, 154–55
Schillebeeckx, Edward, 32
scholarship programs, 15, 173–74
School of Continuing Education, 72,
  131, 148
science, 151–52
scriptural reasoning movement, 18
Season of Creation service, 123
second-generation migrants, 97, 103,
  124, 155
self-sufficient masculinity, 50–51, 64
Seminar Week, 148, 149–50, 151–52,
  161–62
seminars, research, 17, 171–72
Senini, Christine, 181n53
sermons, 164, 175
sexual orientation, 48, 112, 142,
  162–63, 177
Sheridan, Ruth, 182
silagtoga (ritual practice), 106
Slee, Nicola, 181
Smith, Adele, 83, 133
Smith-Christopher, Daniel, 155

Solomon (biblical figure), 169
Solomon Islands, 91, 132
Somasundram, Drene, 182n58
Sonderegger, Katherine, 32
Sorenson, Christine, 52, 60n19
South Korea. *See* Korea and Koreans
South Pacific Association of Theological Colleges (SPATS), 91
space, 71–72, 73–74, 81, 83, 85
The Spirit of the Christian Life course, 28
Squires, John
  in conferences, 149, 153–54
  research and publications by, 178–79, 180, 190, 191
  as research supervisor, 178, 189n102
  as scholarship recipient, 173
St. George's College, Hong Kong, 15
St. Mark's National Theological Centre, 3, 4, 6–8, 10, 14, 16, 20
staff. *See* faculty
Stamp Committee (Uniting Church in Australia), 132
Stanley, Christopher, 154
Statement of Strategic Directions, 128n8
status confessionis, 36
Stellenbosch University, 19, 47
Stephens, Scott, 163
Stockton, Jenny, 83
Stokes, Joanne, 83
Storrar, William, 148
Strathfield-Homebush Parish, 173
Stringer, Robert, 127
Student Support Team (United Theological College), 71, 82–83
Students Association (United Theological College), 9, 58n14
Study Skills course, 71
subdisciplines, 12–14
Sugirtharajah, R. S., 118
Suh, Young Min, 111, 112, 114, 117
Suli, Charissa, 77, 80, 81, 83, 84, 85–86, 90, 104
Summer School in the Arts, 152
Swynny Collection, 135

Sydney College of Divinity (SCD), 1, 171, 178, 184n79
Synod of NSW (New South Wales) and ACT (Australian Capital Territory)
  Camden Theological Library and, 129–30, 134–36, 137, 138–39, 141
  financial support for ministry candidates by, 5, 46
  formation for ordained ministry standards in, 2, 42
  multiculturalism in, 79, 87, 90, 110, 120
  in oversight of UTC, 8–9, 15–16, 21
  reasons for participation with CSU School of Theology, 4–5
  in UTC's intersection of church and university, 20, 21
Synod of Victoria and Ṭasmania, 90, 120
systematic theology
  Ben Myers' instruction on, 29–33
  Clive Pearson's instruction on, 25–29, 30, 36–37, 78, 115, 116–17, 170
  in CSU School of Theology's sub-disciplines, 13
  decline of at UTC, 38–39
  Michael Mawson's instruction on, 33–35, 36
  research and publications on, 26, 29, 30, 32–33, 36–37, 176
  in rise of contextual theology, 98

Tabart, Jill, 150
Tagore, Rabindranath, 190
Tahaafe-Williams, Katalina, 155–56, 186–87
talanoa (storytelling), 91–94, 118, 186
Talanoa Oceania conferences, 91–92, 156, 157
Talia, Maina, 91, 93–94
Tanner, Ian, 150
terrorism, 189n104, 190
Thatcher, Griffithes Wheeler, 149n16
Thatcher Lectures, 148, 149, 165
theology and theological studies

community of the heart in (*see* community of the heart)
CSU School of Theology's curriculum and course profile for, 11–14
demand for programs in, 14
in formation for ordained ministry, 44, 48, 49
multiculturalism in (*see* multiculturalism)
in public universities, 2–4
research and publications on (*see* research and publications)
systematic theology in (*see* systematic theology)
visiting scholars and conferences on (*see* visiting scholars and conferences)
Theology in Global Context course, 37
Thérèse of Lisieux, 164
Thompson, Geoff, 173
Thompson, Paul, 70
Thorn, Lynette, 129n9, 136
Thornley, Andrew, 104
Thornley, Carolyn, 52, 60n19
Tillich, Paul, 27, 36, 37
Tongan National Conference, 105
Tongans
 in chapel worship, 81
 in contextual theology, 97, 98
 as faculty members, 78, 91
 hyphenated/hybrid identities of, 95
 "Pasifika" label and, 94
 in student demographics of UTC, 73
 in UCA leadership, 90
Torrance, T. F., 30, 176
Torres Strait Islander Australians. *See* indigenous Australians
transcontextual theology, 25, 98
Transforming Theology project, 182
Trudinger, Peter, 173n5
Tu'iono, Kamaloni, 92, 101
Tulip, Jim, 4
Tupou-Thomas, Sisilia, 95–96
Tupu, Charles Uesile, 106

Turton, Linda, 74, 77, 80, 81–82
Tuvalu, 91, 93, 94

umu (earth oven), 93, 98
undergraduate programs, 1, 3–4, 10, 11, 12–14, 44
United Theological College (UTC)
 community at (*see* community of the heart)
 CSU School of Theology and (*see* Charles Sturt University (CSU) School of Theology)
 diversity at (*see* Korea and Koreans; multiculturalism; Pasifika peoples)
 formation for ordained ministry at (*see* formation for ordained ministry)
 instruction at (*see* systematic theology; visiting scholars and conferences)
 research at (*see* Camden Theological Library; research and publications)
United Theological College (UTC) Council, 128n8, 148n13, 170
United Theological College (UTC) Korean Fellowship, 157
Uniting (human services organization), 15
Uniting Aboriginal and Islander Christian Congress (UAICC), 43, 147
Uniting Church in Australia (UCA)
 archives of, 134–35, 141
 Basis of Union of (*see* Basis of Union (Uniting Church in Australia))
 education level of members in, 16
 historical studies on, 117, 150, 162, 183
 multiculturalism in (*see* multiculturalism)
 National Assembly of (*see* National Assembly of the Uniting Church)
 ordained ministry in (*see* formation for ordained ministry; ordained ministers)

Uniting Church in Australia (*continued*)
  See also Northern Synod; Synod of NSW (New South Wales) and ACT (Australian Capital Territory); Synod of Victoria and Tasmania
Uniting Church Records and Historical Society (UCRHS), 134
Uniting Church Studies course, 70n7, 183
Uniting Church Studies (journal)
  on Australian missionaries in Korea, 157
  on Calvin Quincentenary conference, 159n69
  establishment of, 173
  on faith and atheism, 164
  on Gospel on Sunday conference, 150
  on Hidden Histories conference, 150n18
  on multiculturalism and reconciliation, 156, 160n76
  on neoliberalism conference, 160
  on Validating Violence conference, 154
Uniting Mission and Education (UME), 16, 21, 139, 140, 142
  See also Board of Education (Synod of NSW and ACT); Board of Mission (Synod of NSW and ACT)
universities, 2–3, 5, 9, 14, 15, 19–20
  See also specific universities
University of Canberra, 3
University of Chester, 19, 158n63
University of Divinity, 15, 181
University of Edinburgh, 19, 163
University of Heidelberg, 20
University of Wollongong, 123
Uota, Sulufaiga, 94
UTC Publications (publishing venture), 173

Vaipulu, Sioeli F., 95, 181n53
Vaka'uta, Nāsili, 156–57
vale (fool), 97

Validating Violence—Violating Faith? conference, 154, 160
Vilitama, Matagi, 35, 90, 93, 98, 105, 181n53
visiting scholars and conferences
  at colloquia, 35, 171
  Communitas program for, 58, 91, 155–56, 186–87
  on Dietrich Bonhoeffer, 47, 162, 164–65
  endowed lectureships in, 165 (*see also* Havea Lectures; Livingstone Lectures; May Macleod Lectures; Thatcher Lectures)
  hybrid model for, 161n81, 165
  nurturing and affirming through, 148–51
  questioning and disrupting through, 35, 65, 91–92, 118, 153–60, 190
  in UTC's commitment to lifelong learning, 145–48
  wondering and imagining through, 151–53, 178
Vital Ministry, 9, 16, 17, 21
Vosloo, Robert, 47
vulnerability, 61–63

Walk for Reconciliation, 160–61
Walker, Peter, 35, 79, 158–59, 162, 164, 165, 173, 177
Walking Together conference, 65
Wallace, Howard, 173
Waqa, Adi Mariana, 76
Waterlines, 158
Wednesdays, 45
Weil, Simone, 164
Wendt, Albert, 94
Wesley, John, 184n76
Wesley Centre, 164
White, Rhonda, 45, 52, 179
whiteness, 50–51, 64–65, 160
Wilcoxen, Matthew, 175n10, 176n15
Wildman, Wesley, 173n5
Williams, Andrew, 138
Williams, Rowan, 30, 32, 47, 176
Wilson, Matthew, 178n34, 189n102
Wilson, Ronald, 160–61
Winton-Henry, Cynthia, 152

With Love to the World scholarship fund, 173
Wolfe, Naomi, 33, 35, 187n92
women. *See* gender
Wood, D'Arcy, 150
World Council of Churches, 90
world religions. *See* interfaith dialogue; Islamic studies and Muslim-Christian dialogue; Jews
worship services, 60, 79, 81, 152, 180–82
Wright, Stephen, 176n15
Wright Library (Princeton), 140
Wrightson, Ann, 127
Wymarra, Pearl, 73, 74, 79, 81, 86–87

Yang, Myong Duk, 69, 79, 110, 157, 173, 188
Yeun, Seung Jae, 111, 117, 121, 123
Yoon, DooAh, 111, 112, 114, 123
Yoon, Jin, 157
youth ministry, 161–62, 179
Yu, Jae In, 176n15

Zacchaeus (biblical figure), 164
Zachariah, George, 35
Zachman, Randall, 159
Zhang, Ji, 160n75
Zikmund, Barbara Brown, 150
Zipporah (biblical figure), 92
Zoom, 10–11, 17, 35, 59, 161n81

www.ingramcontent.com/pod-product-compliance
Lightning Source LLC
Chambersburg PA
CBHW062021220426
43662CB00010B/1419